Wings

Over

Persia

By: Lou Martin

Lt.Col. USAF (ret.)

Seventh Edition

2007

A pilot's true story of intrigue and adventure of flying in Iran during the revolution which overthrew the Shah and installed Ayatollah Khomeini as a fundamentalist Islamic dictator

Best wishes to Dorothy McNamara —

Lou Martin 4/08

Printed in Victoria, Canada

National Library of Canada Cataloguing in Publication

Martin, Lou, 1928-
Wings over Persia / Lou Martin.

Includes bibliographical references.
ISBN 1-4120-0107-2
I. Title.
TL540.M28A3 2003 629.13'092 C2003-901773-7

This book was published *on-demand* in cooperation with Trafford Publishing.
On-demand publishing is a unique process and service of making a book available for retail sale to the public taking advantage of on-demand manufacturing and Internet marketing. **On-demand publishing** includes promotions, retail sales, manufacturing, order fulfilment, accounting and collecting royalties on behalf of the author.

Suite 6E, 2333 Government St., Victoria, B.C. V8T 4P4, CANADA
Phone 250-383-6864 Toll-free 1-888-232-4444 (Canada & US)
Fax 250-383-6804 E-mail sales@trafford.com
Web site www.trafford.com TRAFFORD PUBLISHING IS A DIVISION OF TRAFFORD HOLDINGS LTD.
Trafford Catalogue #03-0470 www.trafford.com/robots/03-0470.html

This book is dedicated to my many Iranian friends, Air Taxi Company colleagues and unnamed passengers who were victims of the revolution that terminated the reign of Mohammad Reza (Shah) Pahlavi. I have fond memories of each and everyone of them and wish them well.

Author's Notes

The Minnesota Aviation Hall of Fame designated *Wings Over Persia* the Best Aviation Writing by a Minnesotan for 2004. The notification statement reads, "We enjoyed your exciting personal account of your days flying as a captain for an air charter company in Iran. Your book was exciting and personal, definitely the type of aviation writing the MAHOF wishes to honor and encourage with its annual award." (See Photo # 35.)

Persia refers to the historical name for Iran, which was a thriving country for more than 3,000 years, but in 1935 Reza Shah Pahlavi officially changed its name to Iran.

With the intent of making the book easy to read, it was printed in Font 12, no hyphenated words and no breaks in paragraphs. The services of a "Ghost Writer" were not used. All 95,867 words are those of the author. I did incorporate suggestions and comments from aviation colleagues listed in the Acknowledgment Section, and continually use comments from readers when preparing updated editions, as in edition seven for 2007. This is a nonfiction book; A few liberties were taken with the sequencing of events, but all of them actually happened.

The Cover: The design of the front and back covers were those of the author. The basic background color is "Desert Sand." The aircraft on the front cover is a Turboprop 690A. The photo of a pilot in a cockpit is the author in a YS-11 in 1975. The pictures on either side of a oil drilling site are of Mohammad Reza (Shah) Pahlavi and Ayatollah Khomeini. On the back cover is a photo of the author in the cockpit of a AT-6 in 1996.

The reader will find references to wages and bank deposits expressed in 1976 U.S. dollars. Published inflation rates for the last 31 years, indicates that each 1976 dollar is equal to $3.36 in 2007.

The Author can be contacted at: pilotlou@aol.com or 952-891-1250.

Acknowledgment

The material presented in this book was derived from personal memories of living and working in Iran and by referencing the remarks section of my Senior Pilot's Flight Log Book. However, information relating to some dates, places and events was obtained through Internet research. I was amazed by the quantity of information available from this source. Inserting keywords like the Shah, Khomeini, Iran, aviation, etc. produced an almost unlimited wealth of information. I don't know who is responsible for supplying this vast amount of data, but I am grateful that it's available. I feel fortunate to be living in an age where I can research at such depth, almost any subject, by the key stroke of a computer.

I would also like to give special thanks to my aviation colleagues, Tom Lymburn, my brother Ben Martin and Dorothy (Dottie) Bassett for reviewing and submitting constructive comments during the preparation of this book. I was very fortunate to have such intelligent professionals to call upon for advice.

Tom is the chairman of the English Department at the Princeton, Minnesota High School and was the historian for the former "Planes of Fame Air Museum (East)." His knowledge of aviation facts is unmatched!

Ben holds a Master's degree in Aeronautical Engineering and invented a "Gravity Gradient Attitude Stabilization System" for satellites, and a "Dual Burning Propulsion System" for rockets (which increased payloads and helped produce *Gemini* and interplanetary probes). He led Lockheed's proposal effort for NASA's manned interplanetary studies, and after winning the contract, was appointed team leader for the original and follow-on contracts. Several of Ben's inventions have been displayed at the "Air and Space Museum" in Washington, D.C. He has also been a guest speaker at many science related events.

Dottie worked for Northwest Airlines for 33 years as the manager of Pilot and Aircraft Publications Compliance and the editor of the airline's OnCourse magazine. Tom, Ben and Dottie were a great help in preparing this book, so I extend my thanks to all three of them.

Contents

Introduction

In *Wings Over Persia* I hope to relive for the reader the many interesting and sometimes near disasters that I encountered when flying for Air Taxi, a charter company in Tehran, Iran. The company was indirectly owned by Mohammad Reza Pahlavi, the Shah (King) of Iran. I was a member of a small cadre of foreign pilots approved to fly a fleet of approximately 25 different types of aircraft throughout the Middle East.

Pilots employed to fly these aircraft underwent a thorough background investigation by the Iranian Savak (secret police) and were personally approved by the Shah. The reason for the strict security clearance was that many of my flights were into secret Iranian military installations and involved transporting high-ranking Iranian military and government officials. The aircraft I flew were the Fokker F-27, the American Fairchild FH-227, the French *Falcon* DA-20 and the Rockwell *Turbo Commander*.

In addition to flying as a line captain, I administered flight instruction to young Iranian Navy officers preparing them to qualify as Aircraft Commanders. Many of the aircraft I flew were owned by the Iranian military and bore military markings. A classified operation I was involved in was the flying of long range Fokker F-27s in high altitude photo mapping of the Iran/Iraq border, where my main concern was the threat of being intercepted by Iraqi jet fighters. Flights throughout the Middle East were never boring. Each day would be a different mission and require the flying of a different type aircraft. One day I would be transporting roughnecks to the hot desert oil fields in Southern Iran, the next day, high ranking VIPs to the shores of the Caspian Sea, and possibly the third day, the Shah's twin sister or his younger brother to the Persian Gulf.

I take the reader through my exhausting efforts to obtain a job in Iran after my position as a captain for Japan Domestic Airlines in Tokyo came to an end. The first chapter is devoted to this frustrating struggle.

The reader will share in the excitement of being part of the "Boomtown" atmosphere of Tehran in 1976. During this exciting time there were more than 100,000 foreigners living and working in Tehran. This large influx of expatriates supported the Shah's goal of modernizing Iran, much as Mustafa Ataturk, the founder of the Turkish Republic, did in Turkey in 1923 when he overthrew the Ottoman Dynasty. Ataturk's success was much admired by the Shah, who sought the same transformation in Iran.

Readers interested in aviation will find the Iranian system of aircraft qualification quite unique, and much different from what pilots go through in the United States. The level of expertise of Iranian pilots ranged from poor to excellent, depending on their training and their mental approach in mastering the skills required to pilot modern aircraft. Persuading many of them to adopt sound safety habits conflicted with their Muslim belief that everything is fixed in advance and human beings are powerless to change events.

The Middle East philosophy that "nothing is a lie if the story is believed" was a difficult concept to accept, but once understood, made everyday life a game of telling a better story than your boss, merchant or Iranian pilot colleagues. This interesting concept of traditional life in Iran is prevalent throughout the book.

The troubling days of 1978 made life in Iran interesting and sometimes dangerous especially when Islamic hard-liners rioted in the streets of Tehran demanding the Shah's removal. The demonstrator's goal was the creation of a fundamentalist Islamic State with the exiled Ayatollah Ruhollah Khomeini as their firebrand leader. Many of my flights during these difficult days were in support of the Iranian military in their fading attempt to prevent the overthrow of the Shah. Even though I was wearing a civilian airline uniform, I often felt that I was back in the U.S. Air Force flying combat support missions in South Vietnam.

The Shah's goal of modernizing Iran resulted in the expenditure of vast sums of Iran's oil wealth, but the benefits did not trickle down to the working poor. Anyone who disagreed with the Shah was forced to leave Iran or face the Savak, the Shah's brutal secret police force.

The Islamic fundamentalists did not agree with the Shah's 1960s "White Revolution," which allowed women to vote, hold jobs, discard the long black "head-to-toe" chadors, and modernize Iran's infrastructure. In fact, they were morally offended in his attempts to import Western culture. They considered it an affront to their Muslim principles. The militant fundamentalists seized on this discontent and preached to the masses that the Shah's goals were in violation of the Koran and "Sharia" (Islamic Law). When this discontent was manifested in street riots, attempts to control them by the Shah's army resulted in the deaths of thousands.

During the initial phases of the revolution my busy flight schedule was maintained, including humanitarian flights to the earthquake-stricken city of Tabas-e-Golshan, where 25,000 people died. I also flew cases of whole blood to the survivors of a tragic theater fire in the Southern Iranian City of Abadan, which had been set ablaze by rioters. During this late night flight my copilot became unconscious, due to a lack of nourishment, as a result of daytime fasting during the Muslim holy month of Ramadan.

Several chapters are devoted to the struggles the Shah and his faithful followers exerted in attempting to maintain control, and how these efforts affected me personally. However, in late 1978, Islamic militants took over most government buildings and attacked Western-owned businesses. In November 1978, a day known as "Black Sunday," Tehran went up in flames. With the city under martial law, and much of the infrastructure destroyed, it became clear that my own life was in jeopardy, especially after an American friend of mine, living in the city of Kerman, was murdered in his apartment by unknown assailants.

I hurriedly left Tehran two weeks before the Shah made a hasty departure for Cairo, Egypt. During my unplanned exodus, I abandoned a Volkswagen, personal property and several months of unpaid wages. I was, however, able to retrieve $30,000, (close to $102,000 in today's value), from an Iranian bank under siege and convert it, after considerable effort, into currency of several different Western countries.

Following the Shah's forced departure from Iran on January 16, 1979, the popular religious leader Ayatollah Ruhollah Khomeini triumphantly marched into Tehran. His arrival created a new round of riots as followers of the deposed Shah attempted to regain control. Under these conditions, I didn't feel it safe to return to Iran to reclaim my losses, especially after the Iranian Revolutionary Guards summarily executed, by firing squad, several of my former VIP passengers and Iranian pilot colleagues.

However, in May 1979, during a visit to Rome, Italy, I thought the internal situation in Iran had stabilized sufficiently to allow me to return. I visited the Iranian Revolutionary Guard Consulate office in Rome and applied for an entry visa. After a three-day wait my visa application was approved. However, an extraordinary lucky event occurred that convinced me that returning to Iran was not a wise move. I returned to the United States with my unused Iranian visa intact.

Author's Historical Note

When the prophet Mohammad, the founder of the Muslim religion, died on June 8, 632 A.D., his followers were sharply divided as to who would succeed him as their Iman (prayer leader). The majority felt his disciple "Abu Bohr" should be chosen. This group became known as "Sunni Muslims." The minority declared his son-in-law as their new Iman. This group became known as "Shiite Muslims."

These two Muslim sects have fought bloody battles for fourteen hundred years over which group should lead the Muslim faithful. Followers of both sects feel they have Allah (God) on their side and that it is an honor to fight and die for their beliefs as they are assured a place in Paradise. This religious struggle is not unlike the bitter fight between the Catholic and Protestant Christians in Northern Ireland.

Iran and Iraq are predominantly Shiite nations, (80% and 60% respectively). Sunni Muslims, who dominated Saddam Hussein's ruling Baath Party, commanded Northern Iraq and represent the largest Muslim group worldwide, including: Afghanistan, Algeria, Egypt, Jordan, Kuwait, Libya, Pakistan, Saudi Arabia, Syria, Turkey and United Arab Emirates.

The Author

Lou Martin was born and raised in Ladysmith, a small Midwest farming town in Northern Wisconsin. Following his birth in 1928, he lived through the worst years of the worldwide economic depression. He was the ninth of ten children of hard working German, Scottish, Irish parents. The hardships of the times instilled a sense of independence, confidence and a will to succeed, no matter what the odds. This characteristic was maintained throughout his childhood and adult life.

He was 13-years-old when the Japanese attacked Pearl Harbor, and along with other young boys his age contributed to America's victory to the extent possible. He collected scrap metal, delivered Western Union telegrams at age 14, worked as a railroad laborer at age 16, and in a defense plant in Chicago Illinois, at age 17.

His stint as a telegraph delivery boy was during the troubling war year of 1942, and recalls riding his *Flyer* bicycle to deliver telegrams to family members informing them that their sons or husbands were killed, missing or prisoners of war. This was an emotional experience for a 14-year-old.

When the war with Japan ended in 1945 he was working in Detroit, Michigan, and recalls the unprecedented victory celebrations with clarity. He obtained a Private Pilot's Certificate at age 17, and for the next 62 years continued his dream of flying. After graduating from high school in 1947, he worked as an apprentice photographer and engaged in commercial flying by performing aerial mapping flights from a Piper *Cub*.

Three years after the end of World War II, the U.S. Air Force was once again accepting young men for training as military pilots. However, entering the Aviation Cadet Program required a minimum of two years of college. With only a high school education it appeared he would not be able to meet the basic education requirements to fulfill a boyhood dream.

However, as a gift from the gods the Air Force began accepting young men for pilot training if they could pass a two-year college equivalency exam, be in perfect physical condition and be approved by a board of commissioned Air Force pilots.

Along with 11 other young men from the Midwest, he reported to Chanute AFB in June 1948 to compete in preliminary testing for an appointment as an Aviation Cadet. Only four of the 12 candidates examined were approved, with only two graduating as Second Lieutenants, and Air Force pilots in September 1949.

After graduating from pilot training he spent the next 21 years as an Air Force pilot. His active service included two three-year tours in Germany, one three-year tour in Japan, and five years flying combat cargo support missions during the Vietnam war, where he was credited with 169 combat flight hours. His military experience ranged from piloting large four engine transports to supersonic single engine jets.

Years attending night school allowed him to achieve his secondary goal of obtaining a college education and graduated from the University of Maryland with a Bachelor of Science degree. He retired from the Air Force in 1970 with the rank of Lieutenant Colonel.

After leaving the Air Force he flew from 1970 to 1975, as a captain and Chief Pilot for Japan Domestic Airlines. His flying experiences in Japan were unique in that he lived in Yokohama and flew a Japanese manufactured YS-11 turboprop transport, with Japanese copilots and Japanese flight attendants. On most flights he was the only foreigner on board, yet was the Pilot-In-Command flying the aircraft.

His years with Japan Airlines included flying with senior Japanese pilots who had participated in the December 7, 1941 attack on Pearl Harbor, and former members of Kamikaze squadrons. When in Japan, he met and later married Chieko Hara, a Japanese senior flight attendant.

From 1976 to 1979, he flew as a captain for Air Taxi an air charter company in Tehran, Iran. In this capacity, he traveled throughout the Middle East and was stranded in Karachi, Pakistan during the demonstrations preceding the overthrow of Zulfikar Ali Bhutto, the Prime Minister of Pakistan, who was later hanged.

He was working and living in Iran during the Islamic revolution that overthrew the Shah and made a hasty exit when his life was in danger. After returning to the United States in late December 1978, he worked as a *Falcon* Fan jet instructor in Napa, California. In 1980 he accepted a position with the Federal Aviation Administration (FAA) as an Air Carrier Inspector. His first assignment with the FAA was in Valley Stream, New York, where he supervised new start-up airlines.

In 1983 he transferred to the Minneapolis, Minnesota FAA Office with duties as a DC-9, B-727 and B-747 pilot examiner. He held the position as Chief FAA Inspector for Northwest Airlines for nine years.

To round out his vast aviation experiences, he became an active volunteer warbird pilot with the Planes of Fame Air Museum (East) in Eden Prairie, Minnesota where he specialized in flying restored World War II aircraft. At the "young age" of 62 he checked out in the nimble single seat U.S. Navy FM-2 Wildcat fighter, an aircraft he built models of when he was 12-years-old.

From 1992 to 1996, he was attached to the U.S. Consulate Office in Frankfurt, Germany, where he served as the FAA Operations Unit Supervisor for the European International Field Office. In this position, he traveled throughout Europe representing U.S. aviation interests, worked closely with numerous foreign aviation authorities and made two trips to Moscow, assisting Russian airlines in operating United States registered DC-10s and B-757s.

Lou Martin retired from professional flying in January 1999, with a total of 19,000 accident-free flight hours. However, he still flies his privately owned single engine Cessna to fly-ins throughout the Midwest and gliders with the Minnesota Soaring Club. He holds an FAA Flight Instructor's and Flight Engineer's certificate, is type rated in nine different aircraft, possesses Airline Transport Pilot Certificates from the United States, Japan and Iran, and is a proud member of the Experimental Aircraft Association. During EAA's Air Venture Oshkosh 2006 he was interviewed for entry into their "Timeless Voices of Aviation."

List of Illustrations Following Chapter Ten, Page 135

19. A caravan of camels in front of author's apartment in Tehran.

20. Author and daughter Lynn on Caspian Sea Coast.

21. Author and son Michael on Khark Island in the Persian Gulf.

22. Chieko in front of brass shop in Tehran.

23. Typical brass shop in downtown Tehran.

24. Author's son Mike in copilot's seat of an F-27.

25. Chieko overlooking the Imam Square in Isfahan, Iran.

26. The Alborz Mountains as viewed from the author's bedroom.

27. View of narrow mountain road en route to the Dizin ski area.

28. Chieko and author after returning from skiing in Dizin.

29. Author with Flight Systems instructor enjoying last flight in F-100.

30. Author enjoying a Beefeater martini in his apartment in Tehran.

31. Chieko enjoying a Beefeater martini in author's apartment.

32. Author in cockpit of F-27 somewhere over Iran in 1977.

33. Author enjoying a ski trip with friends in Austria in 1995.

34. Author's Iranian Air Taxi identification card.

35. Chieko and author during book signing in Oshkosh, Wi. in 2006.

Chapter One --- Obtaining the Job

In the spring of 1975, my position as a captain for Toa Domestic Airlines, formerly Japan Domestic Airlines, in Tokyo, Japan was coming to an end. For the past four and a half years, I had flown a Japanese YS-11 transport throughout Japan. The YS-11 was a popular 64 passenger turboprop aircraft, built by the Nihon Aircraft Company and operated by several airlines throughout the world. It was a great job, but the 1974 worldwide fuel crisis caused a reduction in pilot needs and it was no surprise that foreign pilots were the first to be (technically) furloughed.

I was 47-years-old, possessed nearly 14,000 hours of flight time, and was actively seeking a flying assignment somewhere else in the world. I had prospects of flying YS-11s in Papua, New Guinea, or as a copilot in B-707s for Trans America. My employment search came to the attention of Captain Troy Dafferin, who was the Chief Pilot for the foreign pilots flying DC-8s for Japan Airlines. (Troy, being an instructor pilot, was not affected by the foreign pilot cutbacks.)

Captain Dafferin contacted me stating that he had heard I was looking for a job, and inquired if I would be interested in flying for Iran Air? Troy added that the Chief Pilot of Iran Air, Captain Abdullahi, was a personal friend of his and thought he could help me in my job search. According to Troy, his first civilian flying assignment, after flying B-52 bombers for the Air Force, was as a B-727 instructor pilot for the Boeing Aircraft Company. His specific job was assisting airlines throughout the world in their transition into the B-727. Representing the Boeing Company he would fly with various airlines for a period of time as a line captain and flight instructor. It was in this capacity that he met and worked with the Chief Pilot of Iran Air in Tehran, Iran during their initial introduction of the Boeing 727 in the Middle East.

I told Troy I would appreciate any help he could provide in my finding another job as an airline captain. He said he would write a letter of introduction to Captain Abdullahi which I should send to him along with a copy of my resume. Troy said he would also send a personal note to Abdullahi, recommending me for a position with Iran Air.

With Captain Dafferin's help, I felt a prompt response from Tehran would be forthcoming. After hearing nothing, I sent an international cable to Captain Abdullahi inquiring if he had received my resume. I received an answer the next day consisting of one word, "Yes." Armed with this bountiful and informative message, I waited for further word while continuing preparations for my move from Japan back to the U.S.

By mid June 1975, I had heard nothing more from Tehran and the pickup date with a Japanese moving company was less than a week away. As a last ditch attempt, I sent a second cable to Tehran stating, "Since my contract with Japan Airlines has ended, I'm preparing to return to the United States. Would it be advantageous for me to visit your office in Tehran for a job interview before departing Japan? A quick response would be appreciated." The next day, I received a one word reply from Captain Abdullahi Stating, "Yes." I was getting the impression he was a man of few words especially when dealing with foreigners.

I purchased a Japan Airlines round-trip space-available employee discount ticket to Tehran and the following morning was onboard a B-747 for Iran. The flight made stops in Hong Kong, Bangkok and Bombay. I arrived in Tehran in mid afternoon of the next day, completely exhausted. I called Captain Abdullahi's secretary and was told to be in his office at 10 a.m. the following morning. From a shabby looking airport tourist office, I arranged for a hotel room in downtown Tehran. Following a death defying 20 minute taxi ride, I was standing in front of a hotel that had obviously seen better days, but I was too tired to be concerned.

I checked in at the front desk informing the attendant that I had made a reservation with the tourist office at the airport. The attendant searched his records, but informed me that he did not have a reservation in my name, and since the hotel was full there were no rooms available. He suggested a seek a room in a different hotel.

I didn't realize it at the time, but a convenient memory loss, or truth stretching, by Iranians, would be something I would have to contend with for my entire three years in Iran.

I insisted that I had made a reservation not more than one hour before, was exhausted after flying all the way from Tokyo, Japan and desperately needed a place to rest. After a series of frowns and sighs he said he could give me a small back room with no windows for one night. After he assured me that it had a shower, I told him I would take it.

After riding a shaky elevator to the fifth floor, I located my room near the back of a dark narrow hallway. I didn't have to use a key to enter as the door was unlocked. Entering, I couldn't find a light switch, but from the dim light shinning in from the hall, I spotted a reading lamp next to the bed. The 40-watt bulb in the lamp provided sufficient illumination to survey my room.

The first thing that caught my eye was a hole in a wall, large enough to walk through. It was obviously an ongoing construction project with piles of loose sheet rock on both sides of the opening. The space on the other side of the opening appeared to be some kind of storage area with stacks of boxes and old furniture scattered about.

I picked up my suitcase, rode the shaky elevator back to the lobby, and told the attendant that the room he had assigned me was under construction. He said that I could take the room as is, or find a room in some other hotel. Realizing he was dead-serious back upstairs I went and considered myself fortunate to have a room, no matter what the condition. After a prolonged wait, I was able to draw a trickle of lukewarm water for a well deserved shower utilizing a previously used miniature bar of soap.

Somewhat refreshed, but very hungry, I returned to the lobby in search of a restaurant to be followed by an evening walk on the unfamiliar streets of Tehran. I paused at the main entrance of the hotel to seek guidance from the large mustached hotel manager who was standing off to the side casually smoking a cigarette.

As I approached him a raggedly dressed teenage street urchin came by and stuck out his hand in an obvious gesture of soliciting. I reached for my wallet with the intent of giving him a dollar but the hotel manager abruptly stopped me. In a harsh loud voice he chastised the young boy in a language I didn't understand, but the meaning was clear. He was ordering the boy to move on. Apparently the young lad didn't move as quickly as the hotel manager desired and his displeasure was manifested by a strong hard slap to the boy's face. The manager, being a large man, nearly knocked the boy off his feet. The young man, minus my intended dollar, staggered off with tears in his eyes as the manager calmly resumed smoking his cigarette. (The harshness of the country was just starting to reveal itself.)

I rose early the next morning after a restless night of severe jet lag and a hard lumpy bed. After a "drip, drip," shower, I dressed in suit and tie, packed my bag, paid my hotel bill, and took a taxi to Mehrabad Airport. I arrived at Captain Abdullahi's office 20 minutes early and was invited, by a very attractive secretary dressed in Western-style attire, to have a seat. She said that Captain Abdullahi would see me shortly. After about an hour's wait, I was ushered into his office.

Captain Abdullahi was sitting behind a large oak desk working on stacks of paperwork. He hardly looked up as I entered. In a dictatorial tone of voice he said, "Show me your log book, Captain Martin." He thumbed through a few pages, and then in the same sharp tone of voice inquired if I had a B-727 type rating. I replied "No." He then asked, "Do you have a B-707 type rating?" When I said no for the second time, he pushed my log book back across his desk and said, "Sorry, I can't use you." He lowered his head and resumed working on his pile of papers.

My job interview with Captain Abdullahi, for which I had traveled 5,000 thousand miles, was over in less than 30 seconds. I was left standing before his desk, dressed in my best business suit, my closed log book sitting before him, and being summarily dismissed. I was somewhat angry and realized I had nothing to lose in displaying my displeasure and disappointment in the treatment to which I had just been exposed.

In a reciprocal harsh voice I said, "Captain Abdullahi, why in the hell did you have me travel 5,000 miles only to dismiss me when determining that I didn't have a B-727 or B-707 type rating? My aircraft qualifications were clearly stated in the resume I sent you, along with a letter of recommendation from your friend Captain Dafferin. In addition I sent you a cable asking if it would be advantageous for me to visit your office before leaving Japan, and you replied yes. Now that I came all this way, you indicate you can't use me after asking only two questions, which you could have answered in reviewing my resume."

Captain Abdullahi looked-up from his desk and seemed surprised at my show-off impertinence, but remained silent. I picked up my log book and started to leave his office. As I was nearing the door he called me back and invited me to sit down. In a much more compassionate tone of voice he asked for a short verbal history of my flying experiences. I briefed him on my 22-year military career and my years of flying a YS-11 as a captain with Japan Airlines.

From his body language it was apparent that he had never reviewed the resume I sent him. He explained that Iran Air only hires foreign pilots who already have type ratings in a B-727 or B-707 and therefore he could not offer me a job. He apologized that I had traveled all the way from Tokyo to find this out.

However, in a conciliatory manner he told me that a good friend of his was the president of an Iranian air charter company and was in need of Fokker F-27 *Friendship* captains. He added that the F-27 was a Dutch manufactured turboprop aircraft and very similar to the YS-11 I had been flying in Japan. He said that if I was interested, he would call his friend to inquire if he would like to interview me. I said I would appreciate any help he could provide. He asked me to wait in his outer office while he made a phone call. A few minutes later he called me back into his office and said that he had talked to a Mr. Djahanbani, the Managing Director of the Air Taxi Company, who would like to meet me. He said one of his drivers would take me to Djahanbani's office.

The Air Taxi Company was located on the western side of the airport, and surrounded by a high steel meshed fence. My driver had to enter through a military style security gate, where the guard checked the driver's and my identification before raising the barrier and allowing us to proceed. The driver stopped in front of a modern-looking two-story office building and indicated, through sign language, that we had reached our intended destination.

With my suitcase in hand, I walked in the front door and was immediately stopped by a guard who spoke no English. (It was obvious, he didn't want me to go any farther until he knew the purpose of my visit.) Fortunately, in a matter of a few minutes, a well dressed man appeared and in fluent English asked if I was Captain Martin. When I answered in the affirmative, he introduced himself as Mr. Montpass and said, "Mr. Djahanbani is expecting you."

I entered a large expensively-furnished office equipped with rich overstuffed white leather furniture, a large polished conference table and a huge oak desk in the far corner. Sitting behind the desk was an immaculately dressed man in his early forties. He stood up to greet me and while extending his hand said, "Welcome, Captain Martin, have a seat and tell me about your flying experiences."

As I sank nearly to the floor in a white leather easy chair his secretary handed me a cup of chay (tea). Mr. Djahanbani said that his friend, Captain Abdullahi, had called stating that I was looking for a flying job in Iran. I told him that this was true and that I had flown in from Tokyo the day before with that in mind. He asked if I had a *Falcon* Fan Jet type rating. When I said no, he asked if I had a Fokker F-27 type rating. Stating no once again he said that he was sorry, but couldn't offer me a position with his company.

I had just gone through this merry-go-round routine an hour before with Captain Abdullahi, so thought I would take a different approach this time.

I told Mr. Djahanbani that for the past four and a half years, I had flown YS-11s transports for Toa Domestic Airlines, and that the YS-11, even though a little larger than the Fokker F-27, is powered by similar Rolls Royce Dart engines, equipped with nearly identical Dowty Rotol propellers, and its flight characteristics are very similar to an airplane in which I have over 3,000 hours of Pilot-In-Command time.

His facial muscles reflected an interest and he asked me how much time I thought it would take for me to check out in the F-27 *Friendship*. I replied with confidence, a couple days of self-study of the aircraft manuals and two training flights, not to exceed five hours.

He seemed impressed and said that if I could guarantee I could perform as stated, he would offer me a job as a Fokker F-27 captain. However, after a short pause added that if I couldn't check out in five hours, I would have to pay for the flight time wasted. I gave my assurance that this stipulation was acceptable.

He offered a starting salary of $3,000 a month, plus $100 a day per diem when on trips, and time-and-a-half ($250) for each hour flown beyond 75 per month. (This basic monthly salary was equal to $11,300 today when adjusted for inflation, not a bad starting salary.) I indicated that the salary was acceptable and asked when he would like me to report for work. He chuckled and said, "Not so fast. You will first have to complete a detailed job application form, followed by a security background investigation by the Iranian Secret Police (Savak)." He further stated that if my job application was satisfactory, I would have to complete an F-27 check out before he could put me on the payroll. He called for Mr. Montpass (who I had met earlier) to walk me through the job application process. I thanked him for offering me a job and as we shook hands he told me he would look forward to seeing me in three or four months!

I followed Mr. Montpass to his office and began filling out several pages of job application forms. I worked through the lunch hour and hoped my rumbling empty stomach wouldn't disturb his office workers.

I presented my completed job application to Mr. Montpass who, at a snail's pace, meticulously checked each entry. Finding no errors or omissions, he told me that after making copies of my FAA Aviation Medical and Pilot Certificates, the only thing remaining was the taking of passport-type photos, and the signing of a two-year provisional contract.

In reviewing the contract, I noted completing two years of service would entitle me to a bonus of two months pay, one for each year. I also noted that during the life of the contract I would not be allowed to own or drive an automobile in Iran. I asked Mr. Montpass the reason for the automobile restriction. He said that driving in Tehran was a life-threatening experience, and if a foreigner became involved in an accident with an Iranian, the police would take him directly to jail and it might be a week before he would be allowed to contact representatives from his respective government or company of employment. Consequently, Air Taxi did not wish to expose themselves to this potential problem. He added that community city taxies were plentiful and should be used and transportation to and from the airport would be furnished by the company.

Around 2 p.m., I had completed all the employment application forms and inquired if it was necessary for me to remain in Iran any longer. Mr. Montpass said no, but that it was important to keep him informed of my address in the United States. He added that it would probably be at least four months before the Savak (secret police) completed my security background check, and gave approval for my employment. I asked him why such strict security was required to fly their aircraft. He said that the Air Taxi Company was owned by the Shah and consequently operated into restricted Iranian military installations. They also flew high ranking military and government officials, including the Shah's wife and siblings, plus flights into airports he wasn't at liberty to disclose at this time.

I told him I had movers scheduled to pack up my personal household goods in Japan in two days, and it was important for me to get back as soon as possible. I added that if he could provide me with transportation to downtown Tehran, it may be possible for me to catch the evening Japan Airlines flight to Tokyo. He said this would be no problem and reached for his telephone.

He said I was in luck as a company car was going downtown to pick up some flight attendants and that I could ride along. I was escorted to a waiting Iranian manufactured automobile called a *Paykan* and stowed my suitcase in the trunk. I said good-bye to Mr. Montpass and while shaking hands, said I looked forward to seeing him in three or four months when I would be eager to start flying for his company.

The driver departed the area as if he had just received the green flag at a NASCAR sanctioned auto race. With a constant honking of the horn, he accelerated down a highway crowded with bicycles, donkey carts, trucks of every description, walking pedestrians and people hanging onto the sides of crowded busses. I attempted to convey to him that it wasn't necessary to drive so fast, but since he didn't speak English, and I didn't speak Farsi, I just gritted my teeth and put my faith in Allah (God). I just hoped that the 20-mile ride to town would pass quickly!

About five miles from Mehrabad Airport, he started taking a northeast course which I thought would take us away from downtown Tehran. As we headed into the suburbs, I realized we were not driving toward the city. Through the use of vigorous sign language, I attempted to get the driver to change direction, but he was either ignoring me or didn't understand. He just kept on driving as if he were overdue at a pit stop.

My repeated gestures of displeasure in the direction he was going apparently upset him, and he decided to rid himself of the agitation. He slammed on the brakes and pulled off the road unto a narrow gravel shoulder. After stopping he got out, removed my suitcase from the trunk, and kept repeating "Enja." (I learned later that “Enja” literally means you are here.)

He was very vocal in informing me that he was taking me no farther. Recognizing his displeasure in me as a passenger, and that we were not heading downtown, I waved him off. With rear tires spinning, he sped off giving me the impression that this pit stop was longer than he desired, and hurried off to make up the time he lost in catering to me!

I was stranded on a rural two-lane highway with little traffic. Figuring there was no other option, I began hitchhiking in the direction of downtown Tehran. I sensed that passing Iranian motorists didn't know what to make of a 47-year-old male foreigner, dressed in a business suit, carrying a suitcase, and raising his thumb in the direction of Tehran. Most cars passed without so much as a curious "rubber-necking" slow down. With sweat beginning to show through my suit, I began losing hope of reaching Tehran anytime soon. (I later learned that the American symbol for hitchhiking is considered an obscene gesture in Iran. This undoubtedly was the reason I was being ignored by passing motorists.)

Unexpectedly, a late model black Buick sedan pulled to a stop. The driver, dressed in a tie and business suit, inquired in English if I was an American. When I answered in the affirmative, he asked me where I was headed. I replied, "Downtown." He said, "Jump in, as that is where I'm going and I would be happy to have you ride with me."

Settling down in his air-conditioned automobile, I explained how I found myself hitchhiking on a rural road in Iran. He didn't seem surprised and told me he would be happy to drop me off in front of the Japan Airlines downtown ticket office. I asked him where he had learned to speak English. He told me that he had attended college in the United States and was always treated well by Americans. Consequently, he welcomed the opportunity to reciprocate. As I exited his automobile, I felt refreshed and thought a job in Iran might not be so bad if there were more Iranians around like him.

I presented my space-available ticket to the Japan Airlines agent and inquired if I could get a seat on their evening flight to Tokyo. Without hesitation, he said that the flight was oversold, that there were about ten full-paying revenue passengers on standby, and my chance of obtaining a seat was zero. I inquired about the availability of a seat on the next day's flight. He responded by stating that all flights for the next several days were oversold and didn't see any chance of me obtaining a seat, even if I was willing to pay full fare! It looked like I would have a difficult time in returning to Japan anytime soon!

However, I knew that Iran Air flew daily B-707 flights to Tokyo, after making a refueling stop in Peking, China, so I thought this might be an alternative way of getting back to Japan, although it didn't come without a potential problem. At the time China did not have diplomatic relations with the United States and required Americans to have a visa when transiting China, even on refueling stops. However, recognizing my pressing need to get back to Japan, I decided to push my luck.

I asked the Japan Airlines representative if he would endorse my JAL ticket over to Iran Air. He said he was willing, but would first have to obtain permission from Tokyo. At my request, he sent an electronic message to Japan and permission was forthcoming within a few minutes. The agent stamped the back of my Japan Airlines ticket and I headed for the Iran Air office just a few doors down the street.

The Iran Air agent said that their evening flight to Tokyo was only about half full and assigned me a seat straight away. I knew it was the responsibility of international carriers to check passports for proper visas, but the only check the agent made was my entry visa for Japan. I'm quite sure he wasn't aware that Americans required a transient visa for refueling stops in China. However, as far as I was concerned, the "don't ask, don't tell" policy was the proper action in my situation.

I boarded an Iran Air B-707 without incident and, as predicted, noted many empty seats. We flew directly over the Himalayan Mountains and in spite of our altitude of 37,000 feet they seemed to almost scrape the bottom of the aircraft. Mount Everest was especially spectacular since it was free of clouds, a rare occurrence according to the captain's cabin announcement.

The pilot made a smooth landing in Peking, and taxied to an almost empty terminal ramp. The most striking object in sight was a huge colored poster of Premier Zhou Enlai. It seemed to dominate the entire airport landscape. As the boarding steps were being positioned, I observed four military-style vehicles racing toward the aircraft.

When the aircraft door opened five armed Chinese soldiers marched through the cabin and came to attention about every ten feet. A Chinese Army officer began working his way down the aisle asking passengers for their passports. When he reached my seat, I was purposely gazing nonchalantly out the window at the poster of Premier Zhou Enlai. The officer, standing no more than two feet away, barked, "Passport, Preeze." I handed him the requested document and returned to my window gazing. I noted him thumbing through my passport, page by page, several times obviously looking for a Chinese transient visa. His task was difficult due to the many entry/exit visas I had accumulated.

Finally, after being convinced he could not find what he was looking for he barked, "You have no visa for China. You must come with me." I told him in an equally authoritative tone of voice that I was not going to China, but Japan. He countered with, "You are in China now!" We went back and forth in this verbal "Ping-Pong" game, with him insisting that I leave the aircraft and go with him, and my insistence that I was going to stay where I was. During his demands, two of his armed guards moved closer to my position and I sensed that my ignoring their officer's orders, in front of them and foreign passengers, was making them very uncomfortable.

When I observed sweat starting to appear on the forehead of my demanding Chinese friend, I figured it was time to state my case. I told him that I was a United States citizen, onboard an Iranian aircraft, and even though China and the United States did not have diplomatic relations, China and Iran did. I also stated that the only way I would leave the aircraft would be by being physically dragged off by him and his armed guards. Without responding, he and his guards left with my passport clutched tightly between his fingers. When they reached the ramp they boarded their vehicles and were last seen speeding toward the main terminal building. What was going to happen next, I wasn't sure. But one thing was certain, I wasn't going to step off the aircraft and become a hostage pawn between China and the United States in their dispute over formalizing diplomatic relations, which they had been arguing over since the end of the Korean War.

Hi Dorothy hope you
enjoy the book. It is
a gift from my
sister-in-law Betty
Martin in South Carolina.
Lou Martin

About 30 minutes later the aircraft refueling trucks were beginning to pack up, and I observed that the catering vehicles were nearly finished with their restocking. We were just minutes away from continuing on our flight to Tokyo, but the Chinese had still not returned with my passport. I pushed the flight attendant call button and told the male purser that it was important that I speak to the captain before the aircraft door closed.

A tall mustached Iranian pilot came to my seat and I told him what had transpired between me and the Chinese. I pointed out that it appeared that I was the only American on his flight, and Iran Air in Tehran never informed me that I needed a transient visa for the refueling stop in China (a true statement). I also mentioned that it would be very difficult for him personally if he landed in Japan without me being in possession of a passport, as the Japanese were very fussy about this potential problem. He said he would return to the cockpit and make a radio call.

A few minutes later an army vehicle could be seen speeding across the ramp toward our aircraft. My Chinese army officer friend came marching down the aisle and stopped next to my seat. He handed me my passport and barked, "We gave you one-time visa to visit China, but Preeze never come back to China again!" He made an about face and left the aircraft. The aircraft door closed and the rest of the flight to Tokyo was uneventful.

The movers arrived to pack my household and personal belongings the day after I got back to Japan. The Japanese in their traditional measure of efficiency prepared my authorized three thousand pounds in two parcels. Two thousand pounds for immediate shipment to the U.S. and one thousand pounds in storage for later shipment to Iran. I established temporary residence in my hometown of Ladysmith, Wisconsin, while I waited for instructions from Tehran to report for work.

Three months went by without receiving any word from Tehran, when without prior notice, I received an international telegram. The message, however, was not what I expected or planned on hearing. The cable stated that the Air Taxi Company had reevaluated their pilot needs and were not able to offer me a position at this time.

By return cable, I stated that I was very disappointed in their decision, and that by not offering me the job promised during my job interview in Tehran had caused me great personal loss and a disruption of future plans. I added, that I had passed up several good flying positions based on their commitment (not true) and requested they reconsider.

Within a few days, I received another telegram stating that they had reconsidered their pilot needs and were now able to offer me a position as captain. In late December 1975, I received a packet containing airline tickets to Iran, along with instructions to proceed to the Iranian Consulate Office in San Francisco to obtain an Iranian work permit and visa.

When I presented my passport, work contract and visa application to the San Francisco, Iranian Consulate Office the waiting room was crowded with people of many different nationalities. Clerks were scurrying about and desks were overflowing with what appeared to be hundreds of visa applications. When my application was finally reviewed the attending clerk told me to come back in three or four weeks. I told him that this wouldn't do as I had reservations for a flight to Tokyo and Tehran the next day.

My comment was not taken seriously, so I asked to see a senior consulate representative. A bespectacled middle-aged man soon arrived and inquired as to my problem. I told him that I was hired as a captain for the Air Taxi Company in Tehran and didn't think he was aware that it was owned by the Shah. I added that foreign pilots hired to fly for Air Taxi were personally approved by the Shah himself, after receiving security clearance from the Savak. I told him that I was expected in Tehran within the next couple of days, and if they were going to delay my departure for several weeks he should send a telegram to the Shah and Savak Headquarters explaining why I could not report for duty. He asked if I would mind waiting a few minutes. While waiting, I was served a cup of chay (tea). I had my visa about 30 minutes later.

I left the Iranian Consulate Office walking past rows of people who hadn't moved since I came in. The next morning I was on a flight to Tokyo and looking forward to my job in Iran with great excitement.

Chapter Two --- Reporting for Work

Following stops in Tokyo, Hong Kong, Bangkok and Bombay, I arrived in Tehran, Iran during the early hours of January 3, 1976. After clearing customs, I was disappointed that there was no one at the airport to greet me. I called the Air Taxi Company to notify them that I had arrived and requested they send someone to pick me up. I talked to several different English speaking employees, but no one knew of me or what my purpose was in requesting to visit their company. I finally gave up and, with the assistance of the airport information desk, hired a taxi to drive me to my new place of employment.

The taxi was required to stop at the company security gate and not allowed to proceed into the compound. I paid off the driver, retrieved my two bags from the trunk, and stood waiting while a non-English-speaking guard made a telephone call for guidance.

About ten minutes later Mr. Montpass (the personnel manager I had met six months earlier) arrived and welcomed me to Tehran. He said that if I had advised them of my arrival date and time he would have had someone meet me at the airport. I told him that I had sent several messages regarding my pending arrival and that I was on schedule. His response, "Insha Allah," as he helped me place my bags in his Volkswagen van.

The expression "Insha Allah" was to become very familiar during my life in Iran. A literal translation would be, "If Allah wishes," or "as Allah commands." Except for the reference to Allah, the connotation is similar to the song made famous by Doris Day called, "Que Sera, Sera," whatever will be will be.

In contrast, an amusing expression employed by many men, when they wish to imply disagreement to a thought or idea, is a snapping sound from their lower lip in concert with an abrupt upward movement of their chin. I asked my copilots to explain the meaning of this gesture, and with a chuckle, they said it meant, "Kiss the camel's ass."

Mr. Montpass drove me to the Flight Operations building and escorted me to the Chief Pilot's office. I was introduced to a Captain Mamoud Ayoubkahn who thrust out a hand shake of welcome. Captain Ayoubkahn was about six feet four and weighed at least 230 pounds. His deep baritone voice boomed out beneath a large flowing black mustache. He instructed me to pick up my bags and follow him. He led me into a large opulent furnished room which he said was their VIP waiting lounge, but not in use at the moment. He told me to make myself comfortable and he would be back in a few minutes.

About ten minutes later he returned carrying three large manuals. He presented me with a Fokker F-27 Flight Manual, an F-27 Performance Manual, and an Air Taxi Company Procedures Manual. He said that since the VIP lounge was not in use, I could make myself comfortable and begin a self-study program and if there was anything else that I needed he would be in his office. He abruptly left without providing any guidance on lodging, company identification badges, uniforms, flight checks, or transportation to a hotel. I sat for a few minutes in a huge overstuffed white leather chair, with my rumbling empty stomach demanding food, and my eye lids fighting to stay open for lack of sleep.

I didn't want to be caught sleeping on the job within an hour of reporting for work, so I decided I should explain my dilemma to Captain Ayoubkahn. I went to his office and told him that I had not slept more than a couple hours in the past three days, hadn't eaten a good meal for the last 24 hours, was in a desperate need of a shower and didn't have a place to stay. Captain Ayoubkahn looked up from his desk and said, "What do you have in mind, Captain Martin?"

I suggested that I proceed to downtown Tehran, secure a hotel room, eat a hardy meal, and after a good night's rest commence my self-study program in the privacy of a hotel room. He thought this was a good plan and instructed his dispatch office to provide me with transportation. He recommended I try the Tehran International Hotel and to call back with a telephone number where I could be contacted. Before being dismissed he wanted to know how much time I needed before I would be ready for testing on the material contained in the manuals he provided. I told him two or three days should be sufficient. He nodded in agreement.

I obtained a room in the Tehran International Hotel and was pleased to find it comfortably furnished with Western-style furniture. As the name implied, it was truly international with guests from many different nationalities registered. The lobby and dining room was a mirror image of the United Nations, but English was the prominent language spoken.

Abadan, Bandar Abbas, Esfahan, Kerman, Shiraz and Tehran and other major cities in Iran were overflowing with expatriates from most advanced western countries. Tehran, as the capital, was the main distribution point for this foreign labor force.

Finding adequate Western-style living quarters was a problem, but high salaries compensated for many of the hardships encountered. When I arrived in Tehran there were approximately 35,000 Americans living and working in the city, along with thousands of British, Canadians, French, Germans, Indians, Japanese, Pakistanis, etc. It was exciting to be part of transforming Iran from a backward 17th century country into a modern state. (More on this in a later chapter.)

After three days of self-study, I called Captain Ayoubkahn and informed him that I felt I was sufficiently versed in the operation of the Fokker F-27 aircraft and Air Taxi procedures to undergo a company checkout. He said a crew bus would pick me up at 6 a.m. the following morning to transport me to his office. He would then make arrangements for me to start the process of obtaining company work documents. (See Photo No. 34.)

Captain Ayoubkahn was waiting for me and after a vigorous handshake briefed me on my first day's schedule. The morning would be spent with members of his personnel staff in obtaining identification badges, and completing the forms for obtaining an Iranian Air Transport Pilot's Certificate and an Iranian/FAA Medical Certificate. In the afternoon I would visit the Iranian Civil Aviation Office to complete the F-27 Fokker written exam. He explained that in Iran a closed-book written exam, administered by the government, is given in lieu of the American-style oral exam when obtaining an additional aircraft type rating and License.

The morning was a routine paper mill and after a company lunch of rice, lamb, pita bread, and hot chay (tea), I was ready for the Iranian Government office. Captain Ayoubkhan arranged for a company car to drive me there and wait while I completed the exam. He added that accompanying me would be an older Iranian copilot, by the name of Mohammad Ahmadi, who was also scheduled to take the F-27 written exam as he was hoping to upgrade him to captain.

The government testing room was a standard secure area designed for aptitude testing of aircraft mechanics and pilots alike. The room consisted of two long tables with a testing monitor's desk off to one side. The monitor, after comparing name identification with a prearranged testing schedule, issued the proper exams. The Iranian copilot and myself were issued 100-question multiple choice exams along with answer sheets and sharp number two lead pencils. We were told a 75 percent passing grade was required for successful completion. With that, he invited us to take a seat. I sat down at one of the tables, and my Iranian colleague took a seat right next to me.

I considered the exam straight forward and didn't feel I would have any problem in passing. I first addressed only the questions I was confident I knew the answers to, and bypassed the others. I then counted the number of questions I had answered correctly to compute my score up to that point. I determined that I had already achieved a passing grade of 77 percent and could therefore leisurely work on completing the questions I had bypassed.

I glanced over at Mr. Ahmadi's position to check on his progress and noted, with surprise, that his answer sheet was a mirror image of mine. The questions I had answered he had answered identically, and the questions I had bypassed, he also bypassed. It was obvious he had copied my answer sheet question by question.

Not wishing to be accused of "cooperating to graduate," I covered my answer sheet with my elbow while answering the remaining 23 questions. This did not meet with Mohammad's approval and he started whispering louder and louder for me to move my arm so he could see my answer sheet. His whispers were starting to draw the attention of the test monitor who put down his magazine and began staring in our direction. I quickly answered the remaining questions and submitted my exam to the test overseer. He said my company would be informed the next day regarding the results of the test. As I left the room, I told my copilot buddy I would wait for him outside in the hall.

About 30 minutes later he emerged and was obviously upset in my shielding my answer sheet while answering the last 23 questions. I told him that it was obvious that he had marked his answer sheet exactly like mine and I didn't want our test results to reflect a 100 percent similarity so I left the room when I finished my exam.

He started to grill me on how I had responded to several questions that he was forced to answer on his own. By the nature of his questions it became readily apparent that although we both had been issued F-27 aircraft exams, they were not identical tests. This explained why the test monitor allowed us to sit next to each other during the examining process.

I explained to my Iranian pilot friend that it was clear that we had been issued different F-27 exams. He started to turn pale as the reality of it sank in. He asked me what I thought he might have scored on the test. I told him that since it was obvious we had different exams, and that since he had marked his answer sheet exactly like mine, he would be lucky if he made 10 or 15 percent.

With the color in his face now almost gone he wondered out loud what the Chief Pilot would say if he completely bombed the exam. Not being able to answer his question, I suggested we head back to the company as our driver was waiting. In a weak voice he told me to go ahead without him as he was going to hang around and see if the test monitor could grade his exam before giving the results to the company Chief Pilot.

The next morning I rode the crew bus to the company to find out what I was scheduled for next in my check-out program. The Chief Pilot saw me and extended congratulations on my passing the Fokker F-27 written exam. He said I had passed with a score of 87 percent, very impressive. He added that the next step was to secure a First Class Medical Certificate from an FAA approved Iranian doctor in downtown Tehran. He said that he would call for an appointment and in the mean time I could relax in the pilot's lounge.

As I entered the lounge, I spotted my F-27 written test buddy, Mr. Ahmadi, standing with a group of Iranian pilots drinking chay and eating fresh pita bread smeared with copious amounts of cream goat cheese. He seemed to be in good spirits so I assumed he had passed the exam, although I couldn't understand how.

As I walked up to him he thrust out his hand while greeting me with Salam-U-Alaikum (God be with you). I asked him in a subdued voice how he made out with the test monitor the day before. With a big smile he pulled me aside stating that the luckiest thing happened after I had left.

He said he talked to the test monitor in the hopes of obtaining his test results, but the monitor couldn't find his answer sheet. He said they looked all over for it, but it was obviously lost and no report could be sent to the company. He said he would have to take the exam again at some later date. It was clear to me that he had entered into a Bakhsheesh ("under-the-table") bribe arrangement with the test monitor to trash his answer sheet. I congratulated him on his good fortune and he happily returned to his tea drinking Iranian pilot colleagues. (This was my first exposure to the long established system of Bakhsheesh "payola" which I was to learn was a standard way of doing business in Iran.)

The Chief Pilot sought me out and said he had made an appointment with their local flight surgeon, Doctor Beyrami, to examine me for the issuance of a First Class Medical Certificate. He wrote the doctor's name and address (in Farsi) on a piece of paper and said a company driver would drop me off in front of the doctor's office on the way into town to pick up a couple flight attendants.

My driver on this trip was not an aspiring NASCAR driver, but as before spoke no English. Somewhere in the bowels of Tehran, he stopped and said, "Enja" (Get out). I found myself standing on a busy sidewalk with scores of bearded men and chador-shrouded women shuffling back and forth. Their head-down movements were accompanied by a steady cadence of horn-blowing, smoke-belching, lawnmower-size automobiles.

All the signs on the various business places and shops were in Farsi, as well as the note given to me by the Chief Pilot. Assuming the driver had let me out close to my intended destination I started going from door to door attempting to match up the scribbling on my note with the scribbling on the various windows and doors.

After a frustrating search, I finally found a sign on a door which I thought matched the hieroglyphics on my directions. I opened it and saw a stairway leading to second floor offices. I proceeded up creaking steps that emptied onto a semi dark hallway illuminated by a single low wattage naked light bulb. I again started comparing the writings on my note with the signs on the office doors. To my amazement, a door in the middle of the hallway matched the Farsi writings on my Chief Pilot's note and underneath, in English, "Dr. Beyrami, Welcome."

With a feeling of great accomplishment, but unsure of what to expect, I entered Dr. Beyrami's office. The waiting room was sparsely furnished, dimly lit, and had two rows of straight back chairs for waiting patients. Acknowledging my entrance were six women dressed from head to toe in flowing black chadors. Only their piercing black eyes were visible. As if connected together, all six heads turned toward me as I entered the room.

A receptionist's desk was in the far corner, but there was no one sitting behind it. I stood like a statue next to it while the six Muslim women raised their eyes and stared in my direction. Their looking directly at me was unusual as Muslim women customarily drop their eyes in the presence of men, but I guess their curiosity in seeing a foreign male in their midst triumphed over adhering to Muslim custom. There was complete silence, as no one spoke and the room was void of background music. I could hear sounds of activity in the next room, so I just stood there waiting.

After a few minutes a nurse, dressed in a white Western-style uniform, appeared stating, "Salam-U-Alaikum" (God be with you), and in broken English asked me my name? After responding, I was told that the doctor was expecting me and to follow her into his examination room. A tall well groomed man, dressed in a white smock and sporting a thick black mustache, stood and greeted me as I entered. I was pleased when in strongly accented, but understandable English, he invited me to sit-down.

While checking my pulse rate he asked how I was feeling. As he strapped the blood pressure cuff around my arm I said I was feeling fine. Satisfied with my blood pressure, he asked me to open the front of my shirt so he could listen to my heart. Passing the stethoscope test he asked if I wore glasses. Receiving a "no" answer he inquired as to my hearing. I told him my hearing was excellent and with that he proclaimed me in excellent health and proceeded to complete the FAA First Class Medical Certificate form. I asked if he was going to need a urine sample and was told no. I informed him that I had been holding off on emptying my bladder and it was about to burst. He pointed to a room which I could use while he completed the paperwork.

Within ten minutes of entering his office I walked out with a current First Class FAA Aviation Medical Certificate and an empty bladder. Back on the noisy busy street I hailed an orange colored community taxi which I hoped was going in the direction of my hotel.

(I updated my FAA Medical Certificate every six months, with the same doctor, but in future visits arrived with an empty bladder. I don't know what Air Taxi paid for each medical renewal, but whatever it was, it was too much!)

Chapter Three --- Aircraft Checkout

Following my successful completion of the Fokker F-27 Written Exam, and the Iranian Aviation Medical Exam, the Chief Pilot proclaimed me ready for a check out in the aircraft. He reminded me that when I was hired I had stated I could qualify in only two training flights, not to exceed five hours, so that was all he was prepared to offer. (See Photo No. 2.)

Although the Air Taxi Company was ostensibly a civilian organization, it had close ties with the Iranian military. In fact, many of their 25 plus aircraft bore Iranian military markings. The Air Taxi fleet of aircraft included the French *Falcon* Fan-jet DA-20, the Dutch Fokker F-27 *Friendship*, the U.S. North American Rockwell *Turbo Commander* 690A, the North American *Shrike* Commander, and later the U.S. Fairchild FH-227. I was told that a Colonel Madnia, from the Imperial Iranian Air Force, would be my instructor and examiner for my check out in the F-27.

I arrived at the airport early and the company dispatcher informed me that the aircraft to be used in my first training flight with Colonel Madnia was EP-52601, one of their newer F-27s. A young Iranian copilot would be occupying the jump seat as observer. I had about three hours to kill before engine start so I decided to devote a couple hours sitting in the cockpit reviewing normal and emergency operating procedures. I felt this exposure would be helpful as I had never been in the cockpit of a F-27.

Except for a few minor exceptions, I was pleased to discover that the actual aircraft controls, instruments and switches matched the description outlined in the flight manual I had been studying in my hotel room. Being a turboprop aircraft, it was quite similar to the YS-11 I had flown in Japan, but in addition possessed many differences and required a separate aircraft type rating endorsement by the FAA and the Iranian government.

The Iranian military Fokker *Friendship* I was to fly this day was an F-27-200. It had a 95-foot wingspan, was 82-feet long, powered by two Rolls Royce Dart turboprop engines producing 2000 HP each, had a 42,000 pound gross weight, a seating capacity of 44, and cruised at 275 miles per hour. After two hours of concentrated cockpit self-study I found I could locate most controls and switches without too much “hunt and peck.” I figured I was ready for the colonel! After a short "pee and tea" break, I and my young Iranian jump seat observer were standing at the front of the aircraft awaiting Colonel Madnia.

From a distance, I observed a blue military staff car speeding across the airport ramp and heading in our direction. Its headlights were on bright and a red rotating beacon was warning onlookers to get out of the way. The brightly polished car came to an abrupt stop next to the aircraft and the driver rushed to open the rear door. With a mechanical like movement, he snapped open the door, clicked his heels, came to attention, and popped a salute to the emerging colonel.

Colonel Madnia was a dapper man of about 40, six feet tall, a slim 180 pounds, sporting a neatly trimmed black mustache, wearing large dark sunglasses, and dressed in a tailor-made blue flight suit decorated with colorful military unit patches. Around his neck was a white silk scarf. Topping off this eye-snapping appearance was a large garrison style military cap embellished with lightning bolts on the visor and gold rope trim on each side. His feet were encased in brightly polished black Jodhpur style zip-up boots. His appearance was very impressive and would put the Blue Angels and Thunderbird Pilots to shame.

He thrust out his hand while stating "Salam-U-Alaikum" (God be with you, peace). He was surprised when I responded with, "Wa Alaykumus Salam" (Thank you, an expression I had just learned from our jump seat observer). In fluent English he said "You must be Captain Martin, pleased to meet you." I echoed his sentiments and he asked me if an aircraft preflight had been completed. I told him no, as I was waiting to see what his requirements were. He nodded in agreement, while instructing me to preflight the right side while he did the left. He added that when we were finished, we would meet in the cockpit.

I performed what I considered a somewhat thorough, but hasty walk around inspection of the right side of the aircraft, and noted that when I approached the cockpit the colonel was already strapped in the right seat and obviously eager to get going. I positioned myself in the captain's seat and asked for the Before Starting Engines Checklist. The colonel said he had already completed it and requested I perform, by memory, an Auto Feather Check of the propellers.

The Fokker F-27 is equipped with a safety system that will detect a power loss of either engine during the critical takeoff phase of flight. Sensing this power loss, the affected propeller will automatically move to a low drag, feathered position. It is possible to test the operation of this automatic system before starting the engines by arranging the throttles and power levers in such a manner as to fake a power loss. Once each propeller is observed moving towards the feathered position the test is discontinued. This check is normally performed by maintenance personnel and therefore was not part of my self-study program.

Not wishing to attempt a complicated procedure I had not incorporated into my self-study program, I told the colonel I had not committed the procedure to memory. With a grunt, he said he would show me how it was performed. He whipped through the procedure by rapid fore and aft movement of throttles and power levers and declared the system functional. I was then instructed to start the engines, albeit my first time in this type aircraft.

The engine start worked out OK and I felt we were almost ready to taxi. But before I could call for the Before Taxi Checklist the effulgent colonel requested taxi instructions from the tower and was giving me excited hand signals that indicated he wanted me to get moving. Fortunately, I had operated out of the Tehran Mehrabad Airport some seven years previously, when a pilot in the U.S. Air Force, so I remembered that there was only one main 10,000 foot long East/West runway so I knew which way to go without asking the colonel for guidance.

During the rapid taxi Colonel Madnia said he would complete the Before Takeoff Checklist so we would be ready to go upon reaching the end of the runway. Noting that both engines were running and all instruments were in the green, I figured we could safely get airborne even if we hadn't run the Before Starting Engine Check, Before Taxi Check, and the Before Takeoff Check. (The aircraft checklist booklet I so diligently studied remained in my unopened flight bag.)

The tower cleared us for takeoff and in spite of a field elevation of 4,000 feet the acceleration was rapid and we were quickly airborne. I was impressed by the nimble feel of the flight controls and noted that it was much more responsive than the Japanese YS-11. The colonel instructed me to take up a heading of 180 degrees and climb to 10,000 feet.

After level off I trimmed the aircraft for straight and level flight at which time I was instructed to perform a 360-degree steep turn to the left and right. Both steep turns resulted in flying through my own prop wash, which resulted in a nod from the colonel without comment. He then said, "We now do stalls." Without guidance from him I went through a series of turning and straight and level stalls in both a clean, (gear and flaps up) and dirty, (gear and flaps down). These maneuvers produced another nod and grunt from the colonel.

The next command was, "Feather and unfeather the right propeller." Successful completion of this procedure brought another nod. The next long-winded command from the dapper Iranian Air Force colonel was, "Return to the airport for pattern work."

After performing a series of touch-and-go landings, and several simulated engine failures during takeoff, the talkative colonel said, "Make this landing full stop." I taxied back to the Air Taxi Company ramp and as the engines were winding down I observed the colonel's staff car parked near the front of the aircraft. My first training flight of two and one-half hours was history.

While exiting the cockpit, he instructed me to complete the flight logbook, learn the auto feather propeller check procedure, and stated that we would fly again the next day, at the same time. He climbed into his chauffeur driven staff car which went speeding across the ramp with its red rotating beacon flashing brightly.

The post flight debriefing for my first flight was over in 30 seconds. However, my young Iranian copilot agreed to remain with me in the cockpit and for the next hour we went through the auto feather propeller check until I could whip through it blindfolded. I was now ready for day two with the colorful Iranian Air Force bird colonel!

The brightly polished staff car, with its rotating red beacon flashing, arrived on schedule. The colonel was dressed in the same dapper flight suit, he had worn the day before, and as he stepped from his staff car he inquired if the aircraft preflight was complete. I snapped back that the preflight was complete and I was ready to fly. I could see that this met with his approval since he snapped back with, "Let's Go."

He headed for the cockpit in a near trot with me close behind. Before we were strapped in, my faithful young jump seat rider had the main entrance door closed. Without waiting for instructions, I performed a silent before starting engine cockpit check scan without reference to the checklist. I followed this with an auto feather check of both propellers in a whir of positioning throttles and power levers. Still without a word exchanged I inquired, "Right engine clear?" Receiving a nod from the colonel, I started the right engine followed close behind by the left engine. Before the engines had fully stabilized at idle power, I requested the colonel to contact the tower for taxi and takeoff clearance. I advanced power on both engines and had us moving at a quick pace down the taxi way as our taxi clearance was being issued. I sensed the colonel was pleased in what he saw.

I performed a before takeoff cockpit check by memory during the taxi and upon approaching the active runway requested he call the tower for takeoff clearance. Takeoff clearance came back immediately and we went from taxi to takeoff without making a stop at the end of the runway.

The aircraft, being lightly loaded, accelerated rapidly and the colonel's V1 call (takeoff decision speed) was followed by his retarding the right throttle to idle and announcing, "Simulated engine failure." I called for maximum power on the left engine, corrected the yaw to the right with hard left rudder, instructed the colonel to simulate the feathering of the right propeller, declared a simulated emergency with the tower and requested an immediate return for landing. He nodded compliance with my instructions and by hand signals instructed me to execute a single engine climb to the south.

At 9,500 feet he gave a flat hand signal which I interpreted as a command to level off. My dashing colonel, in his first words since stating "Simulated engine failure" requested I perform a 360 degree steep turn to the right and left. This was followed with power off approaches to stall and recovery with minimum loss of altitude. I was then instructed to perform a series of standard rate turns at minimum single engine control speed. Receiving a nod of satisfaction on these maneuvers, he instructed me to return to the airport for a simulated single engine landing. During the landing roll out, I received another nod of approval as he advanced the right throttle to full power while stating, "Touch-and-go."

We remained in the airport traffic pattern for two more touch-and-go landings followed by a full stop. Not a word was said as I taxied back to the colonel's waiting staff car.

After the engines were cut and I completed, by memory, an Engine Shutdown Check, Colonel Madnia turned to me and said, "What do you think about night flying, Captain Martin?" I responded with, "When it gets dark I turn on the lights!" With the first smile I saw on his face in two days he said, "Good answer, congratulations on passing your type rating check in the F-27." True to my promise, I completed transition to the Fokker *Friendship* in two flights for a total flight time of five hours. The last I saw of this flamboyant colonel, he was speeding back across the aircraft ramp in his blue staff car with a siren blaring, rotating beacon flashing and headlights on high-beam!

Chapter Four --- Initial Operating Experience

With an Iranian FAA First Class Medical Certificate and a Fokker F-27 type rating in hand, I reported to Chief Pilot Ayoubkahn stating I was ready to go to work. The flight operations unit consisted of four individual flight sections with a Flight Leader in charge of each. I was introduced to Captain Bokhari, who was to be my immediate boss. He was a retired Pakistani Air Force Colonel and had worked for the company for a year or more. Captain Bokhari was a portly man in his mid forties, spoke English with a pleasing Indian accent, wore his hair in a crew cut style, and sported a pencil thin black mustache.

He welcomed me to the company and said as soon as I obtained a uniform he would start my left seat line training. He suggested I contact the personnel manager for permission to be fitted by their tailor in Tehran. I told Captain Bokhari that obtaining an Air Taxi uniform might take several weeks and I was ready to start line training straight away. His response was that company policy required all pilots to be in uniform. I countered that I was in possession of a Captain's uniform I had brought with me from Japan, and it was almost identical to the uniform worn by Air Taxi pilots. With the assurance of being in proper attire he said I could start flying the next day, and should stop by the dispatch section to ensure they were aware of my Tehran address and telephone number.

However, a few days later I did visit the company's tailor shop and was measured for uniforms. I was issued two tailor-made winter and summer uniforms, six shirts, three black ties, and a three-pound hat the size of a large dinner plate. (No one wore the hat because it was so heavy it gave you a headache!) I then visited a boot maker and was issued two pairs of tailor made jodhpur style zip-up black boots like Colonel Madnia's.

During my first two weeks in Iran, I maintained a room in the International Hotel. However, Matt Matthews, an Air Taxi American pilot colleague from California, invited me to share a three-bedroom apartment he was time-sharing with a Mr. Gibson, an American certified accountant working for a company in downtown Tehran. I jumped at the opportunity and settled down in a spacious private room on the third floor of a new apartment building in the Northern section of Tehran. My bedroom had a splendid view of the Alborz Mountains, which reached heights of nearly 12,000 feet and were usually snow covered year around. On a clear day it was also possible to view the 18,550-foot Mt. Damavand, the highest mountain in Iran which resembled Mount Fugiyama in Japan.

Across the street from the apartment was a vacant lot used as a dumping ground for household garbage. This lot attracted packs of mangy looking wild dogs which roamed at will about the city. It was not uncommon to be awakened in the middle of the night by the sounds of one or more dogs fighting over scraps of food. Needless to say I never saw a stray cat roaming about. (A cat would have been nothing more than an appetizer for my K-9 neighbors.) (See Photo No. 19 and 26.)

Adding to the ambiance was the frequent sound of camel caravans coming down from the hills. The lead camel would wear a string of brass bells around it's neck, while the rest followed the melodic clanking in a nose to tail procession. There was also the occasional bleating of sheep herds being driven to market. I certainly knew I was no longer in Wisconsin and enjoyed the excitement of being in such a strange land.

My alarm clock sprang to life at 5 a.m. and one hour later I heard the beeping horn of the company Volkswagen crew bus. Already in the bus were several half-asleep young Iranian copilots and female flight attendants. They were not bashful in stating that I must be the new American pilot and started peppering me with questions. Before we reached the airport, they knew my life history. I didn't consider them rude, just extremely curious about life beyond Iran.

En route to the airport we stopped at an open-air bakery where the driver purchased a large stack of freshly baked pita bread, along with a large amount of fresh goat cheese.

After arriving at the flight crew lounge, I joined an already assembled group of flight crew members for a breakfast of fresh pita bread, cream goat cheese and strong hot chay (tea). I soon learned that this would be a morning ritual while working in Iran and began looking forward to it.

I met Captain Bokhari at the dispatch counter who informed me that my first line qualification flight would be a round trip to Khark Island.

Khark Island contains a very important deep water crude oil loading facility for the Iranian oil industry. Situated in the Persian Gulf, it provides a secure harbor for giant oil tankers. Oil is pumped through underwater pipes where it is stored in huge tank farms awaiting transfer to tankers from around the world. Because of its importance, it was guarded by the Iranian Navy and access to it was tightly controlled. It was bombed extensively by Iraqi fighter bombers during the Iran/Iraq war from 1980 to 1988. Considerable damage to the oil facility was the result. Khark Island was also famous for the harvesting of shrimp from the Persian Gulf. I could purchase a five-pound box of frozen jumbo shrimp for around 820 rials ($12). (See Photo No. 1.)

After a two-hour flight, we started a descent and a very impressive sight began to fill the windshield. Khark Island stood out like a white jewel in the blue Persian Gulf, but much more startling was the extent of the oil loading facility. There was a seemingly endless number of large white oil storage tanks dotting the landscape, and 20 or more giant oil tankers, riding at anchor, awaiting their turn to take on oil. It was interesting to note how high the empty tankers rode in the water, versus fully loaded ones leaving and slowly making their way toward the Gulf of Oman.

The final approach to the runway was over a fleet of waiting tankers, which provided such an interesting sight it required a concerted effort to keep my eyes on the rising runway. (Flying to Khark Island was to become a routine destination in my years in Iran and it became an interesting game to count the number of tankers waiting for oil, and their countries of origin. It was not unusual to count 20 or more.)

After a quick lunch in the Iranian Navy Officers' Club of "Chelo Kebab" (Baby goat Kebab on a bed of rice) we headed back to Tehran. My first left seat line orientation flight of five hours was history and Captain Bokhari seemed pleased with my performance.

My next qualification flight was to Bushier, a large oil-producing city on the Persian Gulf and just across the bay from Khark Island. The airport was a joint-use civilian and Iranian navy facility. We would spend the night in Bushier before flying back to Tehran. Since this was my first overnight stay, I was curious as to what sort of accommodations would be provided since when flying for Japan Airlines flight crews were always billeted in first class hotels. I was shocked to discover that my accommodation for the night was a steel cot in an Iranian navy enlisted men's open bay dormitory, which I shared with about 20 other men. The shower and latrine were 30 feet down a half-lit concrete hallway. Sleep was nearly impossible, as my throaty Persian room mates held a snoring contest that lasted the entire night. (I would have been hard pressed to declare a winner as they were all champions.)

During our flight back to Tehran, I told Captain Bokhari that I would not accept overnight accommodations like that in the future. He tried to convince me that it was a good deal as we were not charged for sleeping in the Iranian navy open dormitory, and we would still receive our full per diem allowance from the company. I told him he could keep the money, but henceforth I would go to a hotel where I could get a good night's rest.

I made a few more left seat training flights with Captain Bokhari, and Iranian captains to various desert airports and Iranian cities. Every captain I flew with seemed pleased with my performance and proclaimed me close to being qualified to operate on my own. However, before turning me lose the Chief Pilot suggested I fly a few trips with a foreign captain from Holland by the name of McKillen. He said Captain McKillen had flown Fokker F-27s for Athena Airlines in Athens, Greece and I could probably benefit from his experience of flying in the Middle East.

I met Captain McKillen for the first time at the dispatch counter as we were preparing for a series of flights to airports along the Persian Gulf. I noted that he was at least 15 years my junior (maybe 31 or 32-years-old), quite heavy set, and didn't convey the image of airline captains I had known in the past. He said that the Chief Pilot had requested he fly copilot for me for a few trips so that I might gain more experience in flying in Iran. I welcomed his help with a comment that anything he could provide would be greatly appreciated.

Since he was flying as my copilot, it was his task to copy air traffic control clearances, make en route position reports, and coordinate, by radio, with our company dispatch section. I was surprised in his ineptness in fulfilling these simple routine copilot duties and sensed an uneasiness in his completing normal second pilot responsibilities.

During our first few flights together I asked him about his flying experiences in Greece, but he seemed reluctant to provide any details. Since I was undergoing captain line training, I flew from the left seat and made all command decisions, but Captain McKillen was technically the "Pilot-In-Command." I was not informed as to how long I would be "wet-nursed" by my junior instructor, so I just kept pressing on.

Our fifth trip together was a flight from Tehran to Abadan with a full load of passengers. As we approached Abadan the tower informed us that the Instrument Landing System (ILS) was inoperative, but we would be cleared for a non-directional beacon approach (NDB).

A NDB approach is a notorious form of performing bad weather instrument approaches to a landing since the pilot must line the aircraft up on a single radio navigation aid, and use other instruments to maintain proper altitude and adjust for wind direction to stay on course. However, with proper training, an NDB approach can be safely flown, and I had performed literally hundreds when flying for Japan Domestic Airlines.

The control tower stated that the weather was 500 foot overcast with two miles visibility in blowing sand. In checking my airport charts I noted that it was legal for us to perform an NDB approach.

I instructed Captain McKillen to inform the tower that we were commencing a descent and started to reduce power. However, to my surprise, he pushed the throttles back forward to their cruise position. I asked him what he was doing and he said that we were going to return to Tehran as he didn't like NDB approaches. I told him that the weather met our minimums, and that we were going to land at Abadan.

He responded that he was the "Pilot-In-Command" and directed that we return to Tehran. I countered that I was at least 15 years older than he was, had nearly 15,000 hours of flight time, had made literally hundreds of NDB non-precision approaches, and was going to deliver our 44 passengers to the airport they bought tickets for. I again reduced power, executed an approach, and had the field in sight at 600 feet. An uneventful landing followed. The cockpit chatter during our return flight to Tehran was very subdued, which suited me just fine!

After landing in Tehran, I went directly to the Chief Pilot's office and after informing him of my dissatisfaction with Captain McKillen during our flight to Abadan, told him I had been exposed to enough left seat familiarization training and was ready to fly as captain without additional supervision. His response was a simple OK, adding that starting the next day I would fly with regular line copilots. (I was learning more each day that in Iran if you don't speak up you will be trampled by the crowd. Flying for an Iranian Air Charter company was much different from flying for a Japanese scheduled airline. The very nature of the operation was a "you call, we fly" basis.)

The Air Taxi's fleet of 25 aircraft provided support for customers ranging from the Shah's family, high ranking Iranian government officials, the Iranian Navy, oil field rough necks, foreign construction companies and scheduled passenger flights for the National Iranian Oil Industries Company. The procedure for learning my next day's flight schedule was to call the dispatch office each day between 5:00 and 7:00 p.m. The dispatcher would provide me with my crew bus pickup time, flight departure time, aircraft type and destination.

I would normally be scheduled to fly six out of seven days. The uncertainty of the destination, aircraft type and mission made the flying very interesting. One day I would be flying high ranking government VIPs to villas on the Caspian Sea, and the next day transporting burly foreign oil field workers to remote desert sites. (See Photo No. 32.)

The Iranian copilots possessed a variable amount of flight experience, were generally very young, but a pleasure to fly with. Most were eager to enhance their aviation experience and appreciated constructive help in accomplishing this goal. Some had attended flight schools in the United States and their expertise in the cockpit was reflective of this specialized training. Copilots stated that to obtain an Iranian exit visa to attend flight training in the U.S., it was necessary for them to post a $10,000 bond, (About $38,000 in today's dollars) which would be forfeited if they failed to return. Others who had received their flight training in Iran required constant monitoring.

There was a group of young Iranian navy officers, also flying as copilots, who had spent two years in training with the Fokker Aircraft Company in Amsterdam. Part of my job was to help this group of "hell-for-leather" pilots qualify as Aircraft Commanders. To accomplish this task the company operated six military configured navy F-27s.

Although the weather in Iran was generally favorable for flying there were times when, due to rain showers or blowing sand storms, instrument flight was necessary. I and the other foreign captains were provided Xerox copies of Jeppesen instrument approach charts and outdated low and high altitude navigation charts. We were told this system was used to save money, and in addition, we would soon commit to memory all pertinent aeronautical information in Iran, so individual subscriptions to aeronautical approach charts and maps was not considered necessary.

Iranian captains were issued individual Jeppesen publications, but it was apparent they were not inserting biweekly update revisions. I noted that several pilots had stacks of unopened revision envelopes stuffed in their flight bags. Most showed no desire to ensure their publications were current as they considered it too time consuming to bother with inserting changes, every two weeks, when the weather was generally very good.

In spot checking some of my Xerox copies of aeronautical publications I noted that many were outdated by several months. I spoke to the Chief Pilot about the problem of outdated navigation publications, but he wasn't prone to authorize the money, time or effort to provide individual subscriptions to his small number of foreign captains.

I was finally able to persuade him to agree that if the foreign pilots split the initial cost of a limited Middle East subscription the company would pay the balance. I contacted the other foreign captains who readily agreed and we were soon provided with individual current publications from the Jeppesen Company in Frankfurt, Germany. I noted that Iranian captains still stuffed unopened revision envelopes in their flight bags, or between pages of the Jeppesen manual, and the copilots continued using outdated Xerox copies.

Within a couple of months I had flown into most of the airports serving major cities and prominent military bases. My basic salary of $3,000 per month ($11,300 in today's dollars), for 75 hours of flight time, was top of the line in 1976. Our contract called for time and a half pay for anything beyond 75 hours. I soon learned that it was wise to allow my Iranian copilots to maintain the flight logs as their sharp pencils could easily add 10 to 15 hours extra time each month. My total take home pay was generally more than a foreign captain flying a B-707 for Iran Air.

The problem was that my entire salary was paid in Iranian rial bank notes. Each month, I would stand in line at the paymaster's window along with janitors, handymen, and secretaries, who would be drawing a small amount of rials. When it came my turn to be paid, the cashier would count out a huge stack of rials. It was initially somewhat embarrassing, but I learned to live with it. If I was due overtime pay, I generally had to engage in a heated argument with the paymaster over the amount of additional pay due. I soon learned to bring my flight log book with me to reflect the extra hours flown and not leave his window until paid, even if I held up the line. During my first visit to the paymaster I took his word that he would get back to me, regarding overtime pay, but I had a devil of a time in collecting it. Once paid, I would stuff my stack of rials into my flight bag and head for the American Express Office in downtown Tehran.

At the American Express Office, I would stand in line with other foreigners for the purpose of converting my Iranian rials into U.S. dollars. The cost of conversion would be one percent of the total. The Iranian operating the office was flanked by an armed guard and slowly counted out the rials each customer was converting. He would meticulously separate them into denominations of 50, 100, 1,000, and 10,000 notes and when in agreement with the dollar amount to be exchanged, issue crisp one hundred U.S. dollar bank notes.

Once I initialed his pay sheet he would rake all the rials he so carefully sorted into a large open desk drawer. (Obviously they would have to be separated and counted again later.) There were times that my busy flight schedule would not allow me to exchange money at the American Express Office, so I opened a savings account in an Iranian Bank close to my apartment. (More on this mistake in a later chapter.)

After a couple months of sharing an apartment with two not-so-easy to-get-along-with men set in their ways, I decided it was time to find an apartment of my own. There were approximately 100,000 foreigners working in Tehran in 1976, and finding Western-style housing was quite difficult and expensive. The first subject of discussion at social gatherings of foreigners was, "Where did you find a place to live, and how much did you have to pay?"

In the search of an apartment, I visited an Iranian housing agent to inquire if he had a furnished apartment available that would accommodate me and an occasional guest. He told me that he had just come across a small apartment, owned by an Iranian woman whose husband had recently died and was moving to Paris to live with her daughter for a year or more. She was interested in renting her second floor apartment to a foreigner for a minimum of at least one year. However, he added that he didn't think I would be interested in it since it did not have central heating or air-conditioning. I inquired if the apartment had a telephone. When he replied that it did, I told him I would like to see it.

Her apartment was on the second floor of a duplex shared with her brother and sister-in-law, and her 13-year-old (English-speaking) niece occupying the first floor. The agent introduced me to a middle-age Iranian woman by the name of Mrs. Amini. The apartment consisted of a very long and narrow living room in which she had placed a bed at one end. It also had a fairly large dining room, a small, but adequate, kitchen and an Iranian-style bathroom. The toilet was a standard porcelain hole in the floor with two raised foot pads designed for squatting. Most Iranians did not use toilet paper, instead relying on a strong squirt of cold water from a decorative hose for cleansing the derriere. (See Photos 30 and 31.)

This method of personal hygiene was certainly an eye opener on cold mornings, but in spite of this, I preferred toilet paper.

The air-conditioner was a water evaporator on the roof and the heat source was a kerosene (naft) fed space heater. I told them that I would take the apartment if they would install a Western-style toilet. The agent and his non-English-speaking client agreed, and we settled on a monthly rent of 35,000 rials ($1,900 in today's rates) with one month's rent going to the agent, and one month's rent as a security deposit. We agreed to meet to consummate the deal after a Western-style toilet was installed.

A few days later the housing agent informed me that Mrs. Amini was ready to sign the rental lease and requested I attend a meeting in her apartment the next day. When I arrived I was surprised to see about 12 people gathered around the dining room table. Most of the women were dressed in head-to-toe black chador robes, while the men were wearing 1950s-style business suits and soup-stained faded ties. My housing agent introduced me to brothers, sisters, uncles, aunts and friends of my future landlady and invited me to take a seat before a steaming hot cup of chay (Iranian tea). I asked the agent why the mini United Nations meeting, just to sign a rental lease. His response was that my landlady's relatives and friends wanted to meet the foreigner who was going to live in her apartment, as this was their first opportunity of meeting a real American pilot face-to-face.

The agent inquired if I had brought enough cash to cover his commission, one month's advance rent and one month's security deposit. I said I had, but before making payment I wanted to see the Western-style toilet that had been promised. I got up from the table and walked toward the bathroom with the landlady's entire entourage following. Crowded around the toilet my landlady, with the agent acting as interpreter, proudly began explaining the operation of the toilet. It was obvious that she was especially proud of the flushing action when she pulled the chain dangling from the overhead water reservoir. She was joined in this show of admiration by her family members poking their heads into the narrow doorway. She wanted to know if I understood her detailed demonstration.

Without wanting to sound insulting, I thanked her for the "show and tell" while stating that I was sure I could handle it, but wasn't ready to display this knowledge at this time. She blushed in acknowledgment. However, there was one last bit of instruction she wished to convey, but it wasn't filtering through the interpretation. Her embarrassment in providing these instructions was obvious, along with the agent's inability to find English words to make her meaning clear. After additional prying into what she was attempting to tell me, it became clear that she was saying that soiled toilet paper was not to be discarded in the toilet, but placed in a small waste paper basket she had provided. She and her family friends were very much relieved when I acknowledged that I understood completely the operation of the toilet, and what to do with used toilet paper.

Needless to say, I discarded used toilet paper in the same manner as my mother had taught me many years earlier, and the toilet handled the additional burden with no problem.

We then returned to the table for the formal lease signing. After the proper signatures were affixed to a three-page document, (printed in Farsi) cash payments were made. I received a congratulatory hand shake from all members in attendance and was handed the keys to an apartment at 33 Ladan Alley, Tehran, Iran. (See Photos No. 30 and 31.)

My landlady had decorated her apartment with numerous inexpensive carnival-like knickknacks that cluttered every available shelf space. Along with garish dolls and stuffed animals, every room was also decorated with a framed color photo of the Shah. Throughout Iran it was standard policy to display the Shah's picture in every home, shop, place of business or public building. In fact, various business places frequently vied with one another in displaying the largest and most decorative framed photo of the Shah. Considering that I was never very far from one, I was determined that my apartment would not follow this pattern.

I carefully packed my landlady's cheap knickknacks along with the photos of the Shah in a large box for placement in her storage room. Apparently my landlady, in my absence, had visited the apartment and noted that I had packed up her many personal items and disapproved of what she discovered.

Within a day or so after moving in she was at my door with her English-speaking 13-year-old niece. She strongly chastised me for removing her cherished knickknacks, and was especially angry that I had removed the photos of the Shah. With her niece acting as interpreter I told her that her personal possessions were so valuable that I didn't wish to assume the responsibility of protecting them while she was in Paris. This seemed to satisfy her regarding her inexpensive ornaments, but she wouldn't accept this as a reason for removing her photos of the Shah. To get her off my back I replaced the Shah's photos. She left for Paris the next day, and the Shah's portraits went back into storage.

During one of my flights I told an Iranian copilot about my bout with my landlady and how I had removed the pictures of the Shah. Without hesitation he said this was a big mistake. His reasoning was that if the Savak (secret police) visited my apartment, and didn't see photos of the Shah, it would cause suspicion. I asked him why the Savak would find it necessary to visit my apartment. Again, without hesitation, he stated you never know, since you are a foreigner, it's better to be prepared. (This illustrates the fear the Shah's government instilled in the Iranian population in 1976 as most citizens knew of friends or family members locked up in the many prisons throughout Iran.)

I was fast beginning to feel like a real American expatriate. I was regularly flying the line as a qualified captain, had my own apartment, was starting to make friends with other foreigners and had joined the U.S. Army Officers' Club in the exclusive Northern section of Tehran, known as Sultanabad. Life certainly promised to get interesting. (See Photo No. 10.)

I was also feeling comfortable in taking long walks in downtown Tehran, and always found interesting sights, sounds and smells. Street vendors sold tasty boiled red beets, heated over small propane heaters, and provided a common fork to passing customers, but I carried my own.

Sheep herders would bring their flocks into town and go from door-to-door in attempting to sell fresh lamb on the hoof. A black chador robed housewife would select a lamb she wished to purchase and the herder would butcher it for her right there on the street. The sheep selected would give out loud pathetic cries as it was killed with a single cut to the throat as it was forced to face Mecca. (This ritual killing, known as "Halal-killed" is in compliance with Islamic laws and followed by devout Muslims.) The remaining herd, not wanting to be next, would crowd together in the corner of a nearby building. The butchered lamb would be skinned and gutted openly on the public street and its entrails thrown into the gutter, to be eaten by roving packs of wild dogs before the day was over. The dressed carcass would be delivered to the lady of the house followed by the herder stuffing blood-stained rials into his pocket.

Crossing streets was a real challenge as traffic signals served only as a suggestion, not the rule of law. Drivers were apparently convinced that their automobiles would stop dead if the horn was not blowing continuously. Automobiles, to move ahead a few feet, would climb sidewalks and frequently drive the wrong way on one-way streets. A favorite trick in this wrong-way driving at night, would be to back up at high speed with their headlights turned off hoping they would not be seen.

Adding to the din were the shouts of road-rage drivers venting their displeasure at pedestrians, fellow drivers, motorbikes and bicycles. I would often find a safe spot on a busy corner and just watch the bedlam. It was demolition derby, Key Stone Cops and Laurel and Hardy all rolled into one, interspersed with an occasional crash.

I never understood the practice of Persian carpet stores spreading their most expensive rugs out on the sidewalks, and even the streets, which resulted in passing pedestrians and automobiles giving them a used look. According to the merchants, their carpets brought a higher price if they appeared used and weather beaten.

As an on-call charter pilot it was imperative that I have a telephone in my apartment, which if not already installed would take months to obtain. However, I soon learned not to use it for international calls. I made a short three-minute call to Japan which should have cost no more 1,500 rials ($21.00), but when I received my monthly statement the charge for this call was 14,000 rials ($84.00). My protest to the telecommunication office fell on deaf ears and I was told either pay the bill or my telephone would be disconnected. Checking with other foreigners I found out that I was lucky, as others reported inflated charges of several hundred dollars and they were also told to pay up or lose their phones. From then on, I only made international calls by visiting the central government telecommunications office and paying directly for each call made.

Relying on the Iranian postal system was another frustration to overcome. Letters to and from the U.S. could take a month or more and many were lost in a big black hole in Tehran. In contrast the U.S. military operated a post office that was serviced by frequent military flights and provided rapid and reliable state-side-like service.

I thought my status as a retired Air Force officer would authorize me to obtain a military post office box, but I was disappointed when I presented my retired military ID card to the army sergeant in charge. He told me that my **"gray"** colored ID card did not authorize me to use the military post office facilities. He added that only active-duty military personnel possessing **"green"** ID cards were authorized post office boxes.

Fortunately this disappointing news coincided with the Easter season and as I was coloring some Easter eggs my gray retired ID card fell into a dish of hot green dye. By the time I retrieved it, it contained a **"green"** hue very similar to active-duty ID cards. Armed with this lucky break, I obtained a post office box with the military and my postal problems were solved. I held a military post office box for my entire three years in Iran.

Chapter Five --- Tehran the Oil-Rich Boomtown

Iran in 1976 was at the zenith of its program of modernization launched by the Shah's father in 1925. Great Britain established a petroleum-based foothold in Southern Iran in 1919, and in typical British fashion attempted to mold the Iranian countryside to reflect an English way of life. This caused considerable discontent within the Muslim Qajar Dynasty, so England used its political influence to install a military colonel, by the name of Reza Shah Pahlavi (the younger Shah's father), as the dictator of Iran. However, their chosen despotic puppet soon became distrustful of the British and began developing alliances with Adolph Hitler in Nazi Germany and friendly relations with Joseph Stalin in the Soviet Union.

At the start of World War II, England feared Iran's relationship with Germany and the Soviet Union could result in its joining the Axis powers. However, following Germany's surprise attack on the Soviet Union in June 1941, Great Britain and the Soviet Union, now "reluctant" allies, invaded Iran and forced Reza Shah Pahlavi to flee in exile to South Africa, where he died under suspicious circumstances on July 26, 1944 at age 66. They installed as the new dictator of Iran, Mohammad Reza Shah Pahlavi, the 22-year-old pro-Western son of the deposed Shah.

When World War II ended in 1945, the British and U.S. military units (now a part of the occupying force) honored their prewar agreements and withdrew from Iran. However, the Soviet Union took a hard-nosed stand and indicated that they would not leave the Northern section of the country they occupied. President Truman, under the threat of military force (being the only country possessing the atomic bomb), demanded that Soviet Union forces comply with previous commitments and withdraw from Iran. When the Soviet troops finally left, Mohammad Reza Pahlavi declared a renewed allegiance toward the United States.

The Shah's close association with the U.S. was resented by many Iranians and in 1953 he was forced to flee to Switzerland. However, his exile lasted only 24 hours when the CIA forced the overthrow of Prime Minister Mosaddeg. Mohammad Pahlavi returned to Tehran and continued his modernization of Iran at an increased tempo, and with a renewed strong feeling of appreciation toward the United States.

The Shah's "Fast-Track Program" of bringing Iran into the 20th century touched all sections of the country's infrastructure. His plans were to combine the ultramodern with the traditional way of. life. This included implementing or modernizing agriculture farms, airlines, communications, educational institutions, electrical power plants, entertainment facilities, highways, housing, manufacturing plants, medical facilities, railroads, sewers, water purification, etc. This Herculean modernization program required vast sums of capital and large numbers of skilled foreign workers. The rich oil fields provided the capital and ties with the U.S. and other Western countries would provide the competent manpower.

Reminiscent of the gold rush days in America, at least 100,000 expatriates joined 11 million Iranian inhabitants of Tehran in competing for the basic staples of life. To attract the expertise needed it was required that foreign workers receive salaries that would seem astronomical to most Iranians. This inequity, along with the natural introduction of a relaxed Western lifestyle, an abundance of alcohol, American movies, gambling, gaudy dress, pop music and free and easy spending like there was no tomorrow, took a heavy toll on the traditional ultraconservative Muslim culture and beliefs and irritated the Islamic fundamentalists.

Many American professional couples were holding down two jobs, living well on the salary of one, and banking the other. Complementing the civilian workers, Tehran housed thousands of U.S. military advisors and their families. Military personnel were instructed to maintain a low profile and ordered to wear civilian clothes at all times.

Iranian government officials expressed an eagerness to make foreigners welcome and allowed major hotel chains to operate bars and restaurants openly. Evening "half-price-drink happy hour" sessions were as numerous as in hotel bars in the United States.

Uncensored English newspapers were freely distributed, several TV programs were broadcast in English and an English-speaking American-style radio station entertained foreigners and Iranians alike. The popular disk jockey was a colorful American by the name of Ted Anthony. Ted was admired by most expatriates and was also a favorite with young Iranians. He played all the latest American hit songs, including the 1976 hit "Don't Cry for me Argentina" as sung by Julie Covington. (Whenever I hear this song I still think about my exciting life in Iran.)

Mr. Anthony was silenced during the early phases of the revolution that would overthrew the Shah in the fall of 1978.

Wishing to enjoy the fruits of their high salaries, expatriates flocked to the dining rooms and bars of major hotels and engaged in a never-ending parade of home cocktail parties. Once your name was listed in the social register, you were invited to more parties than it was possible to attend. Providing the liquor and exotic foods for these gala events was not a problem. Western embassies, especially the U.S., operated commissaries and liquor stores selling their wares at huge discounts. With high salaries and cheap liquor, frequent noisy parties were a natural aberration. If private parties didn't fit your mood, you could visit the U.S. Army Officers' Club which hosted a lively bar, lavish restaurant and Olympic-size swimming pool. Needless to say, this carefree, cavalier approach to life did not create an image respected in a devout Muslim country. Rubbing salt into the wounds was the unintended lack of respect for Muslim holidays by foreign workers.

Iranian holidays, in contrast to Western days of celebration, do not commemorate memorable birthdays or significant joyous historical events, so are not days of merriment. Iranian holidays commemorate the deaths of eminent religious leaders and are days of mourning. They are marked with the closing of shops and schools for two or three days along with the continuous playing of sepulcher type music on the radio and TV.

It was my impression that Iranians are not happy unless they are sad, and enduring painful lamenting over some long-dead Muslim cleric.

During these religious holidays Iranian women dress in full head-to-toe black shrouds and purple mourning flags are displayed everywhere. In the Western worker's mind these Muslim days of grieving provided extra free time for extravagant parties, spiked with copious amounts of cheap liquor, gaudy dress, games of chance and loud music.

Initially, I was one of six foreign captains hired to augment the Iranian pilots operating the Air Taxi's fleet of aircraft. The foreign pilots consisted of five Americans and one Belgian. The following year two British and one Austrian joined our group. As I became more familiar with the company, it was apparent that this was a coveted position.

Corporate aircraft from other countries were not allowed to operate in Iran giving Air Taxi a total monopoly. Large foreign construction and business firms, desiring to utilize corporate aviation support, were forced to use the services of Air Taxi. This consortium service came at a very high price, and the autocratic control of corporate aviation was to prove very interesting in the coming months.

The Shah's modernization plans were putting a severe strain on the Iranian budget, and by 1974 many projects would have to be curtailed unless additional capital could be found. The relief came as the result of the Yon Kipper War. Syria and Egypt attacked Israel in 1973 and, in support of their Arab neighbors, the Oil Producing Export Countries (OPEC) declared a world wide oil embargo. This put a terrible strain on Western economies that were willing to accept almost any remedy to restore the flow of cheap oil.

The Shah of Iran, during an OPEC meeting, stated that before lifting the embargo the opportunity of boosting the price of oil should not be allowed to pass. He proposed a four-fold increase from three dollars a barrel, to twelve (which would equal $54 in 2007. So it wasn't too far removed from what the West was willing to pay). Other OPEC members were reluctant to agree as they didn't think Western countries would accept such a large increase. The Shah persisted and won the argument. The price of oil was quadrupled without a whimper from the West. The Shah emerged as an OPEC leader and now had the additional capital he needed to continue his Iranian modernization program.

I was oblivious to the fact that my physical presence and high salary were part of the seeds of discontent slowly growing within the Iranian people. I was too busy enjoying myself and developing the skills and reputation needed to be one of the best foreign captains on the company payroll. I didn't have the foresight to recognize that this "Boomtown Economic Bubble" would come crashing down in a little more than two years.

The extent of this collapse will be covered in more detail in subsequent chapters.

The Iranian philosophy of the "best liar wins" prompted me to engage in this mental game of subterfuge myself to see if I could obtain a discount airline ticket for my flight attendant friend Chieko Hara, living in Tokyo.

Air Taxi had interline agreements with Royal Dutch Airlines (KLM), Pakistan International Airlines (PIA) and Iran Air. My work contract authorized me to purchase 80 percent discount tickets on these airlines for myself, spouse and children. However, to exercise this privilege it was required that I obtain a signed statement from Air Taxi requesting a discounted ticket on a trip-by-trip basis. The company request would be presented to the airline's office in downtown Tehran, who would then issue the ticket. I had taken advantage of this interline agreement for myself several times and also in obtaining discount tickets for my daughter Lynn and son Mike to visit Tehran. I figured it was now time to "go Iranian" and branch out. (See Photos 20, 21, and 24.)

I went to see my old friend Mr. Montpass, our personnel representative, and told him I would like to make an application for a round-trip discount ticket on PIA for my daughter living in Japan. He said, "No problem, Captain Martin," as he went to his filing cabinet to retrieve my dossier.

He studied my ticket application, which stated it was for a Miss Chieko Hara, and then compared it with information contained in my personnel file. After a few minutes he looked up while stating, "Captain Martin, I don't understand your request. Your job application file doesn't list a daughter by the name of Chieko Hara living in Tokyo, Japan."

I admitted that this was so, but said that since you have my file in hand you will note that I spent eight years in Japan. The first time was from 1961 to 1964, when I was a pilot in the U.S. Air Force, and the second time was from 1970 to 1975, when I flew as a captain for Japan Domestic Airlines. He acknowledged that this was true and properly documented.

I drew myself very close to his desk and, in almost a whisper, said that when I was in Japan in the early sixties, I was assigned to a jet fighter squadron, was very young and carefree, and a daughter by the name of Chieko Hara was the result of this reckless lifestyle. I would now like to have her visit me in Iran. You will also note that my contract states I'm authorized to purchase a discount ticket for my children, period!

I could see he was mentally digesting my request and without giving him a chance to come back with a negative answer, I added. Authorizing my request will not cost the company one rial so I don't see a problem. Mr. Montpass agreed and issued the required authorization. From then on, obtaining a PIA discount ticket for Chieko (my future wife) to visit me in Iran was treated as a routine request. The die had been cast.

One Western-style recreation activity not anticipated by expatriates in Iran was downhill Alpine-style snow skiing. The Shah and his family were ardent ski enthusiasts and were frequent visitors to the ski slopes in Switzerland and Austria. Realizing that the Alborz Mountain range north of Tehran contained areas ideally suited for downhill skiing the Shah ordered the construction of a winter resort area known as "Dizin."

French downhill ski experts were hired to establish a "state-of-the-art" ski slope on a wide open north-facing mountain, about 50 miles Northeast of Tehran. Cost was not a factor when establishing the site and when completed it included an enclosed "four-man-gondola" cable car and numerous three and four-man chair lifts. A large ski lodge hotel was constructed at the base of the slope. (See Photos No. 27 and 28.)

The elevation of the area was close to 11,000 feet and, when conditions were right, produced large, light, fluffy (powder) snow flakes. Unfortunately, even at this altitude the ski season was relatively short and we felt fortunate if we could begin skiing by mid December but had to find other forms of relaxation before the end of March.

I skied Dizin as often as my busy schedule would allow, but quickly learned to exercise extreme caution when doing so. The trails were poorly marked and under poor visibility conditions it would be easy to unintentionally lose one's way and ski off into oblivion, never to be heard from again. Also huge boulders lying just beneath the snow surface were not marked so it was imperative that you stay on previously skied areas.

Injuries were also a concern as Dizin did not have expert skiers patrolling the slopes as "Ski Patrol volunteers." Slope grooming equipment was not used, but since the snow was usually light powder a useable trail was soon created by the skiers themselves. The slope was not popular with militant Muslims as females were allowed to ski the same slopes as the men and wore sexy Western-style chic ski outfits.

After the overthrow of the Shah, news reports stated that the Dizin Ski area was allowed to operate, but men and women were required to ski separate slopes, and women were required to wear full head scarves with no hair and minimum skin showing.

On clear sunny warm days there was always the possibility that the Shah and his family may decide to spend an hour or so on the slopes. This happened to me one warm February day in 1978. The first sign that the Shah was arriving was the "chop-chop-chop" sound of approaching helicopters.

Three of them landed in a clearing at the top of the slope and within a few minutes Savak security agents on skis started blocking off the most desirable ski area. When the trail was made secure, I could see off in the distance the Shah and Crown Prince don skis and race up and down the slope for about an hour.

They were good skiers and I envied them in not having to wait in long lift lines when taking the gondola back to the top of the hill. While they were skiing we were restricted to a small chair-lift slope on the side of the hill. A couple hours later the Shah and his party boarded their helicopters and left. The main slope was once again available for us peasants, along with the pushing and shoving in long ski lift lines.

The only public access to Dizin was by private auto or a small bus and under good road conditions was approximately a two hour drive. After leaving Tehran the first portion of the drive was via a two-lane paved highway which exposed us to the usual "finger crossed, Allah protect me" type highway adventure. However, driving up the last seven miles was when the fun really began. (See Photo No. 27.)

After reaching the snow line the road was a slippery single lane with few areas set aside for passing. The hope was that all traffic was driving up in the morning and down in the evening. The bigger problem was that the road surface was not salted or sanded and quite often became very slippery from spinning smooth tires. Tire chains or snow tires were not normally used and many "daredevil" drivers with balding tires, but trusting in Allah, hoped they would be able to make the grade to the top.

Quite often a driver would find himself hopelessly stuck and blocking all other traffic from moving up the hill. When this occurred drivers being held-up would leave their vehicles and join together in pushing the stuck vehicle out of its rut. It was not uncommon that uphill drivers would have to repeat this process several times before reaching the cleared parking lot on the top of the mountain. I was always proud of my little Volkswagen *Beetle* in the way it made the last seven miles to the top without a hint of difficulty. After a day of skiing the road downhill was as exciting as riding an Olympic toboggan. I shuddered to think of what I would do if I met a vehicle attempting to drive up the hill, but I never did. (Thanks be to Allah we always arrived at the bottom of the mountain safely.)

After emerging from the narrow one-way mountain road we would usually stop at a popular roadside cafe and bar by the name of "Lady Bird" for a beer and sandwich. It was perched on the edge of a cliff and one could not find a more picturesque setting to unwind after a hard day of skiing and driving a slippery narrow mountain road. On clear days it was possible to see a panoramic view of Tehran off in the distance framed by a far away golden sunset. (Skiing the slopes of Dizin was good practice for European slopes 14-years later.) (See Photo No. 33.)

As the sun sank slowly over Tehran, deep mountain valleys would be in semi darkness while in sharp contrast the Alborz Mountain tops would still be bathed in the red hue of the setting sun. The last mountain top to bid farewell to the sun would be the 18,500-foot-high Damavand Mountain. Shrouded in snow, its majestic peak pointed skyward and appeared much closer than 50 miles away. We would often linger at the Lady Bird cafe until well after sunset. To do otherwise would have been like walking out of a popular Broadway show before the final curtain.

When returning to my apartment I would call an Air Taxi flight dispatcher to obtain my next day's flight schedule. Most likely I would be informed that I was to fly a trip to one of Iran's southern desert oil fields. I would go from snow skiing in the Alborz Mountains to sweating in desert temperatures of 100 plus degrees in a 24-hour period. My job in Iran was certainly varied and never routine.

Driving up the one-way mountain road to the Dizin ski area was not the only time I was exposed to crazy "Allah-protect-me" Iranian drivers. I was confronted with a wild motorist going the wrong-way on a narrow one-way street one night in downtown Tehran. Neither of us had room to pass but since I was driving in the right direction I decided I wasn't going to yield. We faced-off toward each other, with headlights blinking and horns blowing, demanding that the other driver admit defeat and backup. This stand-off continued for some time until I turned off my headlights, took out a book and started reading with the aid of an interior dome light. After about ten minutes of this game of "chicken" motorists behind me began blinking their lights and blowing their horns so my angry opponent finally admitted defeat and backed up into an area that would allow me to pass. As I drove past him he gave me the "finger" and blew his horn but I had won and was learning how to deal with obstinate "bullheaded" Iranian drivers.

Chapter Six --- You Have a Flight

Initially my flights were mostly Fokker F-27 cargo missions in support of the National Iranian Oil Industries Company. These flights usually consisted of transporting food, drilling equipment and oil field roughnecks to established and exploratory oil fields located throughout Southern Iran. The oil workers employed were mostly Iranian but included a mixed bag of nationalities. Americans, Canadians, English, Germans and Russians were all part of the foreign work force. They were mostly an unshaven muscular tough-looking lot who were "overpaid, but not over worked." Their lack of feminine companionship had long erased any sense of gentlemanly respect for women and it was therefore necessary that only male flight attendants be allowed on flights to the rugged desert oil fields occupied by lecherous manly men.

Flights to established airports like Abadan, Bandar Abbas, Bushier, Kerman and Khark Island became quite routine. However, flying into temporary landing strips supporting exploratory oil fields was another story. These sites were identified by numbers, e.g., Field Y 23. I would be given the geographical coordinates which were inserted into an OMEGA navigation computer. Using these coordinates as a guide I would remain at altitude so as to stay above the mountains until the navigation system indicated I was over the designated desert landing site. Peering down through blowing sand, I would search for a 4,000-foot runway created from rolled sand and highlighted by orange rubber cones. Once the runway was in sight, I would spiral down between the mountains and fly a low approach over the airport. This low pass was required to ensure the runway was clear of wandering sheep, goats or camels. If it was free of obstacles, the low pass would be followed by a close-in downwind leg to a sand-absorbing soft landing. (See Photo No. 8.)

The camp site itself would consist of a row of windowless, heavily insulated, air-conditioned buildings that would be suitable for use in the North Pole or in the heat of the desert. One or two buildings would be set aside as recreation halls and this is where I would relax while awaiting departure time. Most of these community centers were equipped with soft ice cream machines, pool tables and other forms of entertainment which were put to good use. (See Photo No. 7.)

On one of my flights to an Iranian desert base, the visibility, due to blowing sand, was very bad and it was all I could do to keep the poorly marked runway in sight as I circled down between the mountains. The runway appeared clear and not wanting to lose sight of it, I decided to land without first executing a low approach. After landing I taxied toward what I knew would be the main campsite but peering through blowing sand I couldn't see any of the familiar rectangular-shaped portable buildings, which were normally located close to the runway.

When I reached the center of the camp area, the only thing visible was a robed shepherd carrying a Biblical-like long curved staff and tending a flock of sheep. Several camels were tied up nearby. It was like a scene right out of the Bible. There was nothing in view that would indicate an oil drilling camp had been located here just a few days before. I was sitting on a piece of empty desert with not a clue as to what to do with the 20 or so oil workers and the fresh food supplies I had onboard.

Keeping the engines running, I cranked up the High Frequency radio (HF) and put in a call to our dispatch center in Tehran. When I was finally able to make contact with the dispatcher, he was just as surprised as I was at the absence of the camp. He requested I confirm my geographical coordinates. When I did he validated that my location agreed with what he had on file for this particular base camp. He instructed me to stand by while he contacted the oil company to obtain instructions as to what I should do with my passengers and cargo. I sat there with engines idling while a very confused shepherd looked on in bewilderment.

About ten minutes later the dispatcher called back informing me that the site, where I was directed to land, had been evacuated two days previously. He said that the oil company's exploratory camp had moved to a new location about 75 miles away, and requested I copy the new geographical coordinates. He further requested I fly to the new site and attempt a landing as he was sure the station manager was in dire need of the fresh food and replacement oil workers I had onboard. He cautioned that he had no information on the status of a runway at the new location or how to contact anyone there by radio or telephone.

I inserted the new coordinates into the OMEGA Navigation System computer, waved good-bye to a confused Biblical sheep herder and climbed above the blowing sand storm. In about 20 minutes I was circling over the location of the new oil exploration site. Fortunately the visibility was much improved and from 500 feet I could see road-grading equipment working on a new sand-rolled runway. It appeared that they had completed about 3,000 feet which would be sufficient for a landing if I could get them to move their machinery off to one side.

I had no radio contact with the construction workers, but after making several low passes, with the landing gear extended, they realized my desire to land and cleared the runway. After an uneventful landing I was warmly greeted as I was the first aircraft to land at their new base, but mostly due to the fact that they were almost out of fresh food and beer.

The foreman told me that the main camp itself was about seven miles away and a vehicle was standing by to drive me and my crew to their newly-opened air-conditioned recreation hall. He added it would be about an hour or more before we would be able to depart for Tehran.

We piled into an English Land Rover with another frustrated NASCAR driver at the wheel. In a cloud of dust we raced down a winding sandy desert trail toward the base camp. After a one-car race of about two miles we skidded around a corner and much to our surprise saw a large pickup truck lying on its side. It appeared the driver had taken the corner too fast and flipped over. We stopped to investigate, but found no one in or around the truck. It was obvious that the accident was recent as a front wheel of the overturned vehicle was still spinning.

We climbed back into the Land Rover and continued on toward the main camp. Approaching it we observed a circle of men gathered between several buildings. With my Iranian copilot in close pursuit, I headed for the group to see what was going on. Lying on the hot sand, in the center of the gathering, was a large bare-chested, full-bearded, Iranian oil worker. He was obviously unconscious and from his blue skin color. I wasn't sure if he was dead or alive. I told my copilot to find out what had happened and was told that he was the driver of the truck we had seen off to the side of the road. He had been brought to the site by another vehicle that was in hot pursuit in a race for the camp.

The men gathered in the tight circle were praying to Allah (God), and shedding large crocodile tears, but doing nothing else. I leaned over the body, but with the noise coming from hysterical praying men and the dust from shuffling feet, I had difficulty in detecting a pulse or any sign of breathing. I shouted to my copilot to have several men pick him up and carry him into one of the nearby air-conditioned huts. He was rushed feet first to a nearby building and as he was carried through the doorway, his outstretched arms banged on each side of the door frame so hard I feared they may have been broken.

Once inside, he was literally thrown onto an empty bunk. I chased most onlookers out of the room and closed the door. Leaning over him, I cleared his throat of sand with a finger, tilted his head back, and began mouth-to-mouth resuscitation. I alternated this with hand compressions to his sand-encrusted hairy chest. The few onlookers still in the room looked on with suspicion while praying to Allah for his survival.

I don't know how long I struggled in attempting to revive him, but after a period of time it appeared that some color was returning to the portion of his face that wasn't covered with hair. I instructed my copilot to get a bucket of ice water as my patient started, albeit weakly, breathing on his own and I thought that perhaps being doused with cold water may force him to recover from his unconscious state.

When my copilot returned, I threw the bucket of cold water on his bare chest and face. The shock caused him to shutter and his breathing became stronger. However, he was still unconscious, his eyes were rolled back and it was apparent that he needed professional medical help. While I was working on reviving him my copilot had determined that the camp, not yet fully established, had no medical help of any kind.

I told my copilot to have the camp manager find or make a stretcher and we would fly him to the nearby Iranian Navy base of Bandar Abbas. Confident that they would find a conveyance of some sort, my crew and I headed for the landing strip to ready the aircraft for immediate departure the minute our injured oil worker arrived.

I went through a "Colonel Madnia-style" Before Start Engine Check and had the right engine running by the time our air evacuation patient arrived. While taxiing out for takeoff, I made a radio call in the blind to any aircraft that could receive my transmission. An Iran Air B-727 flying overhead answered and I asked him if he was in contact with Bandar Abbas tower. Receiving an affirmative answer, I requested he alert them that I was inbound with a seriously injured Iranian oil worker and should be on the ground in about 45 minutes. I instructed him to request an ambulance and doctor to be standing by to meet our aircraft.

After landing at Bandar Abbas, I was pleased to see the rotating beacon of a Red Lion and Sun ambulance and a white-coated doctor waiting in front of the main terminal. Our patient was last seen heading toward a local hospital and we flew back to the desert oil company base to complete our assigned mission.

I heard nothing more about the status of his recovery, but a month or so later, when in Bandar Abbas, I asked the tower if they recalled my emergency medical landing some time back. They said they did and informed me that the man I brought in had fully recovered and was back working in the oil fields. I was pleased to learn that my military emergency medical training had been put to good use.

Flying support missions to the oil fields was always interesting and never routine. In addition to landing on temporary sand-rolled runways, I flew to several small islands in the Persian Gulf. These flights would depart Tehran early in the morning, arriving at the intended destination a couple hours later. After several hours on the ground, I would return to Tehran with about five hours of flight time logged.

Since the support flights provided the majority of the fresh food, mail, replacement workers and other creature comforts, I was bestowed VIP treatment during my hours on the ground. The copilot, flight attendants and I would be honored lunch guests at the camp commander's table and enjoyed the best of what they had in regard to food available. While sitting in an air-conditioned hut, at a large table covered with a white table cloth and fine china, and being served by white-gloved waiters, it was hard to believe I was at some unheard of desert base on a small island in the Persian Gulf.

Following lunch I would usually have several hours to kill and was afforded full access to their air-conditioned recreation hall. Since the oil company employees would be at work, my crew and I would have it all to ourselves. To pass the time we could read, view a current movie in a VCR, play Ping-Pong or engage in my favorite pass time of pocket pool. I taught many a copilot the basic rules of "eight ball" and perfected my own game tremendously. The time I spent with a cue in my hand in oil field recreation halls was golden and put to good use in friendly pool matches at the U.S. Army Officers' Club in Tehran. It was not uncommon to walk away with 20 or 30 dollars of winnings from fellow pilots flying B-727s or B-707s for Iran Air.

My flourishing skills in pocket pool were also profitable when competing against an English pilot colleague who would join Air Taxi some time later and U.S. Air Force and Army Officers who loved to gamble, even when they were sure to lose. (I will outline in humorous detail the circumstances relating to my friendly pool-game onslaught with Captain Bill Aston, an English pilot colleague in Chapter Eleven.)

After landing at a remote dessert base one hot summer day, I observed a bubble-nosed Bell helicopter landing in a swirl of dust, directly in front of my parked aircraft. As the rotating blades came to a stop I noted the pilot emerging from the cockpit. He was a tall man, probably in his mid forties, sporting a long flowing gray mustache, dressed in a half unbuttoned tan short sleeve shirt, white tattered baseball cap, military-style shorts with bulging large open pockets, white socks and weather-beaten sneakers. His skin was a golden tan and he walked with a cocky style gait. (Hollywood would have been hard pressed to find a more perfect example to fill a macho male roll in an *Indiana Jones* movie.)

He took note that I had recently landed and was walking toward my aircraft to extend the usual greeting pilots offer each other, especially in a foreign country. As he approached, I stepped out from the shade of a wing and thrust out my hand in greeting. He did likewise while stating, "My name is Fred Huntington from England. Glad to meet you." His accent left no question that he was as English as the London Bridge. When I said, "Glad to meet you," he countered with, "You must be a yank."

Stepping back into the shade of a wing we chatted for a few minutes enjoying each other's backgrounds and working experiences in Iran. He asked me how long I would be on the ground. When I replied two or three hours, he inquired if I had any plans to kill the time. My response was to try and find some place cool, but since this particular base camp was on the top of a mountain, and could only be reached by a dangerous narrow corkscrew road, I would most likely just camp out underneath the wing of my aircraft. He said that he also had a couple hours to kill and why didn't we jump into his helicopter and fly to the top of the mountain where we could rest in an air-conditioned building and enjoy a soft ice cream cone and a cup of English tea, which he had brought with him.

With just the two of us in his helicopter, which had the side doors removed, we snaked our way up the switch-back road toward the top of the mountain. We flew just 200 or 300 feet above a hastily carved narrow dirt track. The single-lane trail, with occasional wide areas for passing, was void of guard rails and my bird's-eye view confirmed that my decision to pass up motor trips to the top on previous flights was a sound decision.

My dynamic English helicopter pilot friend pointed out the wreckage of several large dump trucks that had failed to make one or more of the hairpin curves. He said most crashes claimed the lives of the drivers, but no effort was made to recover the expensive vehicles.

As we approached the top of the mountain, I was concerned as to where we would land as the small flat space available appeared completely occupied with the standard rectangular-shaped insulated base camp huts. He began to hover over a small bulldozed flat spot jutting out from the side of the mountain. I thought the area he was hovering over was too small for a landing, but he gently lowered the helicopter down like a bird gripping a tree branch. After landing we were staring at shear rock not more than 40 feet in front while our tail rotor was hanging out over empty space.

Exiting the helicopter we followed a dusty foot path to the main camp. We rested in an air-conditioned recreation hall and cooled off over ice cream and English tea while continuing to swap aviation experiences. After a cooling hour or so, we returned to his helicopter for our downhill flight to the main runway. The small pad we were siting on required the pilot to go to full throttle and back off into the valley. I felt like an eagle leaving a mountain-top nest. The return flight was very quick and we landed next to my aircraft which was now loaded and ready for the flight back to Tehran. I thanked my English pilot friend for a very enjoyable two hours and we went our separate ways, never to see each other again.

Bandar Abbas, a large Persian Gulf City in the Southeast section of Iran, was a frequent destination and a moneymaker as far as flight time was concerned. The round trip flight time was normally six hours, but with the Iranian copilot managing the flight log book, we normally logged seven. The airport at Bandar Abbas was a shared civilian/military facility with a large Iranian navy base just a few miles away. When we were required to stay overnight, billeting was always a problem. If we couldn't find a room in a hotel, we would take what we could find at any one of several Iranian navy facilities. The Shah, to alleviate this critical housing shortage, especially for his officers, had come up with a brilliant idea.

The Italians had built two 46,000-ton luxury ocean liners referred to as the "Twin Sisters" and named them *Michelangelo* and *Raffaello*. They had been built with the hope of capturing a large segment of the anticipated post World War II Atlantic Ocean tourist traffic. The Twin Sisters were put into service in 1966, which was about the same time that international jet service was rapidly expanding. The introduction of these magnificent ocean liners not only ran headlong into competition with tourists preferring to travel by air, but was about 20 years before the cruise-ship craze hit the world market. The ships were mothballed after two short unprofitable seasons.

The Shah purchased both ships for about ten cents on the dollar in 1977, and anchored the *Michelangelo* in the harbor of Bandar Abbas and the *Raffaello* in the harbor at Bushier. They were put to use as floating five star hotels for navy officers and visiting VIPs. Both ships were crewed by a limited number of Italian sailors, cooks and waiters who maintained them in full seaworthy status. Each month they were moved to deep water, turned around, and returned to their semi permanent dock. These floating hotels were the pride of the Iranian Navy, especially since the bars, dance halls and swimming pools were kept open. This was a real novelty for a military organization in a Muslim country.

On most of my overnight stays at Bandar Abbas or Bushier, my rank as a Captain for the Shah's Air Taxi company qualified me for a first class state room. Taking a warm shower in an air-conditioned cabin, having a white-coated bartender mix me a martini at a fancy bar, eating a scrumptious dinner prepared by an Italian chef and being served by smartly-dressed waiters with soft dinner music playing in the background was very hard to take. Especially when all this was possible for just a few dollars and still collecting full per diem for each night's hardship.

After the overthrow of the Shah, Ayatollah Khomeini ordered the ships scrapped. The Michelangello was trashed in Pakistan and the Raffaello, a victim of the Iran/Iraq War, remains sunk in the Bushier Harbor.

About twice a month my schedule would include "home standby," where I would be required to remain in my apartment until released at around 5 p.m. If called, I might be scheduled to fly as either a captain or copilot to fill in for a sick or no-show pilot. Since foreign pilots comprised such a small number of the total pilot force, they would not miss a flight if at all possible. Being called in from "home standby" would always be to back-up an Iranian pilot, never a foreign captain! This unexpected crew shift would sometimes come as a surprise to down-line station managers and force them to drastically change their plans.

I was called in from standby to fill-in for a sick Iranian captain on an F-27 flight from Tehran to the United Arab Emirate's city of Abu Dhabi, with an en route cargo pick-up stop at Shiraz. When I emerged from the aircraft at Shiraz, the Iranian station manager's jaw dropped. Obviously surprised he said, "What happened to the Iranian captain?" When I told him that he was sick and that I had taken his place, he shook his head with obvious disgust. At first I thought he was expressing sympathy for the sick pilot, but I knew there must be a more sinister reason.

He asked me how much cargo I could carry to Abu Dhabi. I had computed the maximum allowable cargo load before landing and responded, "10,600 pounds." He said this would never do as he had 16,000 pounds that had to be shipped today as some of it was perishable food. When I repeated what the maximum load would be, he pulled me off to the side and asked how much Bakhsheesh (under-table payment) I required to carry all 16,000 pounds in one flight.

I told him that limiting the load to 10,600 pounds was not up for discussion and I was not demanding a Bakhsheesh payment to exceed it. The limit was to allow for a margin of safety in the event I experienced an engine failure when flying over the mountains. His comment, "I don't understand the problem. An Iranian captain would state, 'Insha Allah,' put some extra money in his pocket and carry the full load without question." I told him this wouldn't work for me and if he needed to transport all 16,000 pounds to Abu Dhabi today, I would have to make two flights after he coordinated this requirement with Air Taxi in Tehran.

He wasn't happy with my decision, especially when he was forced to pay for what he thought was an unnecessary extra flight. (I'm sure he prayed to Allah for a speedy recovery of the sick Iranian captain.)

Being called in from "home standby" sometime later created a problem of a different nature. An Iranian copilot called in sick for a scheduled passenger turnaround flight to Kerman. I was directed to fly as his replacement for an Iranian captain I had never met.

When I checked in with the dispatch center, there was a note from the Chief Pilot attached to the paperwork pertaining to our flight. The note stated that since both pilots assigned to the flight were captains, the Iranian pilot would fly as Pilot-In-Command (PIC) on the leg to Kerman and I would fly the left seat as PIC on the return flight to Tehran.

The initial portion of the flight segment to Kerman was routine and the Iranian captain and I were working quite well as a crew, although I couldn't say that our "Cockpit Resource Management" was sterling. About 100 miles out from Kerman we were flying in a solid layer of stratus clouds at 20,000 feet. We had not been able to receive Kerman's distance measuring equipment (DME) station and, without visual reference to the ground, were utilizing dead reckoning to estimate our position over high mountainous terrain.

Performing as a copilot, I contacted the Kerman control tower and inquired if they had our aircraft in radar contact. They reported that they did not as their radar was off the air for routine maintenance. Without a break in their transmission, they cleared us for a non-precision VOR approach and a descent to 10,000 feet. Upon hearing this, my Iranian captain reduced power and pushed the nose over to start a descent. I immediately pushed the throttles back up to cruise power, and pulled back on the control column so as to maintain level flight.

He seemed surprised by my actions, so I explained the reason I overrode his descent attempt. I said that since we had no way of accurately computing our ground speed we weren't exactly sure of our position over the ground. I referenced the high altitude en route navigation chart and pointed out that the "Minimum En route Altitude" (MEA) for our "estimated" position was 18,000 feet.

My explanation didn't seem to satisfy him. He countered with, "But the Kerman tower cleared us to descend to 10,000 feet." I replied that indeed they did, but since their radar was not working they didn't know our exact location when they issued the clearance. He agreed that this was true, but then commented that he had flown into Kerman many times, knew the terrain extremely well and wasn't concerned about hitting the mountains. "Insha Allah."

He was unhappy with my insistence that we restrict our descent to 18,000 feet until over the station, but complied with a grunt and "under-breath mumbling." When we were over the station we commenced an approach, and broke out of the clouds at 15,000 feet. An uneventful visual landing followed.

Since I was to be the PIC for the return flight to Tehran, I proceeded to the airport flight operations office to file a flight plan while the Iranian captain (now my copilot) went to make a personal phone call. While I was preparing the flight plan, I was informed that we had a full passenger load for Tehran which included many foreigners returning to the U.S. and scheduled for international connecting flights at Mehrabad Airport.

While walking toward the aircraft, I noted that the refueling operation had been completed and the gate agent was loading the passengers. When I was about 50 feet from the aircraft I heard a loud whistle and observed my Iranian copilot (former captain) hurrying in my direction. I stopped to let him catch up.

In an excited voice he told me that he had completed his phone call and that we were going to cancel our flight to Tehran and remain overnight in Kerman. He sensed my surprise and before I could respond, said, "I have some good friends in Kerman who will put us up for the night and take us out for dinner in a very famous first class restaurant." I was still too stunned to respond. Then he added, "We can declare some kind of problem with the aircraft that would prevent us from flying back to Tehran." He was obviously excited about the prospect of spending an exciting night in Kerman and was doing his best to coerce me into being a party to his devious plan.

I turned to my Iranian (former captain) copilot and said in a firm voice, "Since the Chief Pilot directed that I would be the PIC for the return flight to Tehran, I have already filed and signed a flight plan indicating myself as Pilot-In-Command. I don't know what your plans are, but in a few minutes I'm going to climb into the left seat of our aircraft and fly the passengers you see boarding to Tehran, with or without you. If you're not onboard when I land at Tehran, I'm sure the Chief Pilot will wonder why." With that, I did an about face, excused my way past a line of boarding passengers and sat down in the left pilot's seat in the cockpit.

A few minutes later, as I was going through the Before Engine Start Checklist, my Iranian copilot entered the cockpit and asked if I would like him to read the checklist while I performed the required functions. The flight from Kerman to Tehran was uneventful, but somewhat void of cockpit chatter. We delivered our passengers to their destination on time and many were able to make their planned international connections without a problem. Others, who were remaining in Tehran, were able to assume their individually planned activities. "Insha Allah."

Evidence of contrasting procedural standards between foreign and Iranian pilots was not restricted to pilot changes by the call-up of a reserve foreign captain. Many Iranian pilots paid little attention to critical aircraft weight restrictions established by the design engineers. This oversight was especially noteworthy with regard to maximum allowable takeoff weights and maximum allowable landing weights.

Station managers, as previously pointed out, were in many cases allowed to load F-27s and FH-227s as if they were trucks, not aircraft, when working with Iranian pilots. They operated these overloaded aircraft without experiencing accidents because of the outstanding reliability of the Rolls Royce Dart engines and Dowty Rotol propellers. However, there was always the off chance of an engine failure and if this occurred, on an overloaded aircraft, maintaining safe flight over the mountains on one engine would be in doubt. Foreign captains didn't wish to expose themselves to this potential danger, remote as it was, while Iranian pilots protected by "Insha Allah" seemed to have no problem. I suspect they also reaped financial gains in the form of Bakhsheesh by doing so.

Even if they made a halfhearted attempt to honor maximum takeoff weights many Iranian pilots devoted little attention to exceeding maximum allowable landing weights. This oversight was a real problem on short range flights, i.e., from Abadan to Khark Island. The flight time between these airports was approximately 30 minutes and even if maximum allowable takeoff weights were not exceeded on departure, the short flight duration may not allow for sufficient fuel burn-off to reduce the aircraft's weight to its maximum allowable landing weight. The danger in exceeding maximum landing weights was the possibility of causing structural damage to the aircraft. Under certain isolated conditions this could result in an in-flight structural failure on some future flight, especially if severe turbulence was encountered when flying over mountainous terrain. Another potential danger was a tire failing during landing. Complying with this restriction was difficult for many Iranian captains and copilots to comprehend and they therefore ignored the potential danger.

My concerns regarding Iranian pilots over-stressing aircraft was displayed one day as I approached the airport of Bandar Abbas. When about ten miles from the airport I observed an aircraft performing loops and barrel rolls north of the field. At first I thought it must be an aerobatic aircraft which would have been extremely rare in Iran. However, as I drew closer I could see that it was a twin-engine *Turbo Commander*.

After several minutes of aerobatic maneuvers the pilot contacted the tower for landing instructions and his call-sign confirmed that it was an Air Taxi aircraft. I landed a few minutes after he did and observed several giddy male passengers deplaning from the aircraft and shaking the Iranian captain's hand in an obvious gesture of appreciation for an exciting flight.

I reported this dangerous episode to the Air Taxi Chief Pilot but apparently nothing came of it as I saw the same captain flying missions a couple days later in another *Turbo Commander*. However, I did note the "tail-number" of the aircraft I observed doing aerobatics over Bandar Abbas and avoided flying it in the future. But I wondered how many other aircraft were over-stressed by the same or other Iranian pilots that I had no knowledge of.

Chapter Seven --- Flying for the Iranian Navy

Four of Air Taxi's Fokker F-27s were operated on contract with the Imperial Iranian Navy. They were painted a military navy gray and equipped with standard, open-bay, military canvas bucket seats. Since the navy did not have a sufficient number of captains qualified to fly these aircraft, part of my job was to help train a small cadre of naval officers as Aircraft Commanders. The majority of these pilots were navy lieutenants in their late twenties or early thirties who had completed two years of pilot training with the Fokker Aircraft Company in Amsterdam, Holland.

Their training in Holland provided them with only 200 hours of flight time and surprisingly limited knowledge of the aircraft systems. When I asked them what they did during their two years in free swinging Amsterdam, they responded with smiles and glowing comments about great food, good beer and beautiful accommodating women. It was a challenge to convince them that their holiday was over and it was now time to learn the rudiments of becoming an Iranian Navy Aircraft Commander. I found it difficult to rid them of their long-established, carefree, Dutch-holiday attitude, so in spite of my commitment to train them as F-27 captains, I treated them like any other right seat copilot. They seemed content with this arrangement as it didn't force them into a position of having to make critical command decisions.

Once the threat of being pushed into a position that would require the exercising of command accountability was removed, they felt more at ease and were enjoyable to fly with. Since they were naval officers they were well educated, and spoke better English than many of Air Taxi's civilian copilots. However, I felt that their two years in Holland, under the tutelage of autocratic Dutch instructors, implanted a subservient attitude of being more comfortable in taking orders than giving them.

When I flew the Iranian Navy aircraft my cargo and passenger loads were usually military in origin and to and from military bases throughout Iran. It was interesting to see the strict caste system among my passengers. The officers always arrived at the aircraft in separate vehicles from the enlisted men, and along with their chador-hooded female dependents always sat in the front of the aircraft. They all seemed somewhat surprised to see a foreigner as their pilot, but at the same time seemed relieved that they stood a better chance of arriving at their destination safely. "Insha Allah."

The Iranian Navy aircraft were parked in an area of the ramp situated very close to the Shah's private aircraft hangar, where his personal B-727, B-707 and *Falcon* jet were stored. The ramp space in front of this hangar was a restricted area and identified by a wide semicircle red line. It was patrolled by armed guards 24 hours a day. Most of my departures required passing this restricted area, but because of a wide taxiway, infringement into the sterile area was not a problem. However, on one of my departures a transient Japan Airlines B-747 cargo jet was blocking part of the main taxiway so it was necessary for me to taxi closer to the Shah's restricted area than I had in the past.

I taxied through the area very slowly, figuring my left wing tip would be close to the red line, but not over it. To my surprise an Iranian military jeep came speeding in my direction. As a precaution I stopped the aircraft, as the jeep came to an abrupt stop directly below my side cockpit window. An armed guard jumped out, pointed his M-16 directly at my head and charged a live round into the firing chamber.

My copilot said, "What should we do?" I said, "Stay calm, move slowly, and don't do anything stupid!"

I instructed my copilot to call the airport control tower and inform them, in Farsi, that we were parked near the Shah's hangar and being held captive by an armed Iranian military guard with a weapon pointed at us in the cockpit. I sat motionless with a loaded M-16 pointed directly at my head for what seemed like a very long time. An airport security vehicle soon arrived, called off the over-eager guard and waved us past the restricted area. The rest of the day was uneventful.

The Iranian Navy was building a large secret air and seaport base in the Gulf of Oman near the city of Chah Bahar. It was in the Southeast corner of Iran just a few miles from the Pakistan border. When completed it would provide a base for defensive aircraft, submarines and fast destroyers protecting the entrance to Iran's oil distribution ports. Support flights to this base were a full day's schedule of about eight hours with refueling stops at Bandar Abbas. Landing at Chah Bahar was very interesting as the airport runway was still under construction. A temporary landing strip was a narrow blacktop section of highway that was also being used by heavy construction vehicles. (See Photo No. 1.)

When over Chah Bahar, I would make a couple low passes over the makeshift highway runway to alert the construction foreman of my intended landing. I would continue to circle until he was able to clear the road of vehicles and wave a green flag, indicating I was cleared to land. The narrow road provided only about one foot of clearance on each side of the main landing gear. After landing I would taxi to what would be an intersection in the road, turn around and taxi back toward the main construction camp site.

After shutting down the engines, a group of men would hand push the aircraft off to the side so heavy earth-moving equipment could once again have access to the road. The departure from Tehran would be early morning so as to arrive at Chah Bahar around 11 a.m. Scheduled departure for the flight back to Tehran would be just prior to sunset since there were no guidance lights of any kind on the temporary runway.

On this particular flight after the aircraft was secured, the construction foreman drove me and my crew to the supervisor's dining room hut where we were invited to join him and his staff for lunch. After a meal of rice, lamb, pita bread, chay and a mixed salad the supervisor and his staff left for work leaving myself and my crew to relax in their adjacent air-conditioned lounge where we could watch recorded TV shows, shoot pool, listen to music or take a short nap. Checking the time, I noted it would be about five hours before we were scheduled to return to Tehran, so we were free to spend the leisure time in any way we desired.

My two male flight attendants and Iranian Navy copilot were soon curled up in soft leather sofas and sound asleep. As in the past, I retrieved a book from my flight bag and began to read. About 45 minutes later I started to experience severe stomach cramps, followed by a strong urge to go to the bathroom. I made a mad dash down a long hallway reaching the water closet just in time. The toilet was a typical Iranian affair with two porcelain foot pads that required a person to squat when doing their business. The room lacked air conditioning, and with a large window wide open the temperature must have been close to 100 degrees, or more. An overflowing sink resulted in the concrete floor being awash with water which greatly added to the discomfort level.

My stomach pains grew worse, and were so painful that they caused me to double up in a fetal position on the wet floor. I laid there groaning in pain which increased greatly if I attempted to straighten out my legs. I crawled to the toilet opening and vomited until my body was completely dehydrated. I thought of attempting to seek help, but was too weak to cry out or stand up. With my pants down and face hovering over a foul-smelling floor-level toilet, I thought I was going to die on a hot wet floor of a stinking bathroom in far-off Southeast Iran. The heat and pain apparently induced a sedative strong enough to cause me to pass out.

When I awoke, I noted that it had been about two hours since I had entered the bathroom, and although I was still suffering some abdominal pain I was able to straighten out my legs and stand up. My uniform shirt, trousers and underwear were soaking wet. It was obvious that no one had become concerned about me since the door to the water closet had remained locked. I stripped down to my birthday suit and spread out my uniform and underwear on a large bush outside the window. The bush was in direct sunlight and the 100+ degree outside temperature and dry desert air were soon at work in drying my clothes. While my uniform was drying I utilized the time by washing my face, and doing mild bodily exercises. Although not completely recovered, I figured I wasn't quite ready for an undertaker. My clothes and underwear were soon dry enough to put on and I headed back to the air-conditioned lounge.

I discovered my copilot and flight attendants still curled up and sleeping like kittens, with no apparent signs of discomfort. I drank a couple bottles of water, and went for a short walk outside to finish the clothes drying process. When I returned to the lounge I found my crew finally awake. I asked them if they felt OK. They said they felt fine and wanted to know why I was asking. I responded with, "No particular reason, except I'm always concerned about my crew's health."

Sometime later the camp foreman arrived ready to drive us back to our aircraft in his English Land Rover. I noted that construction workers had already pushed the airplane back onto the narrow highway with the standard one foot of space on either side of the main landing gear. The aircraft was loaded for its return flight, and since the sun was sinking low in the West it was time to go.

I was still feeling quite weak, but didn't want to stay in Chah Bahar another minute. There was a stiff crosswind blowing from the left so I knew I would have to make the takeoff, but once airborne I intended to have the copilot fly the aircraft back to Tehran. Fortunately, I had one of the better navy copilots on this trip and since it was going to be a night flight he wouldn't observe me catching a few catnaps en route.

Our landing at Tehran was late at night so I wasn't scheduled to fly the next day. When I arrived at my apartment I defrosted a large filet mignon steak, which I wolfed down along with two martinis and a large glass of red wine. I awoke the next morning feeling none the worse for wear, but several pounds lighter. Another day in interesting Iran was a matter of record, but this was not to be my last bout with food poisoning.

I avoided eating unwashed raw fresh salads, meat unless it was well cooked and drank only canned soft drinks or bottled water. In spite of these precautions, I would occasionally experience an attack of food poisoning that would cause severe stomach cramps and diarrhea, but nothing like what I experienced in Chah Bahar.

In April 1977, Zulfikar Ali Bhutto, the Prime Minister of Pakistan, was fighting for his national survival. His police had opened fire on street demonstrators and many had been killed. In an attempt to restore order he declared martial law and established a 24-hour curfew in most major cities including Karachi. The nature and severity of these demonstrations in this adjacent Muslim country were followed closely in Iran, not only because they shared a common border and religion, but because both countries were controlled by despots experiencing citizen unrest. We had heard reports that several people in Karachi had been killed by Pakistani Army soldiers for violating the government-ordered curfew.

The new Air Taxi Chief Pilot, Captain Sephrizadeh, called me into his office and asked if I would be interested in a semi hazardous Iranian Navy flight that would pay twice my normal salary for each hour flown, plus an extra $200 a day per diem? I told him it sounded interesting and requested the details. He said that 25 high-ranking Pakistani Naval officers, on a goodwill trip to Tehran, were not able to return to Karachi because all commercial flights to Pakistan had been canceled. He said it was imperative that they be returned to Karachi as soon as possible.

To accommodate their requirement to return, the Iranian Government had obtained permission from Pakistan for an Iranian Navy aircraft to fly them there, providing the aircraft land at a military base just south of the city and that the majority of the crew be either members of the Iranian military or civilian expatriates. I told him that it sounded like an interesting flight and when do I leave. He said, "The following morning."

I departed Tehran early the next day with a planned refueling stop at the Bandar Abbas Naval Air Station. My passengers were a mixed bag of high-ranking Pakistani Naval officers with considerable gold braid and hanging ropes decorating their dark blue uniforms. Several spoke English and expressed a very friendly attitude and appreciation toward me and my crew for flying them back home under very tense conditions. My copilot for the flight was an Iranian Navy lieutenant, and my two flight attendants were navy recruits. They all spoke English and said they were looking forward to an unusual exciting trip. (See Photo No. 9.)

After a refueling stop at Bandar Abbas, we headed for the Gulf of Oman and Karachi. Approaching the Pakistan Flight Information Region (FIR), I contacted Karachi radio and gave them a position report along with my foreign clearance entry code I had obtained from our flight operations center in Tehran. Karachi radio instructed me to stand by. A few minutes later they stated that my foreign clearance code was invalid, that I did not have permission to enter Pakistan Air Space and must reverse course and return to Iran.

Since I was already over the Arabian Sea and about 50 miles inside their airspace I decided to press on. I told Karachi radio that my foreign clearance code was indeed valid, that I was continuing on course to Karachi and that I did not have sufficient fuel to turn around and return to Iran. I was again instructed to stand by, but kept pressing on.

A few minutes later Karachi Radio again said I did not have permission to land in Karachi and if I continued, I was risking being intercepted by military jet fighters that would force me to reverse course and return to Iran. I told them that they should be advised that I had onboard several high ranking Pakistani Navy admirals and 20 some other navy officers returning to military duty in Pakistan. The radio was silent for quite some time, but finally came alive with Karachi Radio stating that I now had permission to proceed to my intended destination.

Approaching the city I did not see or hear any other aircraft in the area, either military or civilian and was given a straight-in clearance to land at a military field south of the Karachi International Airport. During the final phase of my approach for landing, I noted a complete lack of vehicular traffic on the streets, which seemed very strange for a city of more than nine million people. After landing I had the airport to myself as I taxied to the terminal. A military bus was waiting for my passengers and they were on their way before we secured the aircraft for the night. A Pakistani Naval officer came onboard and informed me that my crew and I would be staying in the downtown Hilton Hotel and transportation to town would arrive in a few minutes.

A gray navy van pulled up in front of the aircraft and my crew and I climbed in. As we departed the base, two military jeeps --- one in front and one in the rear --- escorted us. Both vehicles were equipped with manned 50-caliber machine guns with belts of ammunition hanging from their breaches. We drove down the middle of what would normally be streets jam-packed with donkey carts, bicycles, trucks, smoky taxicabs, etc., but today not a vehicle was in sight. It was really surreal as, except for an occasional military vehicle, we didn't see any other vehicular or pedestrian traffic on the way into town. The city was truly under a total curfew and martial law.

We were dropped off in the front of the Hilton Hotel and one of our escort officers handed me a piece of paper with a telephone number. He said, "Call this number tomorrow morning and you will be advised as to when you may depart Karachi for Tehran."

Compared to the deserted streets, the hotel lobby and restaurant were alive with foreigners, who appeared frustrated in their unexpected forced imprisonment. I asked the hotel clerk how long guests had been restricted to the confines of the hotel. He told me that this was the third day and he didn't know when the 24-hour curfew would be lifted. He seemed surprised that I was allowed passage from the airport to the hotel. It was close to dinner time, so my crew and I agreed to change clothes and meet in the hotel dining room in about 45 minutes.

The dining room was located on the second floor and we secured a table next to a large picture window. The sun was just setting and the view of downtown Karachi was truly unreal; it was as if the city had died! Shops were closed and sidewalks and streets, with the exception of an occasional military vehicle on patrol, were void of any movement. The only visible lights were street lamps and traffic signals going from red to green in a meaningless sequence.

We enjoyed a normal meal but were advised that the hotel was restricted from serving alcoholic beverages due to the government ordered curfew. My crew and I had put in a long day, so we decided to retire and meet for breakfast early the next morning, at which time I would make a telephone call regarding our return flight to Iran.

The next morning, I called my Pakistani military contact who informed me that our return flight to Tehran was still not approved, but hopefully he would have more information later in the day. I briefed my crew regarding the departure delay during breakfast, but they didn't understand why we couldn't just take a taxi to the airport and leave. I called their attention to the fact that Karachi was under a 24-hour curfew, and how we had been escorted to the hotel by armed military jeeps when we arrived the day before. Also, that we were now under the operational control of the Pakistan military, and they would decide when we would be authorized to depart. I felt they still didn't understand the serious ramifications of the government-directed martial law, and were somewhat unhappy with me as the messenger. I further sensed a frustration on their part as all during breakfast their conversation was in Farsi.

As we were leaving the dining room my Iranian Navy officer copilot informed me that he and the flight attendants were going to go into town to do some shopping and should be back in a few hours. It was obvious that they had discussed this foolish move during breakfast and purposely spoke about it in Farsi, so I wouldn't understand their plans. I told my copilot that this was impossible as the city was under total curfew and violators were being shot. His response was that this shouldn't apply to them as they were Iranian.

While trying to convince him that it didn't matter what the nationality of curfew violators was to trigger happy uneducated soldiers, I took him to a large window overlooking downtown Karachi. I pointed out the empty streets below hoping he would see the futility of his plans for shopping. I felt he still was not grasping the seriousness of my warning, so I told him that the two flight attendants (one male and one female) would not be allowed to leave the hotel. I then demanded he write down on a piece of paper his parents name and telephone number in Tehran. He asked why I wanted information regarding his parents. I said that when he ventured out onto the streets of Karachi he would most likely be shot by Pakistani Army troops. However, I could fly the aircraft back to Tehran alone, but would like to be able to contact his parents to request that they come and pickup his body. He canceled his downtown shopping plans.

The Hilton Hotel housed a very interesting mix of foreign guests seeking ways to occupy their unplanned house arrest. The small supply of magazines and newspapers had all been snapped up and the bar had been closed for several days. Television and radio stations were broadcasting only military directives and Muslim religious music, so consequently they provided little entertainment. The main lobby seemed the place to be, but finding a place to sit was difficult. Guests who only a couple of days before were complete strangers were now gathered in small discussion groups or playing cards. The main topic was when would the airlines be allowed to operate so they could be on their way?

I came across a group of what I was sure were airline flight attendants and pilots stranded like ourselves. Striking up a conversation, I learned they were a B-707 Egypt Air crew from Cairo. Within a few minutes our over zealous pleasure in vocalizing flight experiences started to bother other hotel guests, so I invited everyone to my room for an impromptu party. On the way, I buttonholed a waiter and asked him if he could bring four bottles of wine to my room. He told me of the ban on alcoholic beverage sales, but a $20 tip temporarily canceled this restriction. He said the wine would be delivered in a few minutes.

Gathered in my room were four very attractive female Egypt Air flight attendants, their first officer, my copilot and my two Iranian Navy flight attendants. The combination of the wine and airline crew comradeship made for a very enjoyable group. Past airline experiences were shared in the common language of English and the spirit of friendship increased as the volume of wine decreased. (See Photo No. 13.)

With spontaneous enthusiasm, the Egypt Air first officer and several flight attendants picked up metal waste paper baskets and started beating on them as improvised drums. Several females accompanied the hollow (tin can) beat with a "high-pitch" tongue wobbling sound, usually reserved for weddings or joyous occasions. Other Egypt Air flight attendants picked up the cadence and were soon competing with each other in lively bottom-gyrating belly dancing. Those not engaged in drum beating or belly dancing added to the excitement through loud hand clapping and continuous shrill Arabic sounding off-key singing.

My room vibrated with this spontaneous enthusiastic merriment for some time until we heard a loud knocking on the door. A hotel representative stated that several guests were complaining about the noise and requested we quiet down. Since we had consumed all the wine and the belly dancers were getting tired, we agreed to end the party.

As my guests were leaving I asked the most attractive Egypt Air flight attendant if she would remain to help me clean up the mess left over from the party. She willingly complied. (See Photo No. 13.)

About an hour later, after recuperating from our energetic consensual cleanup chore, we were making the bed when the telephone rang. The caller informed me that the Pakistani government had approved our departure from Karachi and a vehicle would be in front of the hotel at 9 a.m. the following morning to drive us to the airport. My attractive Egypt Air flight attendant got dressed, wished me an affectionate farewell and departed. Our paths never crossed again.

The next morning my crew and I were waiting near the main entrance of the hotel for our transportation to the airport. Total curfew was still in effect and the mood of the stranded foreigners, wandering about the hotel lobby, was becoming more agitated. As I stood waiting in my airline captain's uniform, several people came up and wanted to know which airline I flew for and if I was flying out of Karachi. I became very tired of explaining that I flew for a charter company in Tehran and was only transporting military personnel in an Iranian military aircraft. I finally took off my blouse and folded it so the four gold stripes on the sleeves were not visible, but this did not completely stop the continuous flow of questions from people eager to leave Karachi.

About 9:15 a.m. a gray navy van arrived, escorted by the customary machine gun-armed jeeps in front and back. Once again we raced through deserted streets on the way to the airport. While filing my flight plan I learned that my passengers for the return trip to Tehran would be Iranian Naval officers and their wives who had been stranded in Pakistan.

After receiving my departure clearance I once again had the sky to myself and didn't see another aircraft or hear other radio calls during my exit from Pakistani airspace.

My flight to the city of Karachi when under military siege was very interesting and profitable. I learned after returning to Iran that the curfew and martial law was lifted two days later; however, Prime Minister Bhutto's clamp-down was only a short reprieve from his problems. Later in the year he and his close followers were arrested by military officers loyal to General Zia. Prime Minister Bhutto was convicted of treason by a military court martial and hanged on April 4, 1979.

Following the ending of martial law, Pakistan was eager to resume normal relations with their Muslim neighbor Iran. An integral part of this relationship was joint visits by military officers and enlisted men. The Chief Pilot informed me that a Pakistani submarine was making a good-will port call to the Bandar Abbas Naval Station and Air Taxi was dispatching an Iranian Navy F-27 to support the crew's transportation needs. My mission was to fly about 25 Pakistani sailors to the city of Mashad, and stay with them for two nights while they performed a Muslim pilgrimage in the celebrated Shiite mosque. (See Photo No. 1.)

Mashad is Iran's second largest city and located in Northeast Iran close to the Afghanistan border. It contains one of Islam's most revered Shiite mosques and is a popular pilgrimage site for Muslims the world over. The tomb of Iman Reza, one of the most noted Muslim martyrs, who died in 818 A.D., is located in this elaborate house of god. After checking into the Razavish Grand Hotel my two navy copilots asked if I had ever visited the famous Mashad Mosque. When I replied in the negative, they said that they would take me there after we changed into civilian clothes.

A short taxi ride deposited us near the main entrance to a huge gilded copper-domed mosque easily filling an entire city block. It was protected by a high stone wall and a security guard was overseeing all visitors entering, as only men were allowed and everyone was required to remove their shoes prior to entrance. As an obvious infidel, I was surprised that I was not challenged when I entered this most holy Muslim mosque, as I had heard that the inner sanctum was off limits to all non-Muslims. However, I naively assumed my Iranian Navy copilots knew what they were doing and wouldn't lead me astray.

The interior of the mosque consisted of chambers of glittering mirrors, tiled walls and floors and a huge gold-encrusted sarcophagus in the center of a large cylindrical cupola. It was filled to near capacity with hundreds of male worshipers praying and reciting the Koran in a sort of hypnotic trance. Almost all worshipers were dressed in long black robes, had full beards and were joined in a slow moving, tightly-packed procession toward the mausoleum of Iman Reza.

My escorts and I worked our way toward the rotunda passing men touching and kissing the walls leading to the holy tomb. Some, after being in close proximity to the sarcophagus, were so overcome with emotion that they were rolling on the floor or beating their bleeding heads against the hard marble walls. Most faces were wet with crocodile tears trickling down into thick black beards. Some were in such an emotional state that they had to be held up by friends or other parishioners. The sound of wailing and praying that echoed off the walls and ceiling produced a stereophonic, unearthly, hypnotic effect.

The activity I was observing was strange to my non-Muslim eyes, yet I couldn't help but admire such vivid display of faith. It was obvious that everyone felt a deep sense of devotion to their God (Allah) and were not ashamed of exhibiting this commitment in public.

I was standing off to one side mesmerized by the religious scenes being played out before me when I noticed a group of about eight menacing-looking men encircling me and my companions. Through slow shuffling-foot movements the circle was becoming smaller and soon formed a tight corral. The faces of this unhappy group were contorted with rage as they shouted obvious insults regarding my presence. Their black piercing eyes, dilated with obvious hate, sent a clear message that I wasn't welcome. I sensed a serious concern on the part of my two Iranian Navy copilots. When I asked them what was going on they told me not to speak, or make eye contact with any of the demonstrators, as they were outraged that an infidel had invaded the inner sanctum of their most sacred mosque during the Muslim holy month of Ramadan.

I felt utterly helpless, as it appeared that the situation could turn ugly with the slightest provocation. With a copilot on each arm we started a slow shuffle toward a nearby door. The circle of protesters, still shouting obvious obscenities, moved along with us. When we reached the door, I was literally pushed through it and it closed with a bang behind me. As the door was closing one of the copilots, in an excited voice, said, "Wait here captain, out of sight until we come back with our shoes."

I breathed a sigh of relief in escaping the angry mob inside the mosque, but soon learned that it was only a short reprieve from potential danger from angry Islamic militants. I found myself standing in a small alcove overlooking an open air courtyard.

Marching in unison around a half-darkened flowered center garden were about 25 men, wearing white T-shirts, and engaged in self-flagellation across their backs with small metal whips. Their back strokes were synchronized with a melodic drum beat emanating from a hidden source and painful chants from the participants. The backs of their T-shirts were blood stained and when they passed my position, they gave me a menacing look I'll never forget. I felt like I wanted to melt into the cement wall to escape their stares, but at the same time I had no desire to reenter the mosque.

As they were about to make their second pass, the door opened behind me and my two Iranian Navy copilots appeared carrying our shoes. With backs bent in a slouch position we slowly worked our way around the courtyard, past the euphoric marching mob and escaped through a door which fortunately opened onto a public street. After donning our shoes, we took a taxi back to the Razavish Grand Hotel.

When I entered the hotel lobby I was greeted by an Iranian Navy Lieutenant Commander medical doctor who had been a passenger on some of my previous flights. He extended a warm hand shake while stating, "Salam-u-Alaikum" (peace). He asked where I had been and I told him of my narrow escape from the Reza Iman Mosque. His face turned red as he called my two junior officer copilots to attention. He dressed them down mercilessly in Farsi, and when he was through, they snapped him a salute and headed for their rooms.

After my copilots left, he told me that they had performed a very foolish move in taking me inside the mosque during the holy month of Ramadan. He added that since I was an infidel "nonbeliever," I had exposed myself to the possibility of having my throat slit by one or more of the fanatical Muslims and my body thrown out into the street, where it would have lain until the following morning, or provided a midnight snack for wild dogs.

He stated that a small minority of the Shiite Muslims living in the Mashad area are Militant Fundamentalists who take the writings in the Koran literally. Consequently, my visit to the mosque could have been very dangerous if it had been interpreted as a sin against Allah. He went on to state that some radical Muslims believe it is an honor to fight and die for their religion and believe they are following God's will when they kill infidel sinners. To do otherwise would be to disobey the teachings of Mohammad. Life in Iran was becoming more interesting every day!

At the time I thought the doctor's admonition about the dangers I exposed myself to when visiting the Muslim mosque was overstated. However, in the last 25 years there have been numerous terrorist attacks on Western targets by Islamic militant extremist groups that have killed thousands of people. These attacks ranged from the suicide attack on the Marine barracks in Beirut in 1983 that killed 242 to the World Trade Center and Pentagon attacks on 9/11/01 that killed 3,000.

Terrorist groups like al-Qaida, Taliban, Hamas, Hizballah and Islamic Jihad are familiar names. However, reference to the Internet web page, ***"Terrorist Groups Profiles, Dudley Knox Library"*** *lists more than 60 active militant groups whose goal is to strike against Western countries.*

An excerpt from the web page, ***"Islam and the Shariah"*** *states, "The concept of Jihad, or holy war, is a concept that is interpreted from the Koran and backed up by the Shariah (Muslim law). The holy war to the Shiite Muslims is the war between Muslims and non-Muslims. Many Shiite Muslims believe that it is an honor to fight and die for their religion. They believe they are doing the work of Allah (God) when they kill people who are not Muslim."*

Based on this it appears my doctor friend was providing good advice.

Chapter Eight --- Flying the Fairchild FH-227

In 1976, Air Taxi purchased four FH-227s that were being retired from active service with Piedmont Airlines in Wilmington, North Carolina. The FH-227, built by the Fairchild Aircraft Company in Hagerstown, Maryland, is an American version of the Dutch Fokker F-27. It is similar in appearance to the European model but contains many distinct differences. The fuselage is six feet longer, it is equipped with a freon self-contained air-conditioning system, has different type propellers and the cockpit presentation is totally rearranged. (See Photo No. 6.)

The United States considered the F-27 and FH-227 a common aircraft type rating (license) for pilots, but Iran required separate ratings. I believe Iran's approach was correct as the two aircraft were no more similar than the Douglas DC-4 and DC-6, which do require separate U.S. ratings. All four FH-227s were to be stationed in the southern oil producing city of Abadan and operated by a newly-formed subsidiary of Air Taxi to be called, "Air Service Company." Two of the aircraft were to be retained in the original 44 passenger configuration, while two would be converted to half cargo and half passenger. (See Photo No. 6.)

To operate their fleet of FH-227s, the company hired two qualified Dutch flight instructors for a limited period, with the intent of providing training to an initial cadre of captains from the Air Taxi Company in Tehran. Once a sufficient number of company pilots were qualified in the FH-227, they would be manned on a rotational basis by captains and copilots from Tehran on temporary assignment.

I looked forward to my stint in this interesting southern port city. Abadan is on a delta formed by the Tigris and Euphrates rivers and until 1970 boasted the largest oil refinery in the world. (Both the refinery and city were heavily bombed by Iraq during the eight year Iran/Iraq war.)

In early June 1976, I was dispatched to Abadan and flew my first left seat flight in a FH-227 on June 7th, the day before my 48th birthday. The flight was from Abadan to a nearby oil field with Captain Kuss as my instructor in the right seat. The same day I flew a round trip flight to Khark Island followed by an hour and 20 minute local-type rating checkride. The following day I received an initial captain's line check on a flight to Ahwaz and several small oil supporting airports. When we landed back in Abadan I was a fully qualified FH-227 captain after only two days and five hours flight time in the aircraft. (I considered this a fair birthday present.)

After completing my checkride I returned to Tehran but was told that I would be assigned temporary duty in Abadan shortly to fulfill my share of supporting the southern Iran flight program. Before departing Abadan, I asked Captain Kuss if I could have a copy of the FH-227 flight operations manual so I could review the aircraft systems but was told there was only a limited number available. However, he said he would loan me one for a few days providing I promised to return it.

When I called in for my Tehran flight schedule for June 16, 1976, I was surprised to learn that I would be flying an FH-227 to Abu Dhabi, a city in the United Arab Emirates, with an en route cargo stop at Shiraz. The dispatcher said that an Abadan-based FH-227 would be landing in Tehran during the night and the pilots who flew it would be in crew rest so it would leave the aircraft without a qualified captain. At the time I only had five hours in the FH-227, but the dispatcher stated that I was the only pilot presently available in Tehran qualified to fly this type aircraft. Fortunately, I had briefly reviewed the borrowed aircraft flight manual and figured that in combining my limited knowledge, with the anticipated experience my copilot was surely to have, it would be sufficient to safely fly the trip.

When I checked in with the dispatch center the next morning I discovered, without surprise, that my copilot, Mr. Irampour, had never flown a FH-227. During flight planning he asked me how I liked the Fairchild version of the Fokker aircraft as he was looking forward to flying it. Calling upon my extensive experience, I told him he would enjoy it as it was equipped with a freon air-conditioning system.

I delivered about 30 passengers to Shiraz and took on a mixed load of cargo for Abu Dhabi. My takeoff from Shiraz was on Runway 29 Right. A rising mountain range just to the west of the airport requires a fairly rapid turn to the south (left) after takeoff. On this particular departure I was advised by the tower to exercise caution as a flight of four Iranian F-4 jet fighters were taking off on the left parallel runway. This warning couldn't have come at a worse time, since it was issued just as I was becoming airborne. With a field elevation of 5,000 feet and a fully loaded aircraft, my ability to take evasive action to avoid the jet fighters was limited.

From past conversations with U.S. Air Force instructor pilot advisors, I knew that Iranian fighter pilots had a tendency of not looking out for other traffic, or to put it another way, they had a tendency of keeping their "heads in the cockpit." With the fighters taking off on the parallel runway to my left, and the fact that I would have to be making a left turn to avoid high terrain, I was concerned about the possibility of a mid-air collision.

With my attention directed out the left window, I signaled to the copilot with my right hand thumb to raise the landing gear. I didn't feel or hear the gear retracting and a quick glance at the instrument panel revealed the reason why. The "nose gear not centered" light was on which would prevent the cockpit gear handle from physically moving to the up position.

The pilot's action to correct this condition was simple, but at this precise moment, I couldn't take time to address it. I was busy eyeballing the Iranian fighters converging on my left, the mountains looming up straight ahead and maintaining proper airspeed with the gear extended.

As the fighters disappeared to the south and our altitude rose above the hills, I was able to devote attention to the "nose gear not centered" problem. However, before I could take any action, I felt and heard the landing gear retracting, even though the nose gear warning light was still on. The fact that the landing gear was retracted under this condition was not good and even with my limited experience in the FH-227 I remembered reading about this potential problem in the aircraft flight manual and what must be done when it occurs.

I asked my copilot, who was smiling with a look of proud accomplishment, what he had done to be able to retract the landing gear. With obvious pride, he told me that the reason he couldn't move the cockpit gear retraction handle was that there was a small latch blocking it from moving. However, by using a pencil he was able to reach in behind it and move the latch out of the way. Once he did this, he was able to move the handle to the up position and retract the landing gear.

He noticed a look of astonishment on my face and asked if he had done something wrong. I said, "Mr. Irampour, you may have really screwed up this time!" I told him that since the "nose gear not centered" light was on when he overrode the built-in safety feature, the nose gear might be jammed in the up position and might not extend when we prepared to land at Abu Dhabi.

I engaged the autopilot and took out the aircraft flight manual for a little "in-flight" ground school. I explained to my confused colleague that there were times when taking off in crosswinds that the nose gear might not be completely centered when becoming airborne. If this occurred, we would be alerted to this condition by a light in the cockpit stating, "Nose gear not centered." The corrective action was to move the nose gear ground steering handle back and forth until the light went out. When it did, the latch blocking the movement of the cockpit gear handle would disappear and we would be able to retract the gear. But, by his by-passing the system, he might have retracted a nose gear that was not centered. Consequently, it might be jammed in the up position. (I didn't think there would be a problem, but I didn't want to let my copilot off the hook without a little sweating and a misuse of the expression "Insha Allah.")

While we were en route to Abu Dhabi, my copilot wanted to know what we would do if the nose gear didn't extend. I told him we would have to land on the main gear only and lower the aircraft down onto its nose as gently as possible. He wondered what the Chief Pilot would say if this was necessary. I said I didn't think he would be jumping with joy! He requested permission to extend the gear while en route to see if it was jammed, but I told him that our airspeed was too high. (I also wanted him to think a little longer about the serious mistake he had made.)

After turning onto the downwind leg at Abu Dhabi, I delayed lowering the landing gear as long as possible while my copilot shifted nervously in his seat. When I finally commanded, "Gear down," my copilot breathed a loud sigh of relief when the landing gear extended properly and we had three green lights. His comment, was the expected "Insha Allah."

After a light lunch and some shopping in the airport duty-free store, I let my copilot fly the leg back to Tehran. At the completion of the flight I had 13 hours in the FH-227 and was beginning to prefer it over the F-27. The next day I observed my copilot explaining to his young colleagues in the pilot's lounge the intricacies of the nose gear centering system in the FH-227. (He was now a "nose gear not centered" expert.)

My Iranian copilots, without exception, were fun to fly with and seemed eager to learn. However, their fatalistic philosophy that events are fixed in advance for all time, and that human beings are powerless to change them, was in direct conflict with good flight safety management. Their expression "Insha Allah" seemed to address all unexpected emergencies and deviations from sound safety practices.

A good example of this deterministic approach was demonstrated one day when I was preparing for a passenger flight in an F-27. After starting the right engine, the oil pressure gauge continued to read zero. I rapped on the gauge with my knuckles several times, and when it didn't show any rise in the standard wait of 30 seconds, I aborted the start and called for maintenance support. The mechanics diagnosed the problem as a bad oil pressure transmitter and said it would take about one hour to repair. I gave the flight attendants and passengers the option of remaining onboard, or going back to the terminal. They elected to remain with the aircraft, while the copilot and I went to the dispatch center to update our clearance, check the latest weather and enjoy a cup of hot chay (tea).

While I was sipping my tea my copilot came over and inquired if our aircraft was repaired. I told him no, not yet, but we could expect it to be back in commission shortly and as soon as it was maintenance control would give us a call. His response, "Insha Allah."

With the intent of a little friendly teasing, I asked him what he meant by that remark. He replied that if you are in good graces with Allah, everything will be taken care of and since he was a good Muslim, he doesn't have to worry about problems when flying. I told him that was fine, but presented a hypothetical situation I wanted him to think about.

I called his attention to the lack of oil pressure when we started the right engine, and because of it, I shut it down. I asked him if he agreed with the action I took. He said he did. I said, "OK, let's say that we were racing down the runway for takeoff, but haven't yet reached takeoff speed when we note that the oil pressure on the right engine has dropped to zero. Do we abort, or say, 'Insha Allah,' and continue the takeoff?" I could see that he was puzzled in attempting to answer the question, so I said, "Let me give you a little help."

I said, "Allah Akbar" (God is great), and he said, "Right on, captain." I then suggested that Allah in all his wisdom gave us a brain and if we didn't use this wonderful gift we would "piss him off." So using my example, I said that if we were on a takeoff run and observed a serious problem before reaching takeoff speed, Allah would expect us to use the brain he gave us and abort the takeoff. By aborting, we would avoid "pissing him off" and live to praise him in the future. He seemed to like this approach, but was still a little confused and began scratching his head.

Many Iranian captains also reflected this preordained fatalistic approach when flying between Tehran and the city of Bandar Abbas on the Persian Gulf. The preferred route was to fly the airways depicted on the High Altitude Navigation chart which crossed over Esfahan and Shiraz. The flying time in an F-27 by this route was about three hours, avoided flying over the highest mountains and provided a comfortable altitude margin in the event of an engine failure. It also provided a number of alternate airports to divert to, if the need arose, and radio navigation stations providing accurate on-course guidance, which was a comforting feeling when flying over remote mountainous terrain.

The alternate route was to fly a direct course between Tehran and Bandar Abbas, shortening the flying time by about 20 minutes. However, this direct route was over mountainous terrain higher than a fully loaded F-27 could maintain in the event of an engine failure. I and other foreign captains flew the longer and safer route while most Iranian captains, with "Insha Allah" as their guide, flew the shorter high mountainous route.

Deadheading, especially in the high speed *Falcon* Jet, was another area where I learned not to rely solely on Allah's protection for my safety. (I figured He was quite busy just looking after my Iranian pilot colleagues, so would appreciate all the help He could get.)

One day I was deadheading back to Tehran in a twin-engine *Falcon* DA-20 jet that was being flown by two Iranian captains. They offered me a seat in the cabin, but I said I would be more comfortable in the jump seat. (I preferred the jump seat, so I could keep an eye on my Iranian pilot colleagues.) The flight was uneventful until we approached Tehran.

During the descent we entered the cloud tops at around 10,000 feet and based on the reported weather reports, we could expect to quickly break out in good weather underneath. However, to my surprise, and I'm sure to the two Iranian captains, we were still in the clouds when we leveled off at our interim assigned altitude of 8,000 feet (4,000 feet above the ground). About one minute later Tehran Approach Control cleared us to descend to 6,000 feet and an expedited ILS approach to runway 29 Right. Neither pilot had his approach charts out, since they relied on memory for inserting the correct ILS frequency and heading. In spite of their so-called excellent recollection they became very hurried in setting up the cockpit and while we were still in the clouds, executed a diving high speed dash to intercept the published inbound ILS approach course to the runway.

However, we flew right through the inbound course, doing well over 200 knots, and maintained a heading of northwest. It was apparent to me that both pilots didn't realize we had flown through the inbound course and were now heading directly toward the Alborz Mountains, a few miles north of the city.

I shouted to them that we had flown through the published inbound course and must make an immediate turn to the left. They either didn't hear me, or were in a muddled mental state of confusion and lacked proper situation awareness. I didn't have time to figure out which, so I stood up, gripped a hold of the control column and forced the aircraft into a left bank. About this time we broke out of the clouds and had the airport in sight, well off to our left, and the foothills of the Alborz Mountains uncomfortably close on the right.

They extended the speed brakes, landing gear and flaps, and through some abrupt maneuvers got back on course and made an uneventful, albeit a little hot and long, landing. In discussing this dangerous approach with them later, their only comment was, "We trusted in Allah."

Keeping my passengers safe, and in-turn myself, was always in the forefront of my mind. However, at times this was a difficult goal to achieve. During an early morning F-27 departure from Tehran I was holding in the number one position for takeoff on Runway 29 Right. After completing the Before Takeoff Checklist I contacted the control tower and requested departure clearance. The tower cleared me for takeoff without delay. As I started to taxi onto the runway, I directed my gaze toward the final approach area to ensure that there wasn't an aircraft about to land. Confirming that the area was clear was difficult, as I was looking directly into a rising sun and a hazy sky. Because of the restricted visibility I slowed my taxi onto the runway, and shielding my squinted eyes with a cupped hand, strained to view the approach end of the runway.

Suddenly, without warning, a Pan American B-747 *Jumbo* jet emerged from the haze! I slammed on the brakes as the B-747 landed directly in front of my position. Had I not slowed my taxi to ensure the runway approach area was clear, my relatively small F-27 would have been squashed like a bug by the 600,000-pound jet. Apparently approach control had authorized the B-747 to land without having him switch to the common tower radio frequency. If he had, I would have been aware of his presence on final approach. I wrote a detailed report on the incident and presented it to the Chief Pilot, but never heard another word.

En route to Khark Island with a full load of passengers in an F-27 I was passing over Shiraz at 20,000 feet, heading south. The aircraft was on autopilot and I was enjoying a smooth flight while flying in and out of the cloud tops. My copilot was in the process of transmitting a position report to Shiraz radio when, as we emerged from one of the many cloud tops, a Russian Tupolev TU-154 flying in the opposite direction suddenly appeared at our altitude and directly ahead. It was flying what appeared to be on a direct collision course with our aircraft.

The sighting lasted only a split second and was gone as quickly as it had appeared while missing our aircraft by only a few feet. The sighting was so dramatic that I can close my eyes to this day and still see it. The aircraft that we nearly collided with was a Russian TU-154 operated by the Polish national airline known as LOT. The TU-154 is very similar to a B-727 but has larger cabin windows.

The near-miss was so close that I could see passengers reading newspapers through the cabin windows of the other aircraft. My instinctive reaction when I first saw the aircraft emerge from the clouds was to disconnect the autopilot and take evasive action, but the event was over before I could move. The incident was so fleeting that my copilot never saw it. (See Photo No. 10.)

I called Shiraz radio and inquired about the call sign of the other aircraft passing over Shiraz at our assigned altitude, but was told that they had no knowledge of any other aircraft. About one minute later a LOT pilot, with a heavy Polish accent, reported he was passing over Shiraz at 22,000 feet.

He may have been at 22,000 feet when he made his position report, but was at my altitude earlier when passing over Shiraz.

I prepared a report of the incident and submitted it to the Air Taxi Chief Pilot, but as usual never heard another word. (This near-miss could have resulted in a mid-air collision very similar to the collision of a TU-154 and a B-757 over Germany in July 2002, causing both aircraft to crash and killing everyone onboard both aircraft.)

I believe that the Iranian's rationalistic approach to life was one of the main reasons for their dismal automobile accident rate. I remember one serious incident I came across on my way to work which involved a fire and explosion on a crowded city bus. A passenger boarded a standing-room-only bus with an unsealed can of gasoline. He was standing among a group of heavy smokers and the result was a predictable fire and explosion with many deaths. (Insha Allah.)

The following week the Chief Pilot informed me that I was to go to Abadan for one week where I would fly FH-227s throughout Southern Iran. I called his attention to the fact that this assignment would be during the last week of the month and I had already flown the required 75 hours. Therefore, every additional flight hour would entitle me to overtime pay. I mentioned that if I remained in Tehran I would most likely fly another 25 hours. He said not to worry as I would fly every day in Abadan and would actually make more money (a quintessential Iranian fabrication of the truth). I rode the jump seat in an Iran Air B-727 to Abadan the next morning, checked in with the local dispatcher and secured a room in the Abadan International Hotel. The dispatcher instructed me to check in with him by telephone around 5 p.m. to obtain my next day's flight schedule.

When I contacted the Abadan dispatcher he told me that I was to be a standby captain the following day and would be called if needed. After a non-profitable day of relaxing around the swimming pool, I called the dispatcher for my next day's schedule. I was informed, once again, that I was on standby status, but could expect to be called to fly. However, I wasn't scheduled for a flight on the second day either and spent another non-profitable day lounging in the shade around the swimming pool.

Following two days of inactivity, and lost overtime pay, I called the dispatcher for what I was confident would be a flight assignment on my third day in Abadan. However, the dispatcher informed me that I was to spend another non-productive day on standby. I asked him how many FH-227s were scheduled to fly the following day. He said, "Three, but all were scheduled to be flown by Iranian captains but if one of them canceled I would be called."

I told the dispatcher that I was sent to Abadan to fly, not to sit around a hotel swimming pool like a Maytag repairman, and each day I sat on the ground I was losing money. I added that if I was not assigned a flight the following day I would return to Tehran. No flight assignment was provided so early the next morning I checked out of the hotel and rode the jump seat on an Iran Air B-727 back to Tehran.

I was relaxing in my apartment when the Chief Pilot called and wanted to know what I was doing back in Tehran. I told him I was enjoying a cold beer! He inquired as to why I had returned from Abadan without permission from the company. I told him that my job in Iran was to fly, not sit around a hotel swimming pool. I called his attention to his promise that if I went to Abadan I would fly, not be assigned standby duty while Iranian captains were acquiring overtime. I added that if he sent me to Abadan in the future, he'd better ensure I fly or I wouldn't go!

He didn't disagree with the firm position I took and promised me as many flights as possible in the remaining days of the month. I was finally learning how to deal with the Chief Pilot. Subterfuge and firmness in daily business dealings was the only language he seemed to understand. I could forget the polite and considerate treatment I had been exposed to during my years of flying for Japan Domestic Airlines. Once I learned the Middle East art of only believing what you can see or touch, my life in Iran was considerably more enjoyable and monetarily more beneficial.

One week later I was requested to return to Abadan for ten days temporary assignment. The Chief Pilot promised that this time I would fly almost every day. Making good on his promise, I was assigned flight duty for seven days straight without a break. Most flights originated from Abadan at sunrise in the relatively cool morning air. The flights were to and from the many oil-producing airfields along the Northern coast of the Persian Gulf. The trips were airline-type flying with published departure and arrival times at each stop.

For most of my stay in Abadan I flew with the same copilot and flight attendants which made the experience very enjoyable. This was the first time that I had the pleasure of being teamed up with the same crew for more than one flight. I think they enjoyed the exposure as much as I did.

Air Service Fairchild FH-227s were configured to carry 44 passengers, but more than this number normally crowded around each airport departure area. Company gate agents could be observed holding back passengers pushing to board the aircraft. After one such departure my copilot, after we were airborne, informed me that we had more passengers onboard then we had seats, and several men were standing in the aisle and holding onto the overhead bins as if they were on a bus. I decided to check on this overbooking myself at the next stop.

The gate agent came to the cockpit declaring that the aircraft was ready for departure. I asked him how many passengers were onboard. He said a full load of 44. As I got up from my seat to check the cabin, I could see that he was concerned as to what I might find. Opening the cockpit door I observed about six male passengers standing in the aisle and as before gripping the overhead bins. I told the agent that the people standing would have to be off-loaded. He pleaded with me to reconsider as he had already collected their fares. I insisted that all standing passengers would have to deplane. My persistence created a heated argument between seated and standing passengers as to who would deplane and who would be allowed to remain onboard. The argument became a shouting match, and one burly passenger produced a hammer and was threatening another passenger with menacing gestures, while indicating that he was going to remain onboard.

I grabbed my flight bag and left the aircraft as I had heard that the week before one of our foreign captains was attacked by a standing passenger when he was told he would have to leave. As I left, I told the agent that when he got things settled he could find me in the air-conditioned terminal building enjoying a cold Coca Cola. The agent inquired if a payment of bakhsheesh would solve the problem, but I said no way and kept on walking.

About 20 minutes later the agent informed me that the aircraft was ready for departure and there were no passengers standing in the aisle. (This was factually a true statement, but not the full story.) Entering the aircraft I checked the cabin and was met with 44 sets of eyes, glaring at me with obvious anger.

I was about to enter the cockpit when, for some reason, I decided to check the front lavatory for any possible stowaways. When I opened the door I discovered two bearded men, dressed in black robes and turbans, sitting on the closed toilet seat. I turned to the ground agent, but before I could say a word he pleaded with me to disregard the two men in the restroom. He said he had tried his best to correct the overbooking, but the two in the lavatory had paid more than full fare and had to make this flight. I once again picked up my flight bag and headed for the terminal.

Shortly thereafter the agent said the aircraft was ready for departure and that all passengers were now seated, adding that I was much more difficult to deal with than an Iranian captain who would not make such a big fuss over a few extra passengers. With no passengers standing in the aisle, or hiding in the lavatory, I departed Abadan for the Island of Lavan. Once airborne I activated the freon air-conditioner and enjoyed a comfortable flight along the picturesque North Shore of the Persian Gulf. After a lunch of rice and lamb and a couple games of pool, I flew back to Abadan with all passengers occupying a seat. My prerequisite for proper cabin discipline was not popular with the Iranian ground agents, but was being ubiquitously disseminated.

The Fairchild FH-227 was a welcome addition for flights in the Iranian Desert. The freon air-conditioning system was considerably more effective than the air cycle machine on the Fokker F-27, and cooled the aircraft quickly if it was properly used. However, the system was designed for the East Coast of the United States where temperatures rarely exceed 95 degrees Fahrenheit. But, in Southern Iran with temperatures approaching 125 degrees or higher, the freon air-conditioning system would overheat and pop a circuit breaker if it was activated on the ground, since there was insufficient ram air flow available for cooling. To complicate the problem, in activating it on the ground, was that the circuit breaker was not accessible from the cockpit or in flight. It could only be reset by opening an external hatch in the rear of the aircraft. Also, once popped it required a long cooling-off period before it could be reset.

The trick in proper use of the freon air-conditioning system was to wait until after takeoff before turning it on. After that it would provide cold air for the entire flight. I don't know how many times I explained the appropriate use of it to Iranian captains, but many never seemed to master the technique. Time after time, after enduring a low altitude hot flight across the desert, I would see them opening the rear hatch of their aircraft after landing to reset the circuit breaker.

However, as welcome as the freon air-conditioning system was, it could do nothing to cool the cockpit of an aircraft sitting in the hot desert. Whenever I was required to park the aircraft on a desert airport for more than 15 minutes, I would cover as much of the cockpit area as possible with old newspapers so as to shade the throttles and control column from the searing rays of the sun. There were times when I would don gloves and wear them until airborne because the throttles and controls were too hot to touch with bare hands. With temperatures approaching 125 degrees it was a mad dash to get airborne before the engine oil temperatures exceeded their maximum limits and possibly began to boil. (I believe Death Valley would be a vacation spot in comparison to some sections of the Iranian Desert.)

The extremely high temperatures were not the only discomforting aspect of the desolate Iranian desert. Frequent high-winds would create dust storms that would sting bare skin and irritate unprotected eyes. Close fitting sun glasses were a must and I often covered my mouth and nose with a large handkerchief or white scarf when going to and from my aircraft. However, it was possible to climb above these dust storms soon after takeoff and fly in clear blue skies. Viewing robust sand storms from the air presented colorful mosaic patterns of the landscape that would have been interesting but challenging for an artist to capture on canvas.

Chapter Nine --- Photo Mapping Iraq

In a remote section of the Air Taxi parking ramp, the company kept two unusual Fokker F-27s. They were painted a dull black and had no external markings or numbers of any kind. Hanging from each wing were large extended-range fuel drop tanks which was very odd for this type of aircraft. The area where they were parked was circled by a high barbed wire fence and patrolled by armed guards 24 hours a day. Occasionally, I would see one or both taxiing out for takeoff, but noted that their flight was not posted on the company scheduling board.

I had on several occasions asked Iranian copilots about these strange aircraft, but always received an "I don't know" answer. I would receive the same response from Iranian captains and even the Chief Pilot. Rumors were that they were engaged in some sort of covert activity and the pilots approved to fly them received double pay for each hour of flight. I was intrigued by both the nature of their mission and the reported additional pay received by the pilots. I asked the Chief Pilot several times if he would add my name to the list of captains authorized to fly the "Black F-27s," but he always gave an evasive "maybe some day" answer. I finally gave up and went on flying the standard Air Taxi Company flights.

One summer day in 1977, I was submitting my post-flight paperwork to the dispatch section when the Chief Pilot requested I come to his office. As I entered, he closed the door and asked if I was still interested in flying the "Black F-27s." When I responded that I was, he informed me that what he was going to reveal was top secret and I was not to discuss it with any other pilot in the company or anyone else in Iran. He insisted I agree to his request before proceeding. I assured him I would remain silent since as a former military officer I was familiar with keeping secrets

He said that the two uniquely configured F-27s were photo-reconnaissance aircraft procured from the Fokker Aircraft Company on special order. Their cargo compartments contained high-resolution cameras that took pictures from discretely hidden openings in the bottom of the fuselage. He added that the primary mission of these aircraft was the mapping of the Iran/Iraq border area which the military wanted in the event of an armed conflict with Iraq. For public consumption these aircraft were operated as "Geodetic Survey Flights."

He continued his briefing by stating that these special flights were flown at 20,000 feet and could only be operated on cloudless days in calm winds when ground visibility was not obscured by blowing sand. To obtain both conditions was rare. (This explained the infrequent flying of these aircraft that I had observed in the past.) He also pointed out that both aircraft were equipped with Inertial Navigation Systems (INS) and asked if I was INS qualified. When I answered no, he said he anticipated that and handed me an instruction booklet titled, "INS Instructional Manual." He said, "Study this tonight as I need a special operation's captain qualified in INS in the morning."

INS is a highly complex computerized system which measures spatial behavior through acceleration and movement to provide very accurate geographical positions. When integrated with the auto pilot it will provide a stable uninterrupted platform for the high-resolution airborne cameras.

Before leaving for my apartment I mentioned that it was rumored that pilots flying these special flights receive double pay and inquired if this was true. He acknowledged that it was.

I spent several hours that night reviewing the Inertial Navigation Systems Instructional Manual and felt I had a fair working knowledge of it when I turned out the lights at around midnight and went to bed. As I drifted off to sleep I wondered what type of excitement my special mission flight would generate the following day.

At 6:30 the next morning the company Volkswagen crew bus driver was beeping his horn in front of my apartment. I hurried to a kitchen window to signal that I was up and not to wake up the whole neighborhood. Without a wave from my window, he would just keep on blowing the horn no matter what time of the morning it was. The ride to the airport at this early hour was fast, but on the way we still stopped at a bakery for the customary load of fresh pita bread and smelly goat cheese.

When I checked in with the dispatch center, it was clear that my flight this morning was something special. My briefing folder was in a closed binder and the dispatcher made sure we were in a secluded area of the room when we discussed the flight. My mission had me climbing to 20,000 feet on a westerly heading toward Iraq. My first check point was given in geographic coordinates with additional checkpoints forming a series of concentric loops along the Iran/Iraq border. I was to insert all listed check points into the INS computer and when level at 20,000 feet allow the autopilot to fly the planned course. I was instructed not to communicate with the civilian personnel in the rear of the aircraft operating the cameras. The scheduled flight time for this mission was eight hours (which explained the need for the additional fuel contained in the auxiliary external wing tanks).

The dispatcher was emphatic in stating that I was not to cross the border into Iraq and if intercepted by Iraqi Mikoyan and Guryevich (Mig) jet fighters, to turn immediately to the east, away from the border and not to take any action that could be interpreted as aggressive. I met my copilot for the flight who stated that this was his first special mission flight, was not familiar with the operation of INS or the true purpose of the flight except that he was told that it was classified. (This didn't surprise me!)

Before leaving the dispatch counter we were issued special passes authorizing the guards to allow us access to the restricted ramp area and our assigned aircraft. A crew bus drove myself and my copilot to an all-black F-27, which in itself was different as we normally had to walk to our aircraft. However, I was told this was a unusual mission and so far it took on all the appearances of being just that!

When I approached the aircraft, I observed several white Mercedes-Benz limousines parked under a wing and five or six men in civilian clothes moving in and about the area. One man, who appeared to be in charge, stepped forward and requested my copilot and I provide documentation authorizing us access to the aircraft. After confirming our eligibility, he stated that the pilot's preflight inspection would not allow entrance to the main interior section of the cargo compartment. (This restriction was amplified by the existence of a thick curtain just a few feet behind the cockpit.)

The (no name) geodesist civilian I was talking to asked to review the geographical coordinates of the flight plan and when I handed it to him, he disappeared into the interior of the aircraft. A few minutes later he emerged from the dividing curtain, proclaimed his approval of the plan and stated that it was important for our safety that we not stray from it. I assured him that the flight plan would be followed precisely.

With the INS instructional booklet in hand, I inserted the geographical coordinates listed in my flight plan into the computer keypad. With my copilot looking on in amazement, I checked and double-checked my inputs and was pleased when the enunciator proclaimed the system ready for use.

Takeoff was uneventful and during the climb I engaged the autopilot and instructed it to use the INS for navigational guidance. With the confidence of an experienced INS qualified airline captain, I pointed out to the copilot the wonders of modern technology. My (no name) Iranian geodetic supervisor had been sitting in the cockpit jump seat, but didn't seem impressed in my airmanship. In fact, he hadn't said a word since our taxi out for takeoff.

Leveling off at 20,000 feet in smooth air, the panoramic view of the desert below was beautiful. Visibility was unlimited and ground markings were void of blowing sand. It appeared to me a beautiful day for taking "birdlike" pictures of the Iranian and Iraqi desert area.

About 20 minutes before reaching our first INS check point, my jump-seat rider stated he was going aft and once again cautioned me to fly the flight plan as programmed, as we were very close to the Iran/Iraq border. A few minutes later I noted an amber light in the cockpit labeled "Camera doors open" come on. With nothing to do, but monitor the operation of the autopilot and INS way point countdown, I reflected back on the last time I was engaged in aerial photography.

In 1946, at the age of 18, I flew several aerial survey flights in a 65 horsepower Piper *Cub* near my hometown of Ladysmith in Northern Wisconsin. The government was constructing a Rural Electric Association (REA) hydroelectric dam on the Flambeau River and prior to beginning construction desired a series of aerial photos of the area.

I rented a Piper *Cub* from the local airport operator and opened the side doors so as to provide a construction engineer an unobstructed view to take pictures with a World War II surplus aerial camera. I was paid one dollar for each hour of flight, with the construction company picking up the rental cost of the aircraft. This was my first flight for pay and I didn't realize until much later that I was in violation of Civil Aviation rules as I did not hold a Commercial Pilot's Certificate. At the time I only held a Private Pilot's Certificate and had a total of about 75 hours flight time.

Now, 31 years later, I was flying a photo mapping mission from 20,000 feet in one of the hot spots of the world. Instead of an open-air Piper *Cub*, I was flying a pressurized modern aircraft with a team of Iranian intelligence specialists operating high-resolution cameras in a section of the aircraft I wasn't allowed to visit, while my copilot was straining his neck muscles and eyes searching the sky for Iraqi Mig jet fighters.

About four hours into the mission one of the men in the back of the aircraft brought two gigantic box lunches to the cockpit. They contained fried chicken, fresh salad, rice, yogurt, fruit, fresh pita bread, and of course, a hot cup of chay. I hadn't enjoyed a box lunch of this caliber since flying for the Air Taxi Company and with the aircraft on autopilot we enjoyed a "smooth air" leisurely lunch.

Half way through our lunch we spotted some condensation trails from Iraqi jet fighters high in the western sky. At first they seemed interested in our presence but never came close enough for us to abort the mission or disrupt our meal. About seven hours into the flight I noted the camera door open light go out, which was followed by our unnamed supervisor informing us the mission was a success and we could return to Tehran. An uneventful landing followed and I was credited with 16 hours of flight time with no charge for the box lunch. (Not a bad day's work.)

Within the next six months I flew several more photo mapping missions with several being canceled due to blowing sand storms, making detailed aerial photography impossible. I became quite friendly with several of the camera operators but never learned any of their names.

The importance of these photo mapping missions was brought to light when the Iraqi Army invaded Iran on September 22, 1980. After Ayatollah Khomeini ousted the Shah of Iran in January 1979, he turned his revolutionary talents to assisting Shiite Muslim guerrilla fighters in Iraq in attempting the overthrow of President Saddam Hussein. President Hussein did not wish to find himself in the same predicament as the Shah so considered war with Iran his only alternative. He figured he must strike while Iran was consumed with the U.S. Embassy hostage crisis (November 79 to January 81) and the decline of its military capabilities following Khomeini's purge of high-ranking army and navy officers.

The Iraqi Army, supported by squadrons of combat aircraft, invaded Iran on several fronts with the expectation of a quick victory. However, the Iraqi military's performance did not match Hussein's expectations and they found themselves unable to achieve their planned objectives. In addition their sudden invasion created a unifying effect within Iran sufficient to overcome what was thought to be a country in disarray.

An important factor favoring Iran was that their military leaders had accurate maps of the battlefields, while Iraqi commanders found themselves floundering in unfamiliar territory. The Iran/Iraq war dragged on for eight long years (with over one million casualties) and ended in a stalemate. I believe it's safe to state that the possession of accurate maps by Iranian Generals provided the edge they needed to survive.

Chapter Ten --- Flying the TC-690A and DA-20

The Chief Pilot, for several months, had requested that I check out in the Rockwell *Turbo Commander* 690A and the French Dassault *Falcon* 20 Fan jet. Air Taxi operated several of each type and there were times when captains qualified to fly them did not match demand. I had procrastinated in flying the smaller aircraft as they were generally utilized on short-range VIP flights and consequently generated little flight time. Their flight patterns also involved considerable idle ground time waiting for VIP passengers. Reading magazines in air-conditioned airport lounges, although comfortable, did not produce very many flight hours and therefore had a negative effect on maximizing monthly salary.

I preferred flying the larger F-27 and FH-227 which generated six to seven-hour daily missions. However, I felt it was time I acquiesced in company needs and provide some help in flying the smaller aircraft.

I had learned that everything in Iran was subject to confabulation so, as a trade off with the Chief Pilot, I agreed to check out in the *Turbo Commander* first and the *Falcon* Jet at some later date. He agreed.

The Rockwell Turbo Commander is a six to nine passenger, twin engine, high wing, turboprop aircraft. It is powered by Garret Engines de-rated to around 800 horsepower, providing performance similar to many WW II fighters. It climbs like a home sick angel to altitudes of 30,000 feet or higher and cruises at 260 miles per hour. Being pressurized, flights in the hot desert or high altitude cold were in a shirt-sleeve environment. Air Taxi's Turbo Commanders were configured for five passengers but could carry six if flown without a copilot. They were fully equipped with all the latest electronics, and even though the copilot's station was fully functional, many flights were flown single pilot.

After the standard self-study ground school program, I began flight training with the assistant Chief Pilot, Captain Samini, who was very likable and one of the better Iranian captains. We flew a three-hour training flight consisting of steep turns, stalls, single-engine flight and takeoffs and landings. The following day we flew another three-hour flight involving simulated instrument conditions, single-engine approaches and go-arounds. The third flight was a two-hour check ride. I was a fully qualified T-690A captain after eight hours in the aircraft.

My procrastination in checking out in the *Turbo Commander* was ill advised as it was a pure pleasure to fly. Performance and flight characteristics, as previously noted, were similar to a prop-fighter as it was fast and very responsive to flight control inputs. And, since it was equipped with an excellent autopilot and integrated flight management system, I soon found myself looking forward to being assigned missions in this agile light twin-engine turboprop transport.

Many T-690 flights involved transporting Iranian military or government VIPs to fancy villas on the southern coast of the Caspian Sea. These flights were always interesting as the mix of cold sea air flowing across the warm shore often produced low ceilings of dense fog. Fortunately, these fog banks were only 500 or 600 feet thick, but were dense enough to make it difficult to visually locate the airport. The majority of the Caspian Sea destinations did not possess instrument landing systems so I adopted an improvised method to safely operate in and out of them.

After clearing the 12,000 foot Alborz Mountain range north of Tehran, I would adjust the airborne radar to provide a clear image of the topography shore-line features. I would then determine the location of the intended airport and circle down visually over the obscured field until just a few hundred feet above the fog bank.

I would then fly north over the Caspian Sea and start a descent with gear and flaps extended, while closely monitoring my absolute altitude over the water on the radar altimeter. I would continue descending down through the fog until I had the white waves of the Caspian Sea in sight. (My limit in performing this unorthodox, but interesting type of approach was 200 feet on the radar altimeter.) (See Photo No. 1.)

Once I had a clear view of the water, I would reverse course and fly toward land until I had the coast line in sight. Surprisingly, I would usually locate the airport on my first attempt and sneak in under the overcast to an uneventful, wet runway, smooth VIP-pleasing landing. This type of approach always drew praise from my VIP passengers, resulting in a 10,000 rial tip ($140, or about $500 in today's dollars).

The departure was the reverse of this procedure, in that after takeoff, I would head for open water and in a matter of a few seconds pop out on top of the fog bank. I would then fly back to Tehran in clear skies.

A few days after my *Turbo Commander* checkout, I was scheduled to fly a three-star Iranian Navy Admiral and his aide to the Southern Iranian City of Bushier and remain with them for five days. The mission would be flown single pilot so I wouldn't have to share landings with a copilot. The admiral's mission was to inspect various military bases in Southern Iran and I was to fly him to these locations.

When being assigned the mission, I told the Chief Pilot that I wished to be billeted in the Italian ship *Raffaello*, where I was sure the admiral would be staying. For mission effectiveness, I thought it was important for me to be readily available and close to the admiral The Chief Pilot agreed and said he would ensure reservations were made accordingly.

By the time the admiral's chauffeur-driven white Mercedes-Benz limousine arrived at plane side in Tehran, I had filed a flight plan, accomplished the required aircraft preflight, emptied my bladder and was standing by next to the aircraft. The admiral, dressed in a gold-trimmed uniform, with his aide trailing close behind, issued a good morning smile and inquired if I was ready to go. He seemed pleased when I responded that everything was in order and I was just waiting for his command to start the engines. I added that the flight time was about one and a half hours, the weather en route was forecasted to be smooth, Bushier was clear and hot and there were cold soft drinks in the cooler. A second smile was punctuated with a, "Let's go, Insha Allah."

With only three people onboard, the climb rate was impressive and in no time we leveled off in smooth air at 31,000 feet. After I engaged the autopilot the admiral's aide handed me a cold can of Coke and asked if it was OK for the admiral to sit in the empty copilot's seat for the remainder of the flight. I responded that I would be honored to have him join me up front. The admiral, now in shirt sleeves, settled down in the right seat.

With the Garrett engines and propellers in perfect synchronization we winged over the desolate Persian countryside, six miles below, at close to 300 miles per hour. During the flight I struck up a cordial conversation with the admiral who, in fluent English, told me that he had attended several exchange programs with the U.S. Navy in the United States. He had a working knowledge of aviation which was demonstrated by the many intelligent questions he asked during the flight. The descent and landing at Bushier was uneventful, and the admiral seemed pleased in my assigning him routine copilot duties of extending the gear and flaps during the approach and landing.

Before I completed my engine shutdown check I observed the standard white Mercedes-Benz limousine parked near the nose of the aircraft, ready to transport the admiral and his aide to the *Raffaello* floating hotel. As he was leaving the aircraft he inquired if billeting arrangements had been arranged for me during our stay in Bushier. I responded, "Yes, sir, I'll be staying in the *Raffaello* also." He was obviously pleased and stated that we might have a flight the next day and would inform me of the takeoff time and destination later in the evening. I thanked him for his concern and stated that as soon as I had secured the aircraft for the night I would be following him and his aide to the ship. He pointed out a gray navy staff car waiting for me on the ramp and thanked me for a very enjoyable flight from Tehran. I could see that flying the admiral around Southern Iran for the next five days would be very enjoyable.

After ensuring the aircraft was refueled and secured, I grabbed my roller bag and climbed into the back seat of the waiting Iranian Navy staff car. I noted that my driver was a navy enlisted man who didn't speak a word of English.

After departing the airport it seemed like we were heading in a different direction from where the *Raffaello* was docked, but I figured the driver was aware of my intended destination. However, it soon became apparent, with each rapidly passing mile, that we were heading in an entirely different direction. I tried to convey my displeasure in the course he was taking, but my English objections, punctuated with international sign language, only resulted in the driver increasing his already dangerous pace. I decided to sit back and let Allah determine where we were heading.

About 30 miles from the airport we entered the main gate of an Iranian Navy land base. The guard, observing the four stripes on my airline uniform, waved us right through with a smart salute. The driver stopped in front of a cement-coated two-story building which I thought looked very much like a bachelor officer's quarters (BOQ).

My driver jumped out, retrieved my roller bag from the trunk, opened the rear passenger door, and stated, "Enja" (We are here). I took the bag from him, placed it back into the trunk and slammed it shut. He was obviously eager to get rid of me and attempted to retrieve my bag from the trunk for the second time. I prevented him from opening it by grabbing his arm, which put him in a frozen state of rage mixed with fear.

At about this time, I observed two young Iranian Navy ensigns walking toward us. As they approached they came to attention and saluted. (My four gold stripes were still carrying the day.) After returning their salute, I asked if they spoke English. I was pleased to learn that they spoke passable English and were happy to inform me that they had spent time working with the U.S. Navy in the United States. Relieved, I instructed them to tell my driver that I was to be driven to the Italian ship *Raffaello,* not this "out-of-the-way" navy base.

After a heated and arm waving discussion with my driver, they said that he was only following orders in bringing me to their base. I instructed the young ensigns to issue a counter order by telling the driver to take me to the *Raffaello* **right now!**

We raced back through the main gate where the guard threw me a passing salute which I returned through the rear window. Not a word was spoken as my driver sped through crowded streets and came to a screeching stop at the base of the gang plank of the *Raffaello.*

When I bid farewell to my confused driver the cloudless evening western sky was a bright orange and incandescent lights on the *Raffaello* were starting to flicker on everywhere I looked. Before climbing the ship's gang plank, I stood for a few minutes to soak in the excitement of the activity in play, on and near this magnificent Italian ocean liner. The port holes from the water line to the top decks were ablaze with lights and a string of bare colored bulbs ringed the entire top decks.

Iranian Navy officers, in their bleached white uniforms and family members in Western-style dress, were coming and going everywhere. Taxis and military vehicles were discharging or picking up passengers at the base of the gangplank, which was not unlike vehicles congregating in front of a popular New York Broadway theater opening.

From the interior of the ship I could hear the faint sounds of a Glenn Miller style big band mixed in with sounds of merriment from contented people. With a musical stride in my step, I entered the ship and went straight to the desk labeled "Billeting Officer."

When it came my turn to address the Iranian Lieutenant Commander (Major) seated at the desk, I identified myself as Captain Martin stating I had reservations for an "A Deck" stateroom for the next five days. He politely acknowledged my declaration while scanning a long list of names on his reservation ledger. After a few minutes he informed me that he could not find my name on the list, and since the ship was fully booked, he could not offer me a cabin. My insistence that a reservation was made for me by the Air Taxi company in Tehran did not change his mind and he stated once again that there was "no rooms available."

I was naturally disappointed, but not surprised that my name was intentionally, or unintentionally, not listed on his reservation ledger. However, realizing that nothing in Iran was easy, I decided to resort to contingency plan "Bravo."

From my flight bag I pulled out a small notebook, and with a noticeable action fully visible to the Lieutenant Commander, wrote down his name and serial number printed on his identification badge boldly displayed on his crisp clean white uniform. As I closed my little black book it was obvious I had captured his attention. I asked him if he knew Admiral Shapouri. Without hesitation he replied that he did, since the admiral was a VIP guest on the ship and occupying one of the honeymoon suites on "A Deck." I informed my white-suited desk clerk that I was Admiral Shapouri's personal pilot and had just flown him to Bushier from Tehran.

I added that I was to fly the admiral to various secret military installations during his visit to Bushier and when the admiral asked me where I was staying I told him the *Raffaello.* Before he could respond I said that I had already been on a fruitless search for a place to stay and if he didn't provide me with a stateroom I was going to fly my fully refueled airplane back to Tehran. But, before departing I would leave a note for Admiral Shapouri stating that the reason his personal aircraft and pilot had returned to Tehran was because a certain named Lieutenant Commander did not provide me with a place to stay. His attitude abruptly changed while stating that perhaps he should check the reservation list a second time. After a quick search he apologized for missing my name during his first review and assigned me a stateroom on "A Deck."

The next morning there was a note from the admiral that he wished to fly to a military base about 150 miles east of Bushier, with a departure time of 10 a.m. By 9:30 I had finished the aircraft preflight and was standing in the shade under a wing when the admiral and his aide drove up in a white Mercedes-Benz limousine. The admiral handed me the geographical coordinates of the base he wished to visit, and inquired if I thought I could find it. I told him it would be no problem once I inserted the reference points into the aircraft's flight computer.

Filing a flight plan was not required and we were soon dashing across the desert in our air-conditioned flying carpet. Finding the military base in the desert was not difficult, and after landing on an improvised runway, I taxied to a waiting staff car at the center of the airport.

It appeared that the facility was still under construction with few buildings fully completed. It was around 11 a.m. when we landed and the admiral said he would like to depart about five hours later. I asked him if he objected to me flying back to Bushier for lunch and to rest in their air-conditioned lounge until it was time to pick him up. I added that this would not only provide me with a comfortable area to relax, but would ensure the aircraft was nice and cool when I picked him up later. He thought this was a good idea and told me to go ahead, but be back by 1600 hours (4 p.m.).

Before the cabin cooled off, I was back in the air in my private two engine turboprop near-fighter. As soon as the landing gear was tucked securely into its respective compartments, I leveled off at between 50 to 100 feet and went zooming over the hot desert at 280 miles per hour. I adjusted the cabin temperature to 70 degrees and set the radar altimeter to alert me when I went below 50 feet.

Watching the sand dunes and occasional oases flash by was truly exhilarating, and for this I was being paid more than $3,000 a month ($11,300 when adjusted for inflation). About 20 minutes after takeoff I observed what I first thought was a large oasis starting to fill the windshield. However, as I drew closer, I could see it was a camp site of desert wanderers known as "Nomads." From my low altitude I had an excellent opportunity of viewing the entire group of about 30 men, women and children. The women were dressed in the standard full-length black chador robes, while the men wore colored robes and black head turbans.

I passed directly over their camp at about fifty feet, and to get a second look, executed a tight 180 degree turn. On my second low pass, I noticed that their camels, goats and sheep had bolted and were running across the desert aimlessly, while most camp residents were shaking their fists at me in an obvious gesture of good will and appreciation for an unexpected airshow. However, as an expression of apology, for disturbing their solitude, I decided to make one more low level high-speed fly-by before allowing them time to round up their wandering animals.

I flew out a couple of miles and came back toward their camp right on the deck at about 280 miles per hour. As their tents filled my windscreen I pulled up in a 45 degree climb and zoomed up to about 5,000 feet. I imagine grand kids of this tribe of desert nomads are still being told of the excitement they enjoyed one hot windy day when a crazy bird from the sky dove on them and scared off their camels, goats and sheep.

I landed at Bushier, enjoyed a leisurely lunch in an air-conditioned restaurant and was back at the desert base to pick up the admiral at 1600 hours. He was pleased that the cabin was already cooled and when departing the aircraft at Bushier thanked me for a nice flight.

The rest of the week was more routine with flights to Khark and Lavan Island and other established airports. When the five days were history, I flew Admiral Shapouri and his aide back to Tehran. He thanked me again for a very enjoyable and safe week, stating that he hoped to fly with me again sometime in the future.

I considered the admiral a real gentleman and also looked forward to flying with him a second time. However, this was not to be, and I was sorry to note that he was one of the early military leaders Ayatollah Khomeini had summarily executed after the overthrow of the Shah.

About a week later I flew a *Turbo Commander* on a single-pilot mission to Khark Island. My assignment directed me to spend one week at Khark to provide administrative flights for the Iranian Navy. I would be on stand-by status and free to pursue my own interests unless called.

During my first day on the Island there were no flights, so I spent nearly the entire day at the navy officer's white sand beach house reading and snoozing in the shade of a large umbrella.

The second day involved a flight to Tehran which was uneventful except that upon landing back at Khark Island, the right main gear tire blew out just as I touched down. I tried desperately to keep the aircraft on the runway, but ran off to the right side onto hard crushed coral. Other than the blown tire, there was no damage to the aircraft. The Iranian Navy officers onboard were pleased with my performance and promised to buy me a beer at the Officers' Club later.

The cause of the tire blow out was the frequent deposit of foreign material on the runway from construction trucks. I had complained about this before but my complaint had fallen on deaf ears. The aircraft was towed to the maintenance ramp and was back in commission within a couple of hours.

It's interesting to note that some time later I experienced another main tire blow out after landing and ran off the opposite side of the runway, but this time I had an admiral onboard and he was so scared over the incident that foreign material on the runway at Khark was no longer a problem.

Around noon the next day, I was lounging under an umbrella on the beach when three Imperial Iranian Navy officers, one whom I recognized as the manager of the Officers' Club, approached and wanted to know if I could fly them to Kish Island. I told them that I was certainly capable of flying them there, but could not do so without obtaining permission from our operations center in Tehran. They departed stating they would contact Tehran and obtain the authorization I required. Confident clearance would be forthcoming, we agreed to meet at the aircraft in about one hour. (The reason for my requesting specific authorization to fly them to Kish Island was that access to it was controlled by the Shah as his winter palace was located there.)

I will devote several paragraphs in describing this island paradise in great detail later, but for now will just state that it was apparent that the reason my three navy officers wished to visit Kish island was to shop in its huge duty-free bazaar. Especially inviting would be the well stocked liquor store with its dirt-cheap prices. These so-called non-drinking Muslims were looking to restock their Officers' Club bar.

I readied the aircraft for flight and was standing in the shade of a wing when they drove up in a gray staff car. They handed me the authorization message from Tehran, whereby I told them to hop in so we could get this thing cooled off.

A few minutes later we were zooming along the Persian Gulf at 10,000 feet while sipping cans of iced Coke. One hour later we landed at Kish Island where a navy van was waiting. As my passengers drove off, they said they would be back in about two hours. I told them I would be resting in the nearby air-conditioned airport office.

While I lounged in a white leather overstuffed chair, I had a clear view of my aircraft sitting on the hot bare concrete ramp. When I observed a vehicle approaching I proceeded to the aircraft to assist in loading what I knew would be a large number of liquor boxes. However, I was not prepared for what my passengers had purchased.

The van was crammed full with case after case of scotch, gin, champagne and fine French wines. I was engaged in a discussion with the club manager regarding the ability of loading all the liquor they had purchased, when a gray Iranian government pickup truck came to a screeching stop in front of the aircraft.

A uniformed official stepped out and approached my three navy shoppers. They entered into a heated argument consisting of raised voices and thrashing arms. All seemed to be talking and shouting at the same time with no apparent resolution in sight. It was obvious that the discussion related to the boxes of liquor, but since they were speaking in Farsi, I wasn't exactly sure of what the disagreement was about.

I pulled one of my passengers aside and asked him what was the thrust of the disagreement. He told me that the individual who arrived in the pickup truck was an Iranian customs agent and was requesting a higher bakhsheesh payment than they were willing to make.

The argument seemed to become more heated, when to my surprise, the custom official ripped open a case of Johnny Walker Black Label and removed two bottles. He carried them to the edge of the ramp and smashed them on the concrete. The smell of rich scotch filled the air and a silence fell over the group of verbal combatants. The stand-off was broken when my three passengers gathered in a subdued huddle and emerged with a stack of rials which they handed to the customs agent. He grabbed the wad of bills, jumped into his truck and sped off with the smell of screeching tires blending in with the aroma of 12-year-old scotch.

One of my navy friends told me that the custom agent had threatened to smash every bottle of liquor they had purchased if his payment demand was not met. I helped them load more cases than I wished to count into the aircraft knowing that we were slightly overloaded.

I allowed for 20 knots of additional airspeed in the takeoff roll, and completed an uneventful flight back to Khark Island, while hoping I could avoid another tire blow-out upon landing. That night in the Officers' Club the manager told me my drinks were on the house.

When flying the *Turbo Commander* on high ranking VIP flights, a young Iranian copilot was quite often assigned to fill the right copilot's seat. His primary mission was to cater to the needs of the passengers, not necessarily to assist me in flying the aircraft. The procedure we followed when preparing for the boarding of VIPs was to complete the Before Starting Engine Check right up to pushing the engine start buttons and then await the arrival of our passengers.

The copilot would position himself next to the open cabin door, and as the VIPs stepped from a red Persian carpet into the aircraft, close it and offer them an ice-cold soft drink. When I heard the click of the door handle, I would push the start button for the right engine. Before the copilot finished his cabin service, I would have both engines up and running and be ready to taxi out for takeoff. Most of the time we did not have to file a flight plan, or had pre-filed one, so from taxi to takeoff was usually accomplished without an interim stop at the end of the runway. From start engines to takeoff was usually less than five minutes.

Discharging VIP passengers was handled in a similarly expeditious manner. After a priority approach and landing I would be cleared by the tower to taxi without delay to a parking spot directly in front of the terminal. When approaching the parking ramp, I would shut down the left engine (entrance door side) with the intent of having the propeller stopped rotating by the time I set the parking brakes. The copilot would be standing by next to the entrance door, and after ensuring that the left propeller had stopped spinning, open it and stand at attention outside the aircraft as the passengers deplaned.

Greeting the passengers as they deplaned onto a red carpet would be several local dignitaries, and the usual white Mercedes-Benz limousine. The arrival procedure that required the copilot to be outside the aircraft, as the passengers deplaned, left me alone in the cockpit. This arrangement worked out to my financial gain on almost all VIP flights.

The Chief Pilot had told his captains that he paid his pilots well and that we were not to accept gratuity tips from passengers. However, he had no control over the will of the passengers themselves who were always pleased in being exposed to a smooth flight and a soft "Martin" landing.

I never let the copilot make the takeoff or landing with VIPs onboard.

The ranking VIP, before deplaning, would step forward to the cockpit, thank me for a pleasant flight, and hand me a folded bank note. The standard denomination would be 10,000 rials ($140, or $500 today). I would thank him or her, wish them well, and quickly place the bank note into my left shirt pocket. Quite often I would observe them attempting to offer the copilot a lessor amount, but he would usually refuse to accept it.

After the passengers left the area, the copilot would join me in the cockpit and state in an indignant tone of voice that the passengers had attempted to present him with a tip; however, he had declined to accept it stating the Chief Pilot's directive. I would compliment him on his allegiance to company policy.

There were days when I returned to Tehran with three or four 10,000-rial notes stuffed into my shirt pocket, while at the same time complimenting the copilot for adhering to company rules. The gratuity presented by members of the royal family was sometimes a "Pahlavi Gold Coin" consisting of one-half ounce of solid gold. I still have several of these coins that I cherish as keepsakes.

One particular VIP flight I recall was to fly a *Turbo Commander* to Hamadan, a city in the Western Central Iranian Desert, to pickup the Shah's twin sister, Princess Ashraf and her son. My flight set-up sheet, signed by the Chief Pilot, instructed me to be in place at 10:30 a.m. for a 11 o'clock departure for Tehran.

I departed Tehran at 9 a.m. and one hour later had the aircraft parked in front of the Hamadan airport terminal. The standard red carpet was rolled out onto the ramp as the copilot and I completed the typical VIP Before Engine Start Check, ensured cold soft drinks were on board and retreated to the air-conditioned airport office to await the Princess.

The terminal was awash with smartly dressed men and women waiting to bid farewell to the Shah's sister. Saying good-bye would be "bittersweet" as Princess Ashraf had a reputation of being quite demanding and not a popular guest.

As time drew closer to her expected departure the crowd became more skittish and began shuffling positions to be closer to the red carpet. Unfortunately, it was laid out in the hot sun and the crowd was beginning to show the effects of the heat. However, since it was almost 11 a.m. no one wished to give up their hard-fought position in the receiving line to seek shade. I was positioned in the cockpit and my copilot, as usual, was standing next to the open passenger door.

When at 11:20 the Princess had not yet arrived, I questioned if my stated pickup time was correct. However, a check of the flight set-up sheet clearly stated 11 a.m. When at 11:25 Princess Ashraf had still not arrived, I left the cockpit and headed for the airport office where I planned on calling our flight operations center in Tehran.

A nervous airport manager, who spoke very little English, assisted me in making my call. After going through the usual frustration of completing a long distance call in Iran, I reached our operations center. I told the dispatcher that I was at the Hamadan Airport, but Princess Ashraf and her son had not yet arrived. He took my telephone number and said he would call me right back after checking with the Chief Pilot..

About ten minutes later the telephone rang and a very nervous perspiring airport manager answered it, then quickly handed the receiver to me. On the other end of the line was the Chief Pilot who began berating me for screwing up a very important VIP flight by not following the directions on my special mission set-up sheet.

In an arrogant tone of voice he told me that Princess Ashraf was waiting for me to call her at her hotel in downtown Hamadan to let her know that I was at the airport. He went on to state that if she expressed her dissatisfaction to the Shah, it would be all my fault and he couldn't predict what the consequences would be.

By now I had learned how to deal with excited Iranians and their attempts to shift blame or responsibility for errors, so shot back with the same gusto to which I had been exposed. I told the Chief Pilot that my flight set-up sheet, signed by him, said nothing about.calling the Princess at her hotel. It stated that I was to be in-place at 10:30 a.m. at the airport, which I had beaten by 30 minutes.

I told him that he was not going to blame me for his screw-up. I added that if he persisted in accusing me of messing up, I would show Princess Ashraf the set-up sheet, which he had signed, proving that the mistake was not my fault. His tone of voice changed dramatically and in a near whisper said that the Shah's sister and her son were now on their way to the airport and to do what I could to smooth the waters.

I went back to the aircraft, informed the waiting crowd that the Princess would arrive shortly, and took my position in the left pilot's seat. A few minutes later three white Mercedes-Benz limousines could be seen rounding the airport terminal. The first and third vehicles held Savak Secret Police, while the middle one held the Princess and her son.

The heat-soaked, sweaty well wishers, resumed their places along the red carpet as Princess Ashraf and her son hurried to board the aircraft. When she entered she came directly to the cockpit and apologized profusely for making me wait. She accepted full blame for the screw-up and was not in any way upset. She was very gracious and in perfect English expressed her concern for the error. She asked about the weather in Tehran and the en route time. I told her it would be a smooth flight of about 45 minutes. She apologized again as she took a seat in the cabin allowing the copilot to squeeze past her to gain access to his seat. I didn't talk to her well dressed son, but we exchanged eye contact and a smile.

After arriving in Tehran, the copilot assumed his normal position outside the aircraft as the Shah's sister and her son prepared to deplane. However, before she left she came to the cockpit, apologized once again for making me wait, and handed me a one-half ounce Pahlavi gold coin.

When I turned in my post-flight paperwork to the dispatcher, the Chief Pilot was eagerly awaiting my report on the flight. I told him that I explained everything to Princess Ashraf and assured her that he had no part in the screw-up. He shook my hand and thanked me for getting him off the hook. (Princess Ashraf survived the revolution, but her son unfortunately was assassinated by Khomeini's militant Muslim henchmen on a Paris Street in 1979.)

Soon after qualifying in the *Turbo Commander*, the Chief Pilot requested I check out in the *Falcon* Fan-jet. Air Taxi operated ten of them, with several belonging to the Iranian navy. Others were owned by various corporations doing business in Iran. However, all were flown and maintained by Air Taxi pilots in a very lucrative contract.

The Falcon Dash 20 was manufactured by the Dassault Company in Paris and operated by many corporations throughout the world. It cruises at 450 knots, carries up to eight passengers, has a range of about 1,300 miles and in 1976 cost about $2,500 per hour to operate.

Since Air Taxi's *Falcons* were equipped with all the latest state of the art electronics, many Iranian pilots did not possess the aeronautical experience required to fly an aircraft of such speed and complexity. When the Chief Pilot noted from my resume that I possessed over 600 hours in single engine military jets, and several hundred hours in the North American twin-engine *Saberliner* corporate jet, he stated that I owed it to the company to help them man their fleet of *Falcons*. I couldn't argue with his logic, so I agreed to undergo a company checkout.

The Chief Pilot told me that my flight instructor would be Captain Mohammad Mousavi, one of their high-time *Falcon* pilots. I had not met Captain Mousavi, but had heard from some of my copilots that he was an excellent pilot and a pleasure to fly with. (See Photo No. 29.)

I was issued *Falcon* aircraft flight manuals, for the standard self-study ground school, and after several days of review was ready for the government-administered written exam, which I passed with no problem. I was then introduced to Captain Mousavi who laid out a very detailed and thorough check-out program. We developed an ethical alliance, especially when I learned that he had flown jet fighters with the Iranian military and had attended pilot training with the United States Air Force.

I liked the Falcon DA-20 right from the start and could understand why Pan American Airways and Japan Airlines used it in their advanced pilot training programs. Although relatively small in size it flew like a large jet. Once settled down in it's snug cockpit, you could just as easily be flying a B-727, B-737 or DC-9.

Captain Mousavi seemed pleased in how quickly I grasped the basics of flying the *Falcon* and predicted a quick check-out. Reluctantly, he confessed that instructing Iranian pilots was sometimes nerve-racking and not infrequently downright dangerous.

A perfect example of what he was faced with was illustrated one morning as we were walking towards a *Falcon* prior to a training flight. Not far from where our aircraft was parked, we heard a series of muffled explosions. When we discovered the source, we couldn't believe our eyes!

An Iranian captain was attempting to start the engines of a *Falcon* Fan-jet with the large "day-glow-orange-colored" plastic engine intake covers still installed. These covers are put in place when the aircraft is parked for long periods to prevent birds and other foreign objects from entering the engine intakes. When an aircraft is being readied for flight they are removed and stored, usually by maintenance personnel. However, a pilot conducting an external preflight walk around inspection would have to be blind or stupid, or both, not to note that they were still installed. They are painted a bright day-glow orange so as to make them clearly visible, day or night.

The pilots involved in this screw-up not only failed to ensure that the intake covers were removed, but persisted in attempting to start an engine being starved of air. The suction force from the engine compressor gasping for air had caused part of the plastic cover to buckle inwards, thereby providing some air, but not enough for proper engine operation. The engine was undergoing violent explosive "compressor stalls" with flames and smoke shooting out from the front and rear of the engine.

The pilots didn't give up on attempting to start the engine until several maintenance personnel came running across the ramp signaling them to abort the start. A small crowd soon assembled as maintenance personnel struggled to remove the bent and ruptured intake cover from the smoking engine. Shaking our heads in disbelief, we continued to our aircraft and completed my check-out flight in the *Falcon*. I was now qualified to fly all four aircraft in the company's inventory. (See Photos 2 through 5).

The Chief Pilot, to my surprise, held to his promise in regard to my not being stuck with frequent short flights in the *Falcon*. It was great to be flying a pure jet again, but its high speed and passenger comfort dictated that it be used for mostly high ranking VIP flights. Also, being a required two-pilot aircraft, *Falcon* flights were always flown with a copilot. However, since it was their prestige aircraft, the copilots qualified to fly it were generally well qualified and a pleasure to work with.

Many *Falcon* flights were the transporting of high ranking government officials or senior Iranian military officers to villas on the Caspian Sea. After takeoff from Tehran, it was a simple task to clear the 12,000 foot Alborz Mountains north of the city, followed by a rapid descent with speed brakes extended to one of the larger airports on the Caspian Sea coast.

Flight duration for these missions was never more than 30 minutes and usually involved considerable ground time before returning to Tehran. Catering to the desires of the VIPs resulted in very little flight time and minimum time for pay purposes. Also, *Falcon* flights to the Caspian Sea area were restricted to larger established airports with approved instrument approaches, so the sneak-in fun-type approach practiced in the Rockwell *Turbo Commanders* was not flown.

One *Falcon* flight to the Caspian Sea stands out in my mind and was typical of many to follow. I was flying a high ranking Iranian government official and his aide to Farahbad, a resort town on the coast. My mission was to have them there by 10 a.m., remain with the aircraft and return to Tehran later that afternoon. His high rank was demonstrated by the large size of the white Mercedes-Benz limousine that drove him to the airport in Tehran and the fancy limousine that met him in Farahbad.

As he was departing the aircraft after landing, he inquired as to how I and the copilot would spend the next five hours waiting for the return flight to Tehran. When I told him we would probably wait in the airport office, he proposed a much better arrangement. He said he didn't need his aide to accompany him on his business luncheon, so would instruct him to take us to one of the better hotel restaurants next to the Caspian Sea for lunch. He added that his assistant would pay for everything.

After securing the aircraft, we took a taxi to what had to be a five star hotel overlooking the blue waters of the Caspian Sea. Even though it was July, a cool breeze blowing in from Russia provided natural air-conditioning. We followed our appointed guide to a shaded outdoor second-floor restaurant, and secured a table overlooking a white desolate sandy beach.

Up to this point I had only spoken a few words to our host so I wasn't sure of how fluent he was in English, but from past experience in working with influential Iranians I assumed he would do very well. When I asked him his name, I was pleased to learn that he spoke excellent English, but with a trace of a British accent. I found out later that this was due to his being educated in England.

The waiter brought a menu printed in French and Farsi. I suggested that since we were his guests our host should order for all three. My exquisitely prepared lunch was sturgeon caviar fresh from the sea, a delicious fish cream soup, a refreshing garden salad and grilled sea bass. A fabulous desert was topped off with a strong cup of cappuccino coffee. After dinner my copilot retreated to a shady corner to take a nap as my host and I lingered over more coffee.

He asked me how long I had been living in Iran. When I said two and a half years, he inquired if I had ever met the Shah. Surprised by his question I told him no, but had flown his twin sister, his younger brother and his nephew on several occasions. He then asked me if I had ever met President Jimmy Carter. With a chuckle, I replied no and asked if he had. I was astonished when he said yes, several times.

He went on to tell me that he had been the Shah's interpreter during his visit to the White House and attended all the meetings the Shah had with President Carter. He added that he had also assisted the Shah when the President and Lillian Carter visited the Shah and Queen Farah at the Niavaran Palace in Tehran. When I asked why the Shah needed an interpreter, when he spoke very good English, he said that he didn't wish to take a chance on missing certain words and needed someone loyal to him who spoke and understood English to take notes.

I asked my new friend what he thought of President Carter, and without hesitation he told me, not much! When I asked him why, he said that President Carter didn't have a very good grasp of world politics and presented very simplistic solutions for solving difficult and complex international problems. When he asked how I felt about Jimmy Carter, I told him that as far as I was concerned he described him quite well. I asked if the Shah shared his opinion, to which he replied, most certainly, adding that the Shah understood international politics better than any world leader he knew, and was misunderstood by most of them.

We had switched our drinks to iced tea, loosened our ties and were becoming comfortable in our frank discussion about world leaders and world problems. I suggested we play a game of three questions that we could pose to each other that would be answered truthfully, or not at all. He thought this was a good idea and suggested I go first.

I asked him if the Shah was aware of how destitute many Iranians were, and that during his efforts to bring Iran into the twentieth century the oil wealth was not filtering down to all levels of society. I felt I had struck a nerve, when with gusto, he said that he didn't think so since the Shah only hears what his surrogates tell him, and that their self interests often take priority and are usually in conflict with the needs of the country.

He added that the Shah, like all world leaders, was not able to move freely amongst his people to discern their thoughts, but must rely on others for keeping him informed. Utilizing secondhand information he was doing the best he could in improving human rights for the citizens of Iran.

With passion, he said that the Shah, like his deceased father, was striving to improve the living conditions of all Iranians, be they men, women, rich or poor, with the hope that they would be able to enjoy the fruits of Iran's new found oil wealth. He thought the Shah was especially interested in removing the shackles placed on women by Islamic militant fundamentalists. In this regard he was promoting women to important positions within his government, but was running into considerable resistance from the followers of Khomeini. My luncheon host continued in his vocal support of the Shah by stating he is a stabilizing force in the Middle East, and if he is deposed it would have a disastrous destabilizing effect, not only in Iran, but in adjacent Muslim countries. He was convinced Iran's Western allies were not aware of the importance the Shah played in the world. [I found myself in complete agreement with his profound statements which have proved remarkably prophetic in describing the Middle East situation in 2007.]

His first question was did I think the United States would support Iran in its growing struggle with the militant hard-line followers of Ayatollah Khomeini? My answer was that I thought the U.S. had no option but to support Iran as they had in the past when they helped kick out the Russians after World War II, and had supported him during the attempted overthrow of his government in 1953. (Obviously I was dead-wrong.)

My second question was about the Iranian Air Force having the only B-747 refueling tankers in the world. Who was Iran's potential enemy to justify tankers of such size and long range? He declined to answer.

His second question related to the hiring of foreign workers to foster the Shah's modernizing plan. This practice involved many nationalities, but the Americans, especially the Bell Helicopter employees working in Esfahan, displayed a wanton disrespect for Iranian customs and religion. This irreverence provided fodder for Khomeini's followers in their efforts to overthrow the Shah. What can be done to improve this situation?

I told him that I thought Iran had made a mistake when they allowed Bell Helicopter, and other large foreign corporations, to pay their workers their full salaries when working in Iran. I suggested a much better approach would have been to pay them 50 percent up front, with the remainder being deposited in a bank in their home country. The fact that most male employees were in Iran without families, and being in possession of large amounts of cash, set the stage for rowdy behavior. Especially during Iranian holidays (days of religious mourning). He thought my response had merit and would discuss it with the Shah.

My third question related to Tehran having the highest automobile accident rate and worst traffic congestion in the world. How was Iran going to solve this problem? With a chuckle, he shrugged his shoulders while stating that the problem had no solution and would probably get worse unless they could devise some system of fast mass transportation.

Lastly, he asked if he should feel safe when flying with Iranian captains. I felt a little uneasy in commenting on Air Taxi pilot colleagues, but suggested he have the company prepare a resume of all captains, both foreign and Iranian. Once prepared, these resumes would be available on demand. I suggested he fly only with captains with a minimum of 5,000 hours or more of flight time. This would ensure he would fly with pilots with at least five years of experience. I also suggested that he not rely totally on "Inaha Allah" for a safe flight, but to exercise good sound judgment in crew selection. With a smile he seemed to agree.

The time passed faster than I realized and it was soon time to wake up my copilot and head for the airport. However, my host wished to make one more point regarding the Shah. He said that he was aware that many Western governments thought the Shah was a harsh leader and abused basic human rights. However, this was not true, adding that Iran was a rough country and only a strong leader would be able to survive.

After landing in Tehran, I thanked my passengers for a very enjoyable day and said I hoped I would have the pleasure of flying them again. However, this was not to be and unless they escaped Iran before or during the revolution, I suspect they were pretty much at the head of the summarily execution list when Khomeini took over as the leader of Iran.

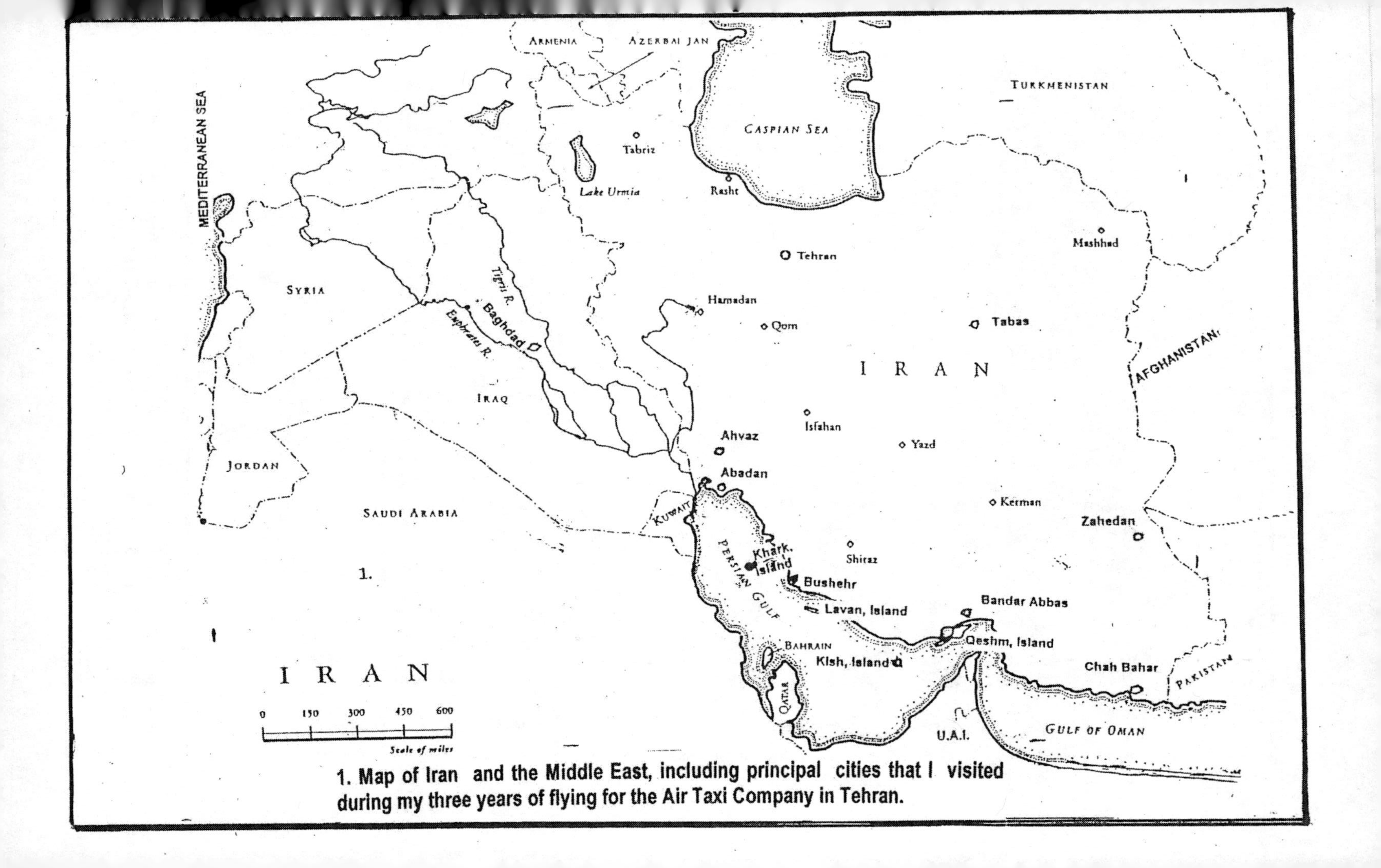

1. Map of Iran and the Middle East, including principal cities that I visited during my three years of flying for the Air Taxi Company in Tehran.

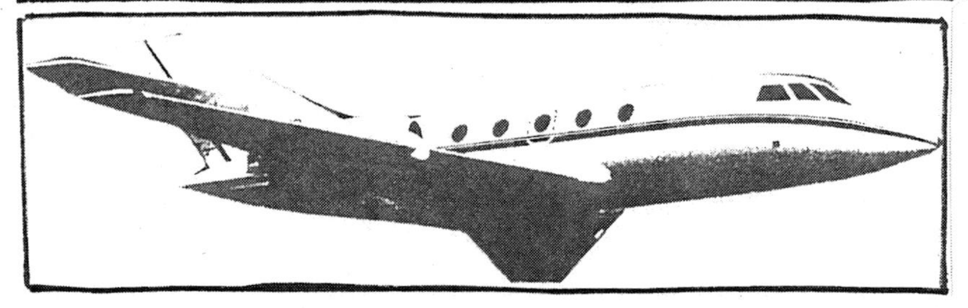

2, 3, 4, & 5. The four aircraft I flew for the Air Taxi Company in Tehran, Iran. From the top: Fairchild F-27 & FH-227, Rockwell 690A, & French *Falcon* jet.

6. Former Piedmont Airline's Fairchild FH-227, operated by the Air Service Company in Abadan. I flew this type aircraft to Desert sand-rolled runways in support of the National Iranian Oil Company. Note passengers standing in the shade under a wing and the copilot entering the aircraft.

7. View of buildings used on desert oil field base camps. Several of these windowless enclosures, with thick insulated walls, would be used for living quarters while others for dinning and recreation. They were located adjacent to the sand-rolled runway and within walking distance of my aircraft.

8. Construction workers maintaining a sand-rolled desert airfield. They required constant attention to ensure that they were capable of supporting FH-227s, which supplied food, water, replacement workers and oil drilling equipment. Desert winds created sand dunes that had to be removed daily.

9. Author with flight attendants in hotel room in Karachi, Pakistan. We were required to spend three days in Karachi during the overthrow of Prime Minister Bhutto. The two male and female attendant sitting next to me were from Tehran. The other female flight attendant was from Egypt Air in Cairo.

10. Author and young Iranian copilot in Cockpit of Air Taxi F-27 somewhere over Iran. He was trained in the U.S., spoke excellent English and was a joy to fly with. He obviously came from a wealthy family. Note mustache which was a common male tradition in the Middle East.

11. Bill Aston, Chieko Hara and Fred Jamerson attending a dinner party in my apartment in Tehran in 1978. They were a fun group!

12. Author in cockpit of F-27 with Air Taxi flight attendant sitting on his lap. Photo was taken by copilot somewhere over Iran.

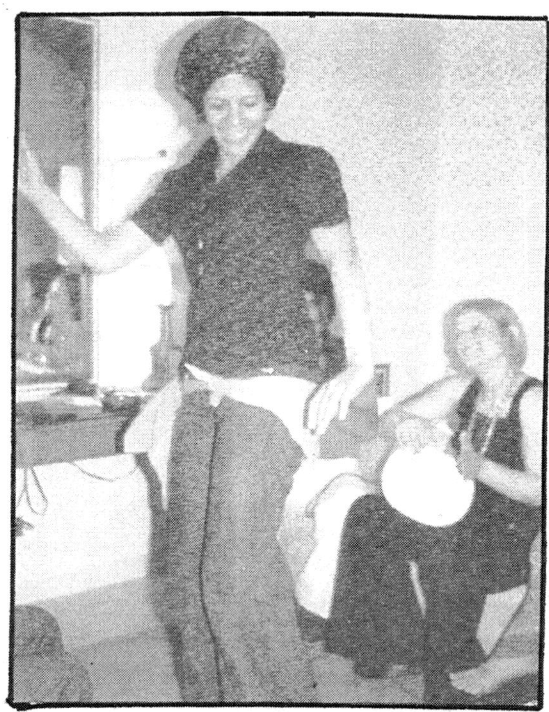

13. Egypt Air flight attendant performing impromptu belly dance in author's hotel room in Karachi, Pakistan while her colleague uses waste paper basket as a drum. When hotel guests complained about the noise the party was discontinued but the belly dancer remained to help me "clean-up" the room.!

14. Author with two Air Taxi flight attendants in Southern Iran . They both spoke fairly good English, were fun to fly with and pleasing on the eyes. They were typical of young Iranian women who cast off their full-length black chadors and sought a Western life-style, which was resented by Islamic fundamentalists who wanted to keep women in the 14th century.

15. Author and Chieko in front of the Volkswagen that was abandoned when making a quick exit from Tehran in late December 1978. We are standing in the parking lot of the U.S. Army Officers' Club in Tehran. All the cars pictured were abandoned by Americans when forced to leave Iran.

16. Jim Wallace and his wife Lynn. Jim was a Falcon fan jet captain but left Iran in early 1978. After returning to the U.S. he flew as a captain for United Airlines. He now lives in Florida.

17. Rich Reeves and his Iranian wife. Rich was an Air Force pilot stationed in Tehran , but took a discharge to fly for the Air Taxi Company. He left Iran before the revolution and became a corporate pilot in Ohio.

18. Chieko in front of the 148 foot Shahyad tower. This magnificent structure was built by the Shah in 1971 to commemorate the 2500th anniversary of the Persian Empire. It is located adjacent to the Mehrabad Airport on Azadi Square and is presently a rallying center for demonstrations against the U.S.

19. A caravan of camels in front of the author's apartment in Tehran. Only the lead camel wears bells while the others follow close behind. The sound of approaching camel bells always created an "Arabian Night's impression."

20. Author and daughter Lynn , in 1977 during a flight to the Caspian Sea in a FH-227. Lynn rode the jump seat and was concerned about our ability to top the 12,000 foot Alborz Mountains after departing Tehran. She was on an around the world trip after graduating from the University of Guam..

21. Author and son Michael next to an Imperial Iranian Navy F-27 at Khark Island in the Persian Gulf in December 1976. Mike was a junior in high school and on a visit to Iran. He was impressed in being able to fly in an Iranian Navy aircraft. He cut his hair when he became a U.S. Air Force pilot.

22. Chieko in front of a brass shop in Tehran. The Iranians were amazed when a Japanese joined them in their game of bartering over the price of goods. Normally, Japanese tourists if interested in an item purchase it at the stated inflated price and were a desirable customer for Iranian merchants.

23. A typical Tehran brass shop. Most of the items were hand-made, very attractive but overpriced. The standard practice was to offer the merchant 50% of his asking price and then start haggling. Even if we didn't make a purchase the verbal contest was a interesting way of spending a few hours.

24. Author's son Michael in copilot's seat of an F-27 en route to Khark Island in the Persian Gulf. Khark Island is a prime deep-sea Iranian oil loading facility and was closely guarded by the Iranian Navy. It was bombed heavily by Iraqi fighter bombers during the eight year Iranian/Iraq war. (1980 to 88.)

25. Chieko overlooking the Imam Square in Isfahan. This magnificent quadrilateral space was built in the 17th century and features celebrated mosques and the entrance to a 3 km long covered bazaar. Isfahan was once the capital of Iran and is now the location of their nuclear weapons program.

26. The Alborz Mountains as viewed from the author's bedroom in the spring of 1976. This picturesque mountain range is only a few miles north of Tehran and reaches altitudes of up to 12,000 feet, or 8,000 feet above the city which is 4,000 feet above sea level. They were usually snow-capped year around.

27. View of the narrow mountain road en route to the Dizin ski area. Traveling on this road was a scary event since it was usually loaded with "Kamikaze" style drivers who trusted in Allah (God) to keep them safe. However, I wasn't sure that Allah was always on our side when going up or down. "Insha Allah."

28. Chieko and author after returning from skiing in Dizin. Our smiles indicate that we were giving thanks to Allah in reaching the relative safety of less dangerous roads. Following each "hair-rising" trip we would vow that it would be our last, but the spirit of adventure forced us to break our pledge.

29. Author (L) and Flight Systems instructor in Northern Germany in 1993. I was attached to the U.S. Consul Office in Frankfurt and was offered a chance at one last flight in an F-100. I flew it from the back-seat and was amazed in how quickly I became accustomed to the jet after an absence of 30 years.

30. Author enjoying a martini in his apartment in Tehran, in 1978. This was obviously before the worst of the revolution because Chieko was still in Iran. What the picture doesn't show is the strong odor of onions coming from my landlords downstairs apartment.

31. Chieko enjoying a Beefeater Martini while toasting to a future of happiness, which I feel was realized when we were married on November 13, 1982. Chieko and her Japanese colleagues left Tehran soon after this picture was taken as their Japanese boss felt they were in danger.

32. Author in cockpit of F-27 somewhere over Iran in 1977. When Chieko obtained a job in Tehran, in January 1978, she had me shave off my mustache.

33. Author enjoying a ski trip with friends in Austria in 1995, when assigned to the U.S. Consulate office in Frankfurt Germany from 1992 to 96. From L -R : Lee Brooks, Eric Elmgren, Chieko and author. (Unfortunately, Lee Brooks was killed in an auto accident after returning to the U.S.

34. Author's Iranian Air Taxi Identification card. Note fully developed mustache which took about a month to grow, but was accepted as the normal facial adornment for an airline captain in the Middle East.

35. Chieko and author attending book signing session in Oshkosh, Wisconsin during EAA's Airventure 2006. I spent most of my time in the "Author's Corner" while Chieko would spend time volunteering to work in the International Tent in assisting Japanese speaking visitors from Japan.

Chapter Eleven --- The Foreign Pilot Brigade

When I joined the foreign pilot ranks of the Air Taxi Company in Tehran in January 1976, I became the sixth member of a unique group of expatriate pilots, consisting of one Dutch and five Americans. Two U.S. pilots were assigned to the Dassault DA-20 *Falcon* Fleet, two Americans and the Dutchman to the F-27 *Friendship* Fleet, and one former U.S. Air Force pilot, who had taken his discharge in Iran and married an Iranian girl, was assigned to fly the Rockwell *Shrike Commander.* Within a year additional pilots were hired, but with varying retention success.

Working and living in Iran was a tremendous cultural shock for pilots who had not previously worked overseas, and several left a short time after reporting for work. On one occasion I noted two, recently hired, American pilots undergoing indoctrination training by the Chief Pilot, but within two weeks both had quit and returned to the United States, even before commencing qualification training and checkout in an aircraft. (I was told that they just couldn't accept the trauma of living in Iran.)

Foreign pilots from European countries, especially England, and older American pilots faired much better. There were two British pilots, who joined the company a year after I did, that I became very fond of. They were both seasoned aviators who had served with the Royal Air Force during World War II and ten years my senior. (See Photo No. 11.)

I was 12-years-old when RAF pilots fought off the German Luftwaffe during the Battle of Britain in 1940. So while I was cutting out pictures of combat aircraft for a scrapbook, my two new British pilot colleagues were 22-years-old and flying combat missions against crack German fighter pilots. They were shooting down Messerschmitt BF-109s and Junkers JU 87 *Stuka* dive bombers, while I was fabricating childhood fantasies of flying Supermarine *Spitfires* and Hawker *Hurricane* fighters.

The Chief Pilot requested that I act as a sponsor for captain Bill Aston and Fred Jamerson, the two new English pilots, in indoctrinating them on company policies and in helping them get settled. I enjoyed this assignment immensely, especially while throwing darts and downing pints of beer in an English-style pub in downtown Tehran. Spending time with them gave life to childhood World War II combat aerial fantasies. They had no problem in becoming accustomed to life in Iran and quickly qualified in the Fokker F-27 *Friendship.*

I became particularly fond of Bill Aston, who rented an apartment close to mine. We became good friends and, when our flight schedules allowed, would visit the U.S. Army Officers' Club in Northern Teheran for dinner and pocket pool. Being British, Bill was an excellent billiard player and was able to transfer a great deal of this talent to the smaller coin-operated six-pocket pool table located in the Officers' Club game room.

We would usually start our nightly pool matches by playing eight ball for a dollar or two per game, plus the loser buying the drinks. Try as I might, I knew I would lose the first few games and, in addition to losing a few dollars, would be required to buy several rounds of cheer.

However, before Bill had arrived in Iran I had become friendly with the Iranian bartender and knew I could depend on him as a partner in my scheme of getting the best of my new English pilot friend. When, as the loser, I would order a triple scotch for Bill and a plain 7-up with a wedge of lime for myself, telling Bill it was a gin and tonic. Surprisingly his regal British breeding didn't allow him to question the honesty of my stratagem.

After losing two or three games, and supplying Bill with two or three triple scotches, our pool playing skills became more evenly matched. After about the fourth or fifth game the tide of battle would turn in my favor. It was great fun to witness the frustration displayed by a former RAF combat fighter pilot being beaten in pool by a Yank ten years his junior. In addition to winning more 7-up than I could drink, I would quite often walk away with 20 or 30 of Bill's dollars in my pocket, even after deducting the cost of paying for his triple scotches. Remarkably, Bill never caught on to my scam and I never tired of using it. His favorite English expression was, "Bloody hell Lou, You've got to be joking."

Bill's apartment was within walking distance of mine and he became a welcomed frequent visitor. We would grill a couple filet mignon steaks, which I purchased at the U.S. Embassy Commissary, while tossing down copious amounts of scotch, gin and wine. Since Bill was not authorized to utilize the U.S. facilities, these steak dinners were much appreciated.

When I knew Bill would be visiting, I ensured I had a full bottle of scotch which would be close to empty by the time he left. My compensation for these social events was being privy to first hand accounts of his combat flying against Hermann Goering's Luftwaffe pilots.

The stories became more vivid and real in direct proportion to the amount of scotch being consumed. At first I secretly questioned some of the daring details. Bill obviously sensed my skepticism, so during one of our dinners he brought over his RAF pilot's log book which supported everything he had said, including an entry documenting the first BF-109 German fighter he shot down.

Bill told me, regarding his first combat victory, that he was sure he was just as scared as the young German pilot who went down in flames. He also showed me the entry in his log book his squadron leader made, when he was shot down over Paris, France, when flying a DeHavilland *Mosquito* bomber and given up for killed in action or taken prisoner.

In reality, after bailing out, he was picked up by the French Underground and made it back to England via Spain. It took him more than two months to return to his squadron.

One evening in the summer of 1977, I was returning to Tehran from a flight to the Persian Gulf when Bill contacted me by radio. He said he was also on a return flight to Tehran and about 30 minutes behind me. He inquired if I was scheduled for a flight the next day. I told him that I had already checked with the company by radio and was scheduled to be off. He said he had also checked and was also off. He suggested I wait for him after landing so we could ride home together and visit the Army Officers' Club for dinner and pool before they closed for the night. I told him that it sounded like a winner, and after landing I would wait for him in the dispatch office.

After turning in my post-flight paperwork, the dispatcher inquired if he should order a company crew bus to drive me home. I told him no, that I would wait until Captain Aston landed and we would ride the same van to town. The dispatcher said that this wouldn't work out, since as soon as he landed he was scheduled to fly the President of the National Iranian Copper Industries Company to Kerman. According to the dispatcher the company president and his staff were already onboard the aircraft and the copilot had completed the preflight inspection and was sitting in the cockpit awaiting Captain Aston. He added that to expedite the departure, a flight plan had already been filed and the release form was just waiting for Aston's signature. (I knew Bill would be pleased with this additional nighttime flight, as he was already on overtime, and this would be four hours extra pay.)

I left a note for Bill congratulating him on the unexpected additional mission, and stated that pool lessons would have to wait until another day. I proceeded to my apartment, mixed a double martini and threw a T-bone steak on the indoor gas grill.

About five hours later, as I was getting ready to retire for the night, Bill called and wanted to know if he could come over as there was something very important he needed to discuss with me. I checked my liquor cabinet, noted a full bottle of scotch, so responded with a, "Sure Bill, come-on over for a night cap."

In record time he was buzzing my front door. As he came up the stairs I noted that he was breathing heavily. Bill was a heavy smoker and always needed a scotch to catch his breath, but on this occasion he seemed more “out-of-breath” than usual. I figured this called for a triple scotch, with no ice! After downing the drink in one gulp he said, “You won't believe what happened to me tonight on my flight to Kerman with the President of the National Iranian Copper Industries Company. It was a complete fiasco and when the Chief Pilot hears about it I'm not sure of what his reaction will be!" Bill went on to state that what happened on this flight was more embarrassing then when he was shot-down by enemy flak over Paris, France in 1944.

As I eagerly awaited to hear his story he thrust out an empty glass for a refill. Bill said that after he landed at Tehran he was told by the dispatcher that he was scheduled to fly the President of the Copper Industries Company and his staff to Kerman in their plush copper-colored F-27. He added that the dispatcher emphasized that the passengers were already on board, a flight plan had been filed, the copilot had completed the aircraft preflight inspection and was sitting in the cockpit ready to go as soon as he signed the dispatch release.

Based on what he was told, he went directly to the aircraft, positioned himself in the captain's seat, performed a quick engine start and taxi check, and when approaching the active runway requested clearance for takeoff. The tower cleared him number one for departure, so he continued to taxi toward the departure end of the runway.

However, just prior to taxiing onto the runway to commence his takeoff, Bill said he attempted to check the flight controls for freedom of movement, a procedure he had performed during his entire flying career. To his surprise, when he tried to perform this check, the (wing) ailerons would not move. Opening his side cockpit window he could see, with the aid of a flashlight, that the external aileron control gust locks were still installed, thereby forcibly locking the ailerons in a neutral position.

Tossing down another scotch Bill stated, "Here I was in the number one position for takeoff with a Pan American Airways B-747 *Jumbo* jet, that was also waiting for takeoff clearance, inching up my ass. When I told the tower I would have to hold my position for a few minutes, the *Jumbo* captain turned on his taxi lights revealing, for the whole world, an F-27 sitting in the number one position for takeoff with red gust lock streamers hanging down from each wing. I naturally couldn't takeoff with the gust locks installed and there wasn't sufficient room for the PAA 747 to taxi around me."

As I refilled Bill's glass with another three shots of scotch, he continued with his tale of woe. He said he had no choice, but to saunter past his confused VIP passengers to the rear of the aircraft and grab the three-piece gust lock removal rods. With the extension rods in hand, he exited the aircraft from an emergency rear exit by jumping onto the ramp.

With the taxi lights from the B-747 illuminating the area, he screwed the rod ends together and reached up and removed the aileron gust locks from each wing. This embarrassing action was in full view of the waiting *Jumbo* jet crew and his perplexed passengers staring at him through the cabin windows. During this whole exercise he said his stringy thinning hair was blowing wildly from the prop blast of his still-turning engines.

After removing the gust locks, he had to throw them and the disassembled metal rods into the back of the aircraft and climb in himself through the waist-high exit. Once inside he had to walk past his passengers, huffing and puffing, his hair in a blow-dry state and his uniform in complete disarray.

He said that the rest of the trip to Kerman and back was routine, but since it was quite late when he returned to Tehran he didn't see or talk to the Chief Pilot. However, he was sure the Copper Company President would inform Air Taxi of his embarrassing screw-up.

When Bill finished his unfortunate inconsolable tale, he asked me what I thought the Chief Pilot would say when he heard about his screwed-up night flight to Kerman. I suggested he have another glass of scotch and just wait to see what happens. He agreed and drank another triple scotch in one long swig. Bill left for his own apartment still mumbling under his breath about how embarrassed he was over the incident. I went to bed, but was awakened early the next morning by an Air Taxi dispatcher informing me that due to a scheduling change I was to fly a turnaround flight to Abadan and the crew bus was on its way to pick me up.

I was signing in for my flight at the dispatch counter the next morning when the Chief Pilot asked me to come into his office. After inviting me to have a seat, he inquired if I had heard about the screw-up Captain Bill Aston experienced the night before when flying the Copper Industries Company President to Kerman. In true Iranian fashion I said, "No, I hadn't heard of any problem, but would be interested in hearing about it and if there was anything I could do to help him, or Captain Aston, all he had to do was ask." (He seemed impressed with my answer.)

Captain Sephrezideh told me about the facts surrounding Captain Aston's misfortune, and to my surprise, the details were just like Bill had described to me the night before. What Bill couldn't have related were the details surrounding the irate calls the Chief Pilot received from the president of the copper company, the Tehran Tower chief, and the Pan American Airways station manager. The Chief Pilot said he didn't know what disciplinary action to take against Captain Aston, and since I had been a Chief Pilot with Japan Domestic Airlines, he wanted to know what I thought would be a proper sanction.

He didn't know that he was asking me what I thought would be a proper penalty for my good friend and pool buddy Bill Aston!

I told him, that the way I saw it, Captain Aston was more or less set-up for this screw-up and his life-long procedure of checking the controls, just before takeoff, averted a serious incident or accident, and this fact should not be overlooked. He admitted that this was true, but emphasized that a proper aircraft preflight was not completed and an item on the Before Engine Start Checklist is "Controls Free and Normal," and regardless of who else was involved, the Pilot-In-Command is responsible.

I couldn't argue with his logic, but suggested he just issue Captain Aston a letter outlining the mistakes made, and state that the letter would be kept on file. He asked me if I thought he should deduct any pay from his salary. I said, "Absolutely not, just issue him a letter." He then inquired if I would write the letter for him. I told him that I couldn't as I was scheduled to fly in just a few minutes. He said, "Don't worry about that, I will delay your flight." I then demanded that he ensure me that Captain Aston not be informed that I was the author of the letter. With his hand over his heart he promised not to disclose that I had anything to do with it.

For once, I believed an Iranian and sat down and wrote a short letter of reprimand in long hand. After presenting it to the Chief Pilot, I emphasized that it was intended as a draft only and whatever he used must be typed on company stationary and signed by him. He agreed and I flew my round-trip flight to Abadan.

After returning from my flight I hadn't been in my apartment more than ten minutes when the phone rang. Bill was on the line steaming mad and said he had to come over right away and talk to me. I told him that I didn't have any scotch as we had consumed it all the night before. He said not to worry, as he would bring his own. From the tone of his voice I was sure the Chief Pilot had issued him a letter of reprimand and gone back on his promise of not informing him that I had written it. I was already contemplating how I would miss his friendship and our frequent pool marathons.

Bill arrived, huffing and puffing, about 15 minutes later. Without waiting for his glass of whiskey, he thrust out a letter in my direction and stated, "Read this insulting letter that S.O.B. Chief Pilot issued to me today!"

A quick glance at the formally typed letter, which was on company stationary and signed by the Chief Pilot, told me that it was "word-for-word" what I had prepared in draft form earlier that day.

I asked Bill how he was presented the letter. He said that the Chief Pilot had called him that morning and requested he come to his office. After arriving, he was told that his night flight to Kerman was an embarrassment to the company and would be made a matter of record. As discipline he was being issued this degrading, insulting letter! He added. "The language used in the letter was typical of those God damn Iranians, who have hated the British ever since we assisted the Soviet Union in kicking the Shah's father out of Iran in 1941."

Bill went on to state that before he headed for the aircraft he was told by the flight dispatcher that the copilot had performed an aircraft preflight, and the only thing remaining was his ass in the cockpit.

I was relieved in Bill's condemnation of the Iranians, as it was now clear that the Chief Pilot had not gone back on his promise of not informing him that I was the author of his outrageous letter, but I still wanted to help lift him out of his depressed angry state of mind!

I asked Bill if the Chief Pilot intended to deduct any pay from his salary. He said no, but this insulting letter was worse than a pay cut. After pouring him a large glass of scotch, I attempted to console him by stating that the letter really wasn't that bad. I pointed out specific phrases that complimented him on his vast experience and how his policy of making a last-minute check of the flight controls prevented the likelihood of a serious incident or accident. I also pointed out that the letter did not threaten him with dismissal or cost him any money. By the time his bottle of scotch was empty, he was feeling somewhat better. In fact, he started to agree with me that the letter was really not that bad and some phrases actually did complimented him on his vast experience and pilotage skills.

Bill and I remained good friends and continued to enjoy dinner and pool to the extent our busy flight schedules would allow. He never found out who the real author of his "insulting letter" was, and he soon forgot that it ever existed and we never talked about it again.

Captain Aston remained in Iran until February 1979. When I last talked to him in 1980, he told me that his last two months in Iran were pure hell. Being an English citizen, he was looked after by the British Embassy after Khomeini marched into Tehran. However, during his last month he was told to remain secluded in his apartment and stay away from the windows. Each night British Embassy personnel delivered food and water. He was finally allowed to leave Iran, but before boarding the aircraft was forced to undergo an embarrassing body strip search. The last I heard, he was working as a Chief Pilot for Gander Airlines in St. Johns, Newfoundland.

Not long after Captain Aston's incident with the Iranian Copper Industries Company President, the Chief Pilot called me into his office again to inform me of a problem he had with Captain Jamerson, the other English pilot. According to his report, Captain Jamerson was slow in placing the propellers of an F-27 into flat pitch after landing, thereby causing both engines to become overloaded and exceed maximum temperature limits. The overheat condition was so severe that the engines had to be removed and sent in for an expensive overhaul.

He requested that I speak to Captain Jamerson, determine the reason for his screw-up and recommend what form of discipline should be administered. The Chief Pilot said that he was inclined to fire him on the spot. I suggested he not be fired, but temporarily grounded without loss of pay, until my investigation was complete. He agreed.

I met with Captain Jamerson in the VIP lounge and told him that the Chief Pilot asked me to inquire into the circumstances surrounding his unfortunate incident. With a long face he said, "What's the use Lou? He's going to fire my bloody ass anyway, so I might as well pack my bags, and buy an airline ticket for London." I said, "Not so fast Fred, let's review what happened, and give me a chance to prepare a report."

Fred stated that after a normal landing on Runway 11 Left at Mehrabad airport, he was preparing to execute a turn off at mid field when the tower began screaming at him to keep it rolling. According to Fred, the tower operator was so excited that his transmissions were in both English and Farsi. He didn't understand what the excitement was all about, especially since he couldn't understand the tower's heated Farsi instructions. Figuring there was another airplane on his ass, he shoved the power levers forward to expedite his movement to the far end of the runway. During his high speed run, the tower operator was still issuing instructions in Farsi and English and his copilot was attempting to translate the instructions into a form of English that he could understand.

He said that between the tower operator issuing instructions in two languages, his copilot attempting to provide simultaneous translation and the increased engine noise, the cockpit was complete bedlam. He said the distraction was so confusing that he didn't hear the cockpit warning signal instructing him to place the propellers into flat pitch, which would unload the engines, until it was too late to avoid an overheat condition.

I asked him what the emergency was that caused the tower to instruct him to keep rolling to the end of the runway. He said he found out later that another aircraft was on final approach, but it wasn't really a problem since he had executed a go-around.

I reported back to the Chief Pilot that the cause of the incident should be shared equally between the tower controller, Captain Jamerson and the copilot. I recommended a letter of reprimand be issued (which I wrote), grounding him without pay for two weeks, and be administered a line check before being allowed to resume captain duties.

The Chief Pilot accepted my recommendations and Fred enjoyed two weeks off, followed by a line check. He was back flying and accumulated enough hours in the remaining days of the month that resulted in very little loss of pay. (He was not aware that I wrote his letter of reprimand.) Each time I saw Fred after this incident he offered to buy me a drink. Captain Jamerson was smarter than the rest of us and left Tehran at the first signs of the demonstrations turning ugly in early 1978.

Another foreign pilot I admired was Robert Davis. Bob was a *Falcon* captain and flight instructor from Fort Wayne, Indiana. I believe he was the first foreign pilot recruited by Air Taxi and he and his charming wife made new foreign pilots feel at home. He was one of the first pilots to check out in Lear jets and flew for Executive Jet in Columbus, Ohio. His boss at Executive Jet was retired Air Force General Paul Tibbets, the Enola Gay B-29 pilot who dropped the atomic bomb on Hiroshima, Japan during WW II. Bob left Iran in early 1977 for a job in the U.S.

Jim Wallace was an early-thirties American pilot flying as a *Falcon* captain. He was a good looking, good natured guy who had a very attractive young wife. I enjoyed several dinners in their small apartment, but it was evident that his wife Lynn didn't share her husband's enthusiasm for living in Iran. When Jim was gone, she would literally lock herself in the house to avoid the lustful stares, or worse, of bearded Iranian men. She was even fondled when just going down the street to a nearby bakery. Many Iranian men displayed little or no hesitance in visually, and sometimes physically, molesting young infidel women. I believe they felt it was no sin if their lust was restricted to infidels. Jim and his wife returned to the U.S. in 1977 and he retired as a United Airlines Captain on September 4, 2004 and now lives in Fort Lauderdale, Florida.

Rich Reeves was a U.S. Air Force pilot stationed in Iran who requested a release from active duty to marry an attractive young Iranian girl he fell in love with. After his discharge, he accepted employment with Air Taxi, flying the North American *Shrike Commander* but later upgraded to the *Turbo Commander* 690A. (See Photo No. 17.)

When I first met Rich, I was impressed by his knowledge of Iran and his ability to drive the chaotic streets of Tehran. At the time he was the only foreign pilot who owned an automobile. Rich introduced me to the ski slopes of Dizin north of Tehran and to several restaurants that I never would have found on my own. He and his pretty wife were great fun and I enjoyed many delightful meals in their spacious third-floor apartment in downtown Tehran. They were a delightful couple who would entertain their guests through playful bantering of each other about their different national customs and ethnic backgrounds.

Rich would remind her that, according to Muslim custom, the husband could divorce his wife by stating three times, "I divorce thee," presenting her with something sweet, a gift of gold and a copy of the Koran. With this in mind Rich would playfully display a lump of sugar on top of a copy of the Koran, a gold coin from his pocket and state all that was needed was for him to say the three magic words.

She would respond that if he opened his big fat mouth she'd knock him off the third-floor balcony. The lump of sugar would go back into the sugar bowl, the gold coin back in Rich's pocket, the Koran back on the shelf and another round of drinks would be offered to their guests. Rich and his Iranian wife left Iran during the early phases of the revolution and now live in Ohio where Rich, until recently, was a captain flying corporate jets.

Captain McKillen was the only foreign pilot from Amsterdam and was the pilot who was assigned to provide me with line experience when I first started flying as a captain. As previously mentioned, I was not impressed with his piloting skills even though it was reported he had flown as a captain for an airline in Athens, Greece. However, there seemed to be some question regarding his reported aviation experience, and he left Iran quite suddenly in the fall of 1976.

Matt Matthews was an American pilot from California assigned to the F-27 and *Falcon* fleets. As I previously mentioned, I shared an apartment with Matt when I first came to Tehran, but moved out as soon as I could find a place of my own. Matt was a capable pilot, but a chronic complainer who loved to openly accuse other foreign pilots of robbing him of overtime flight hours. He was the only foreign pilot who brought his wife and children to Iran, so it's possible his constant whining was a manifestation of the frustration he felt in worrying about the safety of his family.

The difficulties of living in Iran provided the fodder for Matt to openly gripe whenever he could find an audience. It was interesting to watch his listeners disappear, one-by-one, as they found reasons to excuse themselves. His temperament fit in well in Iran, as many Iranians appeared unhappy with the life Allah saddled them with. Matt and his family left Iran during the early phases of the revolution and moved back to California. (The last time I saw Matt was in Napa, California in 1980 when he was seeking employment with a company I was working for as a flight instructor. When my boss asked for my comments he wasn't hired.)

In the fall of 1976, Air Taxi employed a recently retired Pakistani Air Force colonel by the name of Ahmadi. He was to be assigned captain duties in the city of Shiraz operating an Air Service FH-227 throughout Southern Iran. He had considerable flying experience with the Pakistani Air Force, but was not qualified in the FH-227. The Chief Pilot requested that I be posted to Shiraz for 30 days as his flight instructor.

The plan presented was that for the first two weeks Captain Ahmadi would fly as my copilot, and for the second two-week period, he would fly as captain under my supervision. I had no objection with the assignment, but mentioned to the Chief Pilot that since the flights in Southern Iran were of short duration, I would most likely not qualify for overtime pay comparable to foreign pilots remaining in Tehran. To offset this financial short fall, I suggested that the company, in addition to my normal per diem, pay my hotel expenses for the full 30 days, plus a $30 ($115 in 2007) per day food allowance. He said he had no problem with my proposal providing Mr. Djahanbini, the managing director, gave his OK.

I briefed Mr. Djahanbini on my discussion with his Chief Pilot regarding the additional allowance during my 30 day temporary assignment to Shiraz. He said it had his full approval, adding that establishing an operational base in Shiraz was very important and financially beneficial to the company. He shook my hand and wished me an enjoyable and productive month long stay in Shiraz. (See Photo No. 1.)

The next day I rode the jump seat of an Iran Air B-727 to Shiraz and secured a room at the Park Hotel. At the airport I noted an FH-227 parked on the edge of the ramp and assumed it was to be my flying office during my stay in Shiraz. I was looking forward to meeting Captain Ahmadi and beginning the process of flying with a retired colonel from Pakistan. The first phase of my expectation was met when registering at the hotel. The clerk handed me an envelope marked "Captain Martin."

The envelope contained a message from Captain Ahmadi informing me that he was staying with friends in Shiraz and would furnish his own transportation to the airport when scheduled to fly. He also provided an address and telephone number for contact. I thought it strange that a new expatriate to Iran would be staying with friends, but nothing in Iran came as a surprise anymore.

Also in the envelope was a note and flight schedule from the Abadan dispatch office. According to instructions, we were to fly a regular airline type flight pattern from Shiraz for six consecutive days, followed by one day off. If we operated on schedule, and did not require company assistance, there was no need to make daily contact with the flight control dispatch center.

At the conclusion of each week I was to submit a progress report to Abadan with an information copy to Tehran. Reviewing the flight schedule I noted that we would be making frequent flights to oil supporting airports in Abadan, Azadegan, Bandar Abbas, Bandar-e-Lengeh, Bushier, Dubai, Kish Island, and Lavan Island, to name a few. None of the flights were more than an hour or so in duration and provided numerous takeoffs and landings. I figured I was in for a very enjoyable month of flying with nobody looking over my shoulder, a welcome change.

I met Captain Ahmadi for the first time the next morning and liked him right from the start. He was an good-natured man in his mid forties, about six feet tall, very trim and spoke excellent English with a pleasant Indian accent. He had been briefed on our month-long mission and informed me that he had been studying the FH-227 aircraft flight manual sent to him by the company manager in Abadan and looking forward to flying it.

I could see that he would be a quick study and a joy to fly with. Before the first six-day flight schedule was history, we were alternating takeoffs and landings, and he was asking me questions about the aircraft that often sent me scurrying into the aircraft flight manual for an answer.

The aircraft ran beautifully the first week, and without having to make daily contact with the company it was like flying our own personal aircraft throughout Southern Iran, with someone else picking up the tab. Everywhere we landed we were treated royally and I even had a chance to teach Captain Ahmadi the basic rudiments of "Eight-Ball."

I asked him how it was that he was staying with friends versus renting a room at the five star Park Hotel. His answer somewhat surprised me. He said that Shiraz accommodated a large number of Indian and Pakistani professionals and their families working in Iran, and he had several friends who were more than happy to have him stay with them. He mentioned that one of the main reasons he accepted a position with the Air Taxi Company was an opportunity of living in Shiraz where he would have the friendship of many fellow countrymen.

When still on the subject he asked me what my plans were for our upcoming day off. Stating I had no plans, he countered with, "You do now." He said a group of his Indian and Pakistani colleagues were having an outdoor dinner party the following evening, and he would pick me up at my hotel around 4 p.m. in his friend's automobile.

Stating I would be waiting, he politely reminded me that the dress was casual, and since all his friends were Muslim, no alcoholic beverages would be served. If I wished a cocktail before dinner, I should have one at the hotel. I thanked him for the invitation and said I was looking forward to meeting his Shiraz friends.

After a quick dry-martini at the hotel bar, I was standing in front of the hotel at 4 p.m. as instructed. Captain Ahmadi drove up right on schedule in a big black Mercedes-Benz sedan. As I climbed into the passenger seat, I remarked that he certainly had good friends. He commented that the automobile belonged to a medical doctor friend who, along with his wife, were hosting the dinner party we would be attending.

A few miles outside of Shiraz we parked in the private driveway of a large attractive villa, not unlike a house one would expect to find on the French Riviera. We were greeted at the front door by a beautiful middle age woman dressed in a gorgeous silk sari, a diamond in her nose, thick gold necklaces around her neck and a silver bracelet on each wrist. With a slight bow she greeted me with a warm handshake. The smell of sweet incense permeated the air as I entered the house. With a smile, she said her other guests were in the courtyard and requested I follow her.

Shiraz, being 5,000 feet above sea level, provides reasonably cool evenings, and with the sun low in the western sky, the temperature in the garden was near perfect. The perfume from fresh flower beds, combined with the scent from burning torches, produced an atmosphere not unlike Hawaii or other semi-tropical areas.

The party guests consisted of about 20 people casually attired in both western and ethnic dress. Most women were wearing colorful saris and several men were dressed in flowing gowns called kurts. Those in native dress were wearing colorful jewel-studded shoes. All the women were heavily decorated with gold and silver and the men's fingers were adorned with large jeweled gold rings.

I was introduced to the guests as, "Captain Martin, Colonel Ahmadi's instructor pilot." I sensed that this was an equally impressive title as I met several doctors and their wives. They all spoke English with a common Indian accent. I felt that they, especially the women, were just as interested in my American accent as I was in their Indian way of speaking.

The medical doctors were hired by the Shah to update the medical facilities in Southern Iran, but voiced a uniform frustration in the constant theft of valuable equipment and the difficulty of persuading Iranian Muslim females to visit a male foreign doctor.

By the time I had finished a cold Coke, the hostess rang a small crystal bell and announced that dinner was being served. A beautiful buffet-style meal was presented consisting of grilled chicken, roasted leg of lamb, curried tomatoes, sesame eggplant salad, spicy curried chicken chunks with mango sauce and fancy deserts to follow. The beverage was a choice of soft drinks or spiced tea.

Colorful mats were spread out on the grass, which we sat on while eating. The food was delicious, but as expected quite spicy. Captain Ahmadi inquired if I could endure sitting on the ground while eating. I told him that I had lived in Japan for eight years, so sitting on the ground for long periods of time was not new to me. I jokingly asked him if the hostess was going to provide ivory chop sticks, made from elephant tusks. He said, "No, only hand crafted Indian silverware."

After dinner the hostess informed us that we were to be entertained by a local Indian/Pakistan musical group and some ethnic Indian dancing. The music consisted of an Indian-style flute called a Susir, a two-string instrument called a Tantu Vadya and a soft percussion drum. The musicians played a strange sounding, unfamiliar melodic melody, which seemed to repeat, over and over, the same rhythmic cycles with long sustained, never-ending, monotonous tones. (The sounds coming from the musicians reminded me of what you hear when members of a large orchestra are "tuning-up" before a classical concert.)

At first the music was interesting, but soon began to grate on my acoustic senses, which had been anticipating entertainment, not torture! However, when the young girls, dressed in loose flowing split skirts and silk pajama-like pants, started their slow melodic dancing, I was able to ignore the music by staring at the movement of the young female hips. I felt as if I was sitting in a warm garden somewhere in Pakistan or India.

When the "well-intended" entertainment was over, I asked Captain Ahmadi if he could drive me back to my hotel as we had to fly early the next morning. I bid farewell to my gracious host and hostess and new found friends, but secretly decided that once was enough. Back at the hotel I had a stiff night cap before retiring.

The second week of flying went by fast and it was obvious that Captain Ahmadi would have no problem in moving to the left seat of the FH-227. He asked me what I had planned for my upcoming day off, and before he could invite me to another dinner party, I told him I was going to visit the ancient Persian capital city of *Persepolis.* He said he wished he could join me, but had to have dinner with some friends. I wished him "Bon-Appetite."

The next morning, I boarded a bus for the 35-mile trip to the palace known as *Persepolis.* It was built during the height of the Persian Empire around the year 500 B.C. It was nearly destroyed by Alexander the Great in 331 B.C. in retaliation for destruction of the *Acropolis* in Athens, Greece by the Persian ruler Xerxes. Unfortunately the ruins remaining are just a small part of the original palace, but enough still remains to give one the sense of its former glory.

Fortunately after its destruction, it was covered by sand and dust until it was rediscovered in 1930. Still visible are the ruins of the huge *Apadana Palace* complex where the Persian kings received royal visitors who would arrive with gifts of gold, wild animals and slaves. Many stone figures and wall relief panels are still intact, thanks to being covered with sand for over 2,000 years. I spent my entire day off wandering around the ruins of *Persepolis*, which was considerably more enjoyable than fighting heartburn from eating hot spicy Indian cuisine. However, I would miss the gyrating hips of the scantly-dressed young Indian dancing girls.

My third and fourth week in Shiraz went by very quickly and performing copilot duties for Captain Ahmadi was a very easy job. As I anticipated, by the time the month was up, he was fully qualified and a safe Fairchild FH-227 airline captain. He would remain at Shiraz, and in the future, Tehran would send him copilots on temporary assignment. We bid each other farewell and he expressed more thanks than necessary for my help.

I caught an Iran Air B-727 back to Tehran to resume my normal flight duties. It was going to be tough to have to start calling a dispatcher, each evening, to learn what my flight schedule was for the next day.

However, not all of my flights were initiated by a telephone call to a dispatcher. I was returning from a short vacation in the U.S. and after flying all night arrived in Tehran at 7 a.m. dead-tired, experiencing jet-lag and looking forward to a hot shower and a long rest. Departing the jet-way I saw a man holding a sign reading ***"Captain Martin."*** *His message was that I was scheduled for a flight and he was to transport me to Air Taxi. The dispatcher said an Iranian Captain had called in sick and he was about to cancel the flight when he realized that I was scheduled to return from vacation. He called KLM Airlines and when assured I was onboard sent a driver to pick me up. I flew the seven hours flight dressed in a untidy sport shirt and casual trousers, but took frequent catnaps en route.*

Soon after returning to Tehran, a pilot by the name of Fritz Grunt from Vienna, Austria joined the company. He had been flying for Air Zaire in Kinshasa (The former Belgium Congo), was accustomed to working in a foreign country and quickly checked out in the F-27. Fritz and I became good friends and he was amused by my limited ability of communicating with him in broken German. I asked Fritz why he had decided to leave Air Zaire. His answer was quite enlightening! He said that the main reason for leaving was his desire to stay alive. According to Fritz, the few foreign pilots working for Air Zaire, when not flying, were literally prisoners in their hotels. For diversion they would sometimes go by bus to another Western hotel just to have dinner. Other than that, they remained in their own hotels. He said that when scheduled to fly, they were transported to and from the airport in a sturdy crew bus accompanied by an armed guard and advised not to extend their arms through open windows. To do so would expose wrist watches and rings, and they would be taking a chance of having roving gangs of thieves sever their arms with sharp machete.

About a month after returning from my 30-day assignment to Shiraz the Chief Pilot called me into his office and requested I sign a three-page document printed entirely in Farsi. I asked him what it was and he said it was an authorization for the company to withhold 189,000 rials ($2,700, or $10,000 when adjusted for inflation) from my pay to cover the cost of the hotel and meals for my month in Shiraz.

I reminded him that he had agreed that Air Taxi would pay for my hotel and a daily meal allowance. With a straight face, he denied ever agreeing to such a ridiculous compensation arrangement, as I was paid per diem plus my normal salary when in Shiraz. I told him that I wouldn't sign the document and would talk to the managing director regarding this phony charge, which was in violation of a previous oral agreement.

I knocked on Mr. Djahanbini office door and was pleased to find him in. I told him that his Chief Pilot wanted to garnishee my salary to cover the costs of my expenses during my 30 days in Shiraz. I reminded him that both he and his Chief Pilot had agreed that the company would pay for my hotel and meals, in addition to my normal per-diem. He, like his subordinate, denied agreeing to such an arrangement. In a firm voice I told him that they had indeed made such an agreement, and if they took one rial out of my pay, I would resign and catch the first plane to the U. S. I reminded him that he was short of experienced captains, and that many of his VIP passengers were now asking for me by name when scheduling flights. (I felt a strong stance was my only recourse.)

The subject of withholding part of my pay was not brought to my attention again for quite some time, and I figured it was a dead issue. However, about two months later as I was preparing for a scheduled turnaround flight to Abadan, the Chief Pilot said he would like to talk to me. He stated that since Shiraz was in Southern Iran they had transferred the responsibility of recovering the cost of my outstanding hotel bill to Mr. Ayoubkahn. (Mr. Ayoubkahn was the Chief Pilot when I first started flying for Air Taxi, but was now the managing director of Air Service in Abadan.) He requested I discuss the subject with him, as his office is very close to the Abadan airport terminal. He added that when doing so, I should take all the time I needed, and not worry about delaying the return flight.

After landing in Abadan, I instructed my copilot to coordinate the turnaround procedures and proceeded to Ayoubkahn's office. Mr. Ayoubkahn, as I commented on previously, was a very large man, possessed a deep baritone voice and had the reputation of intimidating company personnel in Southern Iran.

Upon reaching his office I walked directly past his secretary and entered it with a slight passing knock on the door. Without giving him a chance to open his mouth, I told him that I was sick and tired of the company screwing around with a so-called unpaid hotel bill for my 30-day stay in Shiraz. Without a pause, I said, "I'll tell you the same thing I told Mr. Djahanbani and the Chief Pilot in Tehran. If the company takes one rial out of my pay for this bogus charge, I'll be on the next plane to the USA to accept one of the many jobs I have been offered flying F-27s or *Falcon* jets." With that I left his office without giving him a chance to respond. The subject of an outstanding hotel bill never came up again.

I was fast learning how to deal with the Iranian practice of adjusting the truth to fit the occasion. At the time I had no prospect of a job in the U.S., but they didn't know it and needed experienced captains. The best way to describe the Iranian approach, be it important or trivial, is their attempt to convince you that what is being stated is the truth. If you accept their story as fact, but later discover you were hoodwinked, you blame yourself for believing it, not the person who persuaded you to accept the fabrication.

I believe this inherit trait of stretching the truth has its origins in the Middle East practice of haggling over every aspect of life. Without arguing and convincing your opponent that you have told the best story, an Iranian or Middle East national would feel that he was somehow a failure.

Haggling to increase passenger loads was even practiced by some gate agents. My procedure to keep them happy, and still not overload the aircraft, was to take full advantage of their inherent propensity for debate.

If, when computing maximum allowable weights, I determined that I could carry 25 passengers, I would inform the agent that he could only load 22. He would come back with a plea to load 28 and would come up with all kinds of excuses why it was essential to do so. I, in-turn, would come back with reasons why it would not be safe to carry more than 22. He would come back with a request to load 26, and I would raise my limit to 24. We would go back and forth in this interchange until we arrived at a compromised number of 25, he felt he had won by being allowed to load three more than my original figure, and I was satisfied since I would not takeoff with an over-grossed aircraft.

Chapter Twelve --- The Revolutionary Crisis

President Jimmy Carter, during his visit to Tehran on New Year's Day 1978, made the following statement in the presence of the Shah, his wife, Empress Farah and senior Iranian Government staff members.

"Iran, because of the great leadership of the Shah, is an island of stability in one of the more troubled areas of the world. This is a great tribute to you, your majesty, and to your leadership and to the respect and the admiration and the love which your people give to you. There is no leader with whom I have a deeper sense of personal friendship and gratitude."

This glowing statement was apparently spontaneous and a surprise to the President's advisors, as well as to the Shah. Subsequent to this unexpected complimentary affirmation by the President of the United States, the Shah felt confident in authorizing the publication of an open attack on his aging enemy, Ayatollah Khomeini, who was in exile in Paris, France. This public attack on Khomeini was the opening salvo in a year-long struggle that would see the eventual overthrow of the Shah.

In the past I had observed Iranian copilots, and some captains, exchanging cassette tapes and pamphlets in shaded corners, which I knew to be anti-government material. This sharing of anti-Shah information was performed in secluded areas, and if I questioned the individuals about what they were distributing, they would clam up and not respond. However, in early 1978 this exchange of pro-Khomeini propaganda became more brazen and more wide spread. On occasion, I would even hear open criticism of the Shah from younger pilots. This would have been unheard of just a few months earlier.

In January 1978, soon after President Carter's visit, there was a large anti-government protest at the University of Tehran. The police moved in to control the crowd and 20 students were killed. In February 1978, 100 demonstrators, led by militant Islamic fundamentalists, were killed in the Northern City of Tabriz, and the following month approximately 100 were killed in the city of Yazd.

Under Muslim belief, the male demonstrators killed were martyrs and their souls would go directly to paradise where they would be warmly greeted by 72 beautiful young female virgins. However, left behind on mother earth were brothers, sisters, fathers, mothers, uncles, aunts, friends and relatives, who now harbored a personal vengeance against the Shah. They demonstrated in the streets in ever greater numbers in seeking revenge without fearing death or the wrath of the Shah's army.

Wildcat strikes throughout the country began to have a crippling effect on the economy, and the Shah ordered the armed forces to take over the operation of the oil fields. Long automobile gas lines were becoming common, and to control the crowds at gas stations, soldiers occasionally fired their weapons into the air. People driving BMWs or Mercedes were often stopped by roving gangs who siphoned their gas tanks and vandalized the drivers and their automobiles.

Oddly enough, these wild demonstrations in early 1978 were sporadic with several weeks of calm in between clashes. It was as if the demonstrators, the police and the soldiers were resting between rounds of a boxing match. The growing uneasiness during the opening months of 1978 did not influence the frequency of my flights. If anything, there seemed to be a heightened eagerness to display, "business as usual."

In the midst of the turmoil brewing in Tehran, I received a most welcome international cable from Miss Chieko Hara in Tokyo, Japan. Chieko was a former flight attendant I had known when we both flew for Japan Domestic Airlines, and the person I obtained round-trip discount tickets for previously. Prior to my leaving Japan, she had resigned from the airline to take a position as a sales representative for the Mitsukoshi Department Store in Tokyo. Mitsukoshi is the largest Department Store chain in Japan and operated stores in New York, Rome, and Paris.

According to the cable, Mitsuhoshi was planning on opening a store in Tehran and Chieko was selected as one of 12 advance sales representatives. In January 1978, I welcomed her arrival at Mehrabad airport and she and her Japanese colleagues took up residence in a large rented house just a ten-minute drive from my apartment. I considered Chieko's arrival an unexpected belated 1977 Christmas present.

However, my joy in her presence in Tehran was not shared by my landlord who occupied the apartment directly below mine. After returning from an Air Taxi trip one day, I invited my copilot in for a beer and to view some snapshots I had told him about during our flight.

Within a few minutes my landlord knocked on my door and when I opened it, launched into in a tirade against me in Farsi. My copilot, acting as interpreter, told me that he was very unhappy because he had observed a young oriental female {Chieko} whom he felt was not my wife visiting my apartment and remaining for several hours. He said that this type of behavior was in conflict with the Koran and an insult to Allah. He demanded that she not be allowed to visit my apartment in the future.

I asked my copilot to inform Mr. Ahmadi that visitors to my apartment were my business and not a concern of his. He was obviously very disappointed in my response and left in a huff. (See Photos 11 and 31.)

When I opened the door to my apartment the next afternoon, I was surprised to see my landlord busily engaged in cleaning the stovepipes to my "naft" (kerosene) space heater. In the cleaning process he had removed them from the wall and was reinstalling them when I entered. Without exchanging a word, or even a nod, I went to my bedroom to change clothes. A few minutes later he indicated, through sign language, that he had finished his job and was leaving.

When the night air began cooling my apartment, I started a fire in the space heater and after a couple bottles of beer retired for the night.

Some hours later I awoke with a terrific headache and a bladder demanding attention. When I rolled out of bed, I was so dizzy that it was difficult to stand-up or walk. Relying on my experience of being exposed to hypoxia during aviation flight training, I knew my body was starved of oxygen, and if I didn't do something fast, I would soon pass out.

I staggered to the large French doors that opened onto an open-air balcony, opened them, and stepped out into the cool night air. Within a few minutes my head began to clear and when feeling that I could walk with a steady gait, reentered my apartment to investigate the cause of the problem.

The prime suspect of the noxious fumes was the space heater and upon inspection, I noted that the stovepipe section entering the wall was slightly ajar. The gap was wide enough to allow odorless, poisonous, carbon monoxide fumes to enter the interior of my apartment.

I turned off the space heater and using some wet towels pushed the hot stovepipe firmly into the wall. I kept the windows open the rest of the night and gave thanks to Allah that the beers I drank just before retiring excited my bladder. If I had not felt the need to relieve myself, I'm sure I would still be sleeping. (Hopefully in Paradise with 72 female virgins!)

When I departed my apartment for work the next morning, I believe my landlord was surprised to see me up and alive. I'm quite sure the misaligned stovepipe was no accident, but I had no proof.

After this incident, I inspected my apartment before retiring for the night and installed an inside night bolt on my front door. Knowing my landlord had a key to my apartment, I also devised a secret indicator which would provide an indication if the front door had been opened during my absence. On several occasions, I noted that this device had been triggered which caused me to check for loose stovepipes or other potential problems before retiring for the night.

January 1978 was also notable as I was starting my second two-year contract with the Air Taxi Company. Prior to renewing my contract, I persuaded management personnel to remove the restriction of my not owning or driving an automobile. I was now the proud owner of a 1966 white Volkswagen *Beetle.* I had convinced the company that I was capable of doing battle with the crazy drivers in Iran and could take care of myself if involved in an accident. One safeguard I adopted was to carry several crisp one-hundred dollar bills to be used as bribes if the need arose. Fortunately, I never had to use them. (See Photo No. 15.)

In February 1978, I was directed to fly a passenger-configured F-27 to Khark Island to transport the Shah's younger brother, Prince Pahlavi and his entourage, to Kish Island and remain with them for three days. I had flown to Kish before and was impressed by its paradise-like atmosphere. However, I had never remained there overnight! I was looking forward to the opportunity of spending a few days on the Shah's private Island as a guest of his younger brother.

Kish Island is located on the Eastern end of the Persian Gulf, close to the Strait of Hormuz and had been hotly contested by both the United Arab Emirates and Iran for several years. (See Photo No. 1.)

This elliptically-shaped island is known as "the Pearl of the Middle East" and encompasses 60 square miles of pristine white beaches. It is 15 miles from Iran's Southern rim, and only 120 miles from Dubai and Saudi Arabia. Its delightful temperatures range from a low of 50 to a high of 82 degrees Fahrenheit.

To bolster Iran's claim to the island, the Shah built an elaborate winter palace with individual private cottages for invited guests. Not far from the palace complex he built a lavish combination hotel and gambling casino. An Olympic-size swimming pool, sheltered by swaying palm trees, was nestled behind the hotel. The hotel and casino were as grand as anything found in Las Vegas, Nevada.

Within walking distance of the hotel was a large duty-free bazaar which featured elaborate Persian carpets, expensive jewelry, rare wine and liquor of every description. To provide access to the island, the Shah built a modern airport and deep-sea water harbor.

Travel to Kish Island was tightly controlled, especially when the Shah, Empress Farah or the Crown Prince were in residence. I assumed that flying the Shah's younger brother and his friends to KIsh indicated that the Shah or his wife and son were not vacationing there at this time.

During previous flights to Kish Island, it was not uncommon to see several Saudi Arabian-registered jets sitting idle on the airport parking ramp. On one of my earlier flights one of my passengers was a British gentlemen who told me that he was the caretaker of a portion of the Shah's Island complex.

I asked him about the Saudi Arabian jets I sometimes observed on the island airport and the occasional bikini-clad young Caucasian women I would see lounging around the hotel swimming pool. He chuckled at my question, and replied that if I took note, I would probably observe that the bathing beauties' presence would coincide with the showing up of Saudi Arabian corporate jets on the aircraft parking ramp.

He called my attention to the fact that the United Arab Emirates and Saudi Arabia were only 30 minutes flying time from Kish Island and had become a favorite rest and recreation destination for Arab Sheiks. He added that when Saudi jets were parked on the airport ramp, I could expect to see the hotel swimming pool flush with attractive young females flown in from Madame Claude's sophisticated call-girl business in Paris.

He explained that the Arab men visiting Kish Island would shuck their turbans and robes before leaving their aircraft and head for the hotel for two or three days of gambling, drinking and enjoying the company of the young French women. When they could take no more, they would don their Arab dress, fly back to Saudi Arabia and resume their pious Muslim life style, where females are not allowed to drive automobiles, forced to wear head scarves (Hajibs), and overall treated as second-class citizens.

On one of my trips to Kish Island there were no visiting Arabs in residence, so my English caretaker friend took me on a tour of the resort complex. It was indeed opulent in every respect, and certainly equal to, or better than anything found in stateside resorts.

After the overthrow of the Shah, Iran touted Kish Island as a tropical tourist spot and converted the hotel into a Muslim university. However, gambling casinos, bars and visiting French bikini-clad females are a thing of the past. In addition there are separate male and female beaches.

When I parked my F-27 in front of the terminal at Khark Island, to pick-up the Shah's brother, the usual red carpet was rolled out from the terminal main gate. A few minutes later, Prince Pahlavi, his wife and about ten high ranking military admirals, generals and their wives, followed him toward my waiting aircraft.

The Prince was wearing a modified Iranian Navy-style uniform similar to pictures I recall of Admiral Horatio Hornblower. His chest was decorated with oversize military ribbons and long strands of gold braid hung from each shoulder. His military assistants were similarly attired, while the women, even though the temperature was near 80 degrees, were all wearing full-length mink coats. As they boarded the aircraft, they appeared to be in a frolicsome mood, which I attributed to their patronizing the Iranian Navy Officers' Club for a lunch of lamb and rice, washed down with generous amounts of expensive French champagne.

After all the passengers were seated, the Prince came to the cockpit, introduced himself in fluent English, and inquired about the weather and en route time. I told him the weather was great and we could expect a smooth flight of about one hour. He shook my hand in acknowledgment and closed the cockpit door as he returned to the passenger cabin. I noted that during the Prince's brief visit to the cockpit my young Iranian copilot turned white with fear, lest the Prince might speak to him.

The takeoff and climb was routine and we were soon cruising along the Persian Gulf coast in smooth air with the autopilot doing the flying. The cockpit door opened and a gold-trimmed Iranian Navy admiral asked me if it was OK for the Prince to sit in the copilot's seat for a while during cruise. Hearing this my copilot exited his seat as if his pants were on fire and was in the cabin before I had a chance to authorize him to leave his position. I told the admiral that I would be honored to have the Shah's brother join me in the cockpit.

Prince Pahlavi was quite a large man and had to take in a few deep breaths to squeeze into the right seat. Once seated, I noted several brown-nosing admirals pushing into the narrow space between the cabin and cockpit so as to be as close as possible to their royal family escort.

As we hummed along the Prince asked a few intelligent questions about aviation and then surprised me with, "Captain Martin, how long have you worked in Iran?" I told him, "A little more than two years."

He asked if I liked living in Tehran. I told him, "Not especially, as the city was very confining, thick with irritating pollution and the traffic congestion murder." He chuckled at my answer and said he agreed.

He then, by memory, discussed my resume in detail which I knew he had been briefed on by his secret police bodyguards. In the discussion he asked why I had abandoned my employment with Japan Domestic Airlines. I responded that when OPEC cut off oil to the West in 1973, and the Shah's subsequent quadrupling of it's price in 1974, it created an economic shock wave that reverberated around the world. Losing my job in Japan was the ressult of this rippling effect. He nodded in agreement.

Coming into view off the left side of the aircraft was a new Iranian Navy harbor and airfield by the name of Zahedan. I noted that this caught the Prince's eye, and even though I didn't understand Farsi, it was clear he was asking his admirals questions regarding this new base. I sat without saying a word enjoying the jabbering of the admirals as they stuttered in trying, unsuccessfully, to answer the Prince's questions.

One of the admirals asked me if I had a map, and in response, I reached into my flight bag and randomly pulled out a high altitude navigation chart and handed it to him. I knew the aviation chart would provide zero help in locating Zahedan and took pleasure in watching him turn it from side-to-side in total confusion.

Finally the Prince lost patience with his babbling admirals and asked me in English if I knew anything about the base that was passing off the left side of the aircraft. I told him with gusto that it was a new Iranian Navy base under construction by the name of Zahedan. When completed it would accommodate Iranian surface ships, submarines and provide a large airport for jet fighters and C-130 transports.

I added that I had made a couple flights into Zahedan and if he wished to land there today we could do so. He thanked me for the information, but said we would press on to Kish Island. He then turned to his admirals, and again without knowledge of Farsi, I knew he was giving them hell for not knowing about Zahedan and forcing him to learn about it from a foreign pilot.

As I taxied to the parking ramp at Kish Island, I noted that it was void of Saudi Arabian jets. This did not surprise me, since the island was to host a member of the royal family, but at the same time I would miss the opportunity of viewing the swimming-pool beauties, albeit at a distance.

After landing, a bus was waiting for my group of VIPs, but before deplaning, the Prince came to the cockpit, thanked me for a smooth flight, and said that I would be billeted in a private VIP cottage. He added that my copilot and flight attendants would be provided adequate, but not similar accommodations. The Prince said we would spend three nights in Kish Island and he planned no flights in between, so we should relax and enjoy our stay. (See Photos No. 12 and 14.)

An air-conditioned limousine deposited me in front of a large round cottage-style bungalow within sound of the pounding surf. Entering my temporary home, I stood in the open doorway for a while to take in the opulence spread out before me. The cottage contained a king size bed, a full white leather sofa with matching love seat, a kitchenette with stove and refrigerator, a dining table, a large screen stereo TV, a fully stocked bar, a huge tiled bathroom with Jacuzzi, and carpets so thick they put a bounce in every step. (I considered them adequate for my short three-day stay.) After a shower, a change of clothes and a Beefeater Gin martini, I met my crew in the guest dining room for dinner. We were served by white-gloved waiters who presented a menu equal to the finest restaurants in Paris. I chose to have a Persian Gulf jumbo shrimp cocktail, another martini, an Australian filet mignon (I could cut with my fork), a glass of fine French red wine and dessert with fresh ground coffee. I was informed that there would be no charge for lodging or meals as we were guests of Prince Pahlavi. This was a real treat as I would collect $100 per diem (about $376 today) for each day to offset the harsh conditions.

Following dinner I invited my crew and two English contract workers to my air-conditioned cottage to enjoy the hospitality of my open bar. When we assembled, I learned that one of my English guests operated the closed circuit radio and television station. He asked if we wished to see a first-run American movie. After presenting an interesting list of titles he disappeared down the street to power-up the TV station. We watched a popular movie (without commercials) while sipping champagne from fine crystal glasses. At the conclusion of the movie we enjoyed surround-sound music from a Japanese stereo set.

I spent the next several days strolling on the white sandy beach, shopping in the bazaar, indulging in great food and drink and just plain relaxing. I flew the Prince and his friends back to Khark Island three days later and headed back to Tehran. This opulent no expense-spared trip took place as Iranians, denied a fair share of the oil wealth, were assembling in Tehran and other major cities to march in violent protest against Prince Pahlavi's older brother, the Shah.

These demonstrations were being led by Islamic Shiite militant followers of Ayatollah Khomeini who was in exile in Paris, France. For some time he had been sending large numbers of anti-Shah cassette recordings and literature into Iran. From all appearances his efforts to unseat the Shah were looked on favorably in France and the United States and According to Donald Wilber's book, "Iran, Past and Present," the French press echoed Khomeini's sentiments by stating that the French government thought the fall of the Pahlavi regime would be in its best interests.

According to Mr. Wilber, the Carter regime was ambivalent to the internal problems brewing in Iran and were very late in realizing the seriousness of the challenge to the Shah. The United States stood by and did little to help correct the deteriorating situation. President Carter's Under Secretary of State George Ball was quoted as stating that the Shah must go. In January 1978 General Robert Huyser, deputy commander of U.S. Forces in Europe, met with the American ambassador in Tehran and his message was to advise the Shah to leave Iran.

It was obvious that Prince Pahlavi and his entourage were oblivious to the reluctance of Western countries to become involved in Khomeini's growing efforts to overthrow his brother and were living on borrowed time.

Less than a year later many members of this carefree gathering I flew to Kish Island would be in prison, executed, or if they escaped Iran early enough, living in exile in various parts of the Western world off their secret Swiss bank accounts.

Chapter Thirteen --- Calm Before the Storm

The spring and summer of 1978 were good times for me in Iran. I was now qualified in all four aircraft operated by Air Taxi and developing a reputation as one of their preferred captains. I was even being requested by name by many of our VIP passengers. I was also free from relying on crowded, smelly, community taxis as I was now driving my own Volkswagen *Beetle*. Adding to the contentment was that Chieko Hara, my flight attendant friend (and future wife) from Japan, was now also working and living in Tehran. (See Photos No. 18, 22, 28, and 31.)

Chieko, as a member of the advanced staff of Japanese representatives of the Mitsukoshi Department Store, had come to Tehran with the intent of assisting in establishing a branch store in Iran. However, while negotiating with the Iranians for a location (a very frustrating task), they opened a Japanese businessman's club and restaurant in a large posh suburban rented house on a tree-lined exclusive housing area.

The club was an immediate success and became a very popular meeting place for the thousands of Japanese expatriates working in Iran. The center was known as "Little Japan" and was not only frequented by Japanese, but also by foreign guests who were familiar with Japanese customs and their culinary delights.

Japan Airlines operated daily flights between Tokyo and Tehran which provided a steady source of fresh sushi quality raw fish, rice, sake, Japanese newspapers and magazines, and videos of the latest TV programs in Japan. Once inside the club it was as if you were in downtown Tokyo. Japanese was the common language spoken and the ladies working there all dressed in the traditional Japanese Kimono. Chieko worked as a cashier and in accordance with Japanese custom put in long hours with very few days off.

Our individual busy schedules did not provide the opportunity of seeing each other as much as we preferred, but it was certainly better than being separated by 5,000 miles. Quite often, I would stop by the "Little Japan" Club on my way home from a flight and, according to Chieko, my airline captain's uniform was much respected by her colleagues and club visitors alike. These stops would usually allow me a few minutes with Chieko and to depart with an obento (box lunch) of sushi and other Japanese delicacies for my take-out evening meal.

I tried repeatedly to have Air Taxi schedule my weekly day off to coincide with Chieko's, but in spite of continuous promises from the Chief Pilot, I frequently found myself scheduled to fly on her day off. With two years of experience in dealing with irresolute Iranians, I emphatically informed the dispatcher that I would not accept flights on specific days of my choosing. The Chief Pilot finally got the message and we worked out a schedule that would allow me to be off one day a week of my choice.

Having the freedom of transportation, Chieko and I explored the Iranian countryside in my versatile Volkswagen and enjoyed the unique strangeness of the Iranian rural areas and the Iranian people. We were always treated with courtesy and respect during these excursions and I'm sure we created more curiosity in the minds of the inhabitants in the quaint villages we visited than we experienced ourselves.

We would sometimes pack a picnic lunch, but could never find a green shady grassy area to lay down a blanket. We learned to accept spreading it out on hot dry sand, wearing large hats, and erecting umbrellas, to provide some shade against the blistering hot sun and dry desert wind.

The only draw back from these excursions was the ever-present danger of Iranian drivers, especially large trucks who would consistently take their half of the road out of the middle. This danger was particularly risky when rounding mountain curves, which in most cases were void of guard rails. Quite often there was nothing between the unguarded edge of a narrow gravel road and thousands of feet of stomach-wrenching open space, overlooking desolate rocky uninhabited valleys. (See Photo 27.)

I was eager to have Chieko visit Esfahan, a culturally rich city 250 miles south of Tehran. Esfahan was in the past the capital of Persia (Iran) and contains magnificently preserved Muslim mosques dating back to the 11th century. It has been said that it is one of the most beautiful cities in the world. I personally don't agree with this claim, but certainly concede that it's a wonderful city to visit. Several of its 400-year-old bridges are still in use by automobiles and heavy trucks alike. Being 4,700 feet above sea level the city enjoys a temperate climate. (See Photo No. 25.)

In preparation for our trip I contacted my immediate supervisor, Captain Bokhari, to coordinate my request for four days annual leave. Recognizing the difficulty in solidifying agreements with my Air Taxi honcho, I started negotiations for my mini vacation two weeks prior to our planned departure date. Captain Bokhari's response when I requested the time off was, "No problem, Captain Martin, just write down the days you want off on a piece of paper and I'll pass it on to the scheduler." I did exactly what he requested, and when I handed him the note he put it into his shirt pocket, while presenting a reassuring nod of his head.

Not wishing to expose ourselves to the hazards of driving, we decided to take a commercial bus to Esfahan and fly back on Iran Air. I purchased the bus and discount airline tickets and made hotel reservations. In the days leading up to our departure, I reminded Captain Bokhari several times about my forthcoming time off. Each time I did, he responded with, "Don't worry, Captain Martin, your leave has been approved."

The evening before our departure we were enjoying dinner and drinks in my apartment. Since I was going on vacation the next day, I didn't make the usual nightly telephone call to the dispatch center to obtain my next day's flight schedule. Around 8 p.m. an Air Taxi dispatcher called and chastised me for not checking in to obtain my next day's flight schedule. Being in a jovial pre-vacation mood, I told him in a light-hearted manner that there was no need for me to call-in, as I was going on four days annual leave the following day. He said he didn't know anything about my going on leave, but just wanted to let me know that I was scheduled for a flight to Bandar Abbas in the morning. I told him, "No way, Jose" as I will be out of town and hung-up.

Additional Autographed Copies of *Wings Over Persia* may be obtained from The author at 13268 Huntington Ter. Apple Valley, MN. 55124. For $17.00, which includes S. & H. Tel: 952-891-1250. E mail Pilotlou@aol.com

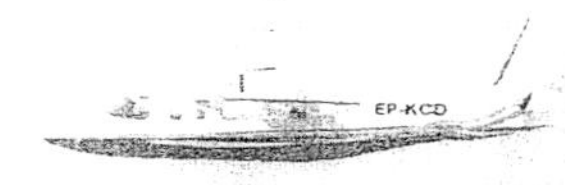

Wings Over Persia

ISBN 1-4120-0107-2

By Lou Martin

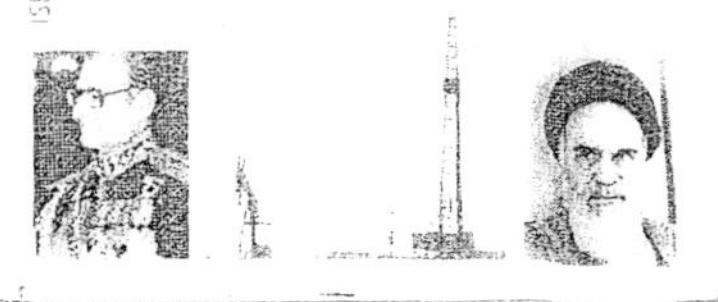

A few minutes later the assistant Chief Pilot called and wanted to know why I had refused to fly a trip to Bandar Abbas. Not wishing to get into a fruitless argument, I asked him under what conditions could I refuse a flight schedule? He said that the most common reason was calling in sick. With that, I told him to mark me down as too sick to fly. He asked me how long I thought I would be sick. I told him, "Four days!"

We left for Esfahan early the next morning by bus, hoping the seven-hour ride would be interesting. The bus was an older Mercedes-Benz which had seen better days and was in dire need of new springs and shock absorbers. We were the only foreigners onboard and were the focus of numerous curious stares from bearded men and chador-dressed women. The bus was not equipped with a restroom, so when the driver finally drove into a rest stop, we anxiously looked forward to the opportunity of relieving the building pressure in our bladders.

The rest rooms were small open-door cement buildings with little separation for men or women. I stood in line behind a group of men and when it was my turn, I had to hold my nose and breathe as little as possible to avoid being overcome by the odor. The smell was overpowering! I looked over at Chieko who was standing off to one side, holding her nose, and too embarrassed to use the open-door stinky women's outhouse. I stood guard while she held her breath and made a quick visit.

We arrived in Esfahan around mid afternoon and were pleasantly surprised to discover that the hotel was actually holding a reservation in my name. (Sometimes things did go according to plan.)

After unpacking, we figured a drink at the hotel bar would be in order and headed in that direction. We found the bar overflowing with countless raucous foreigners, both men and women, whom we soon discovered were mostly American Bell Helicopter employees. It was happy hour and the half-price drink policy drew so many thirsty customers that the crowd flowed out unto the street. (This was certainly not a popular scene in a devout Muslim country, especially in Esfahan which was noted for its many ornate centuries-old Muslim mosques.)

That evening as we were preparing to retire, the telephone in our room rang, and to my surprise it was a call from the Chief Pilot in Tehran. He wanted to know what I was doing in Esfahan. When I told him that I was on annual leave, he said it wasn't approved by him and considered me absent without proper authority. I explained how I had coordinated my time off with my boss, Captain Bokhari, and that he had assured me it was approved. He said he didn't know anything about that, but was short of captains, and if I didn't return to Tehran immediately he would be forced to terminate my employment. I told him to do what ever he thought best, but I wouldn't be available to fly for four days. If he wanted to put me on the flight schedule after I returned, that would be OK with me, and if he didn't, I would return to the United States.

I wasn't sure if I would have a job or not when I returned to Tehran, but it was almost getting to the point that I didn't care. However, the indecisiveness put a damper on our short vacation, and Chieko was concerned that I might be leaving Iran not long after her successful hard-fought effort to obtain employment in Tehran.

After three sight-seeing days in Esfahan, we boarded an Iran Air B-727 for an uneventful flight to Tehran. I was back in my apartment around 4 p.m. and wondered how I would be received when I called the dispatch center for my next day's flight schedule. The dispatcher calmly informed me that I was scheduled for an Abadan turnaround passenger flight. He said nothing about my recent four-day absence, nor did the Chief Pilot mention it when I saw him in the pilot's lounge the following day. I knew at that point, that I had mastered the Middle East game of threat and subterfuge. (I thought perhaps I should change my name to Abdullah, or Mohammad, but didn't dwell on that possibility very long!)

I would occasionally sponsor a dinner party for Chieko's and my colleagues in my apartment. These home parties were not popular with my landlord living downstairs as he disliked seeing infidels enjoying themselves, especially when in the company of unmarried females, but I just ignored his stares of disapproval. (See Photo No. 11.)

Chieko would usually invite one of her non-English-speaking Japanese female colleagues and I would invite my non-Japanese-speaking English friend, Captain Bill Aston. It was very amusing to observe Bill and his Japanese dinner companion attempting to carry on a conversation while we were preparing dinner. Their communication struggles were interspersed with hardy belly laughs so we assumed they enjoyed the experience. I think copious amounts of scotch helped Bill's ability to communicate in Japanese sign language.

Chieko and I would spend some off days lounging around the U.S. Army Officers' Club swimming pool, or haggling with local gold and carpet dealers. I taught Chieko the Middle East art of wrangling over the price of goods, which was in conflict with the Japanese philosophy of complete harmony in every aspect of daily life. (See Photos No. 15, 22, and 23.)

Iranian merchants were overjoyed when Japanese visited their stores. If they were interested in a particular item, they would purchase it at the over-inflated price without question. I explained to Chieko that the standard practice in Iran was to offer the merchant half the price he initially requested and then haggle over the difference.

Successful haggling with merchants was an acquired skill requiring patience and the ability to tell bigger hardship lies than the merchant. It was not unusual for the shopkeeper to fabricate all kinds of stories about mortally sick family members, dead parents, etc., to explain why he could not accept the price I offered for his wares. I would counter with being diagnosed with cancer, not being paid, involved in an auto accident, etc., in explaining why I did not have the money to meet his price.

As the wrangling continued he would generally pour a cup of chay (tea) and offer a seat around a table, where the disagreement over the price could continue in comfort. It was not uncommon to make several trips to a store before a final price was agreed upon for a particular item.

As Chieko learned the art of this Middle East custom, it was interesting to observe the surprise on the faces of Iranian merchants as they encountered this strange Japanese female customer, who would engage them in their own game of fierce vocalized fighting over the asking price of their wares and walk away if they didn't match her offer.

During the summer of 1978, it was obvious that the young Iranian copilots were becoming bolder in their exchange of anti-government cassette recordings and pamphlets, smuggled into Iran from Ayatollah Khomeini and his followers in Paris. I even observed them openly exchanging such items in the pilot's lounge and at layover stations. More adventurous pilots would even openly express their dissatisfaction with the Shah. There seemed to be a lessening fear of the Savak secret police or in other colleagues overhearing their opposition discussions.

Demonstrations in major Iranian cities were becoming more common and crowds seemed to grow in number at each gathering. Accounts of foreigners, especially Americans, being physically threatened when walking on the streets were becoming more frequent. It was even said that it might be wise to replace your personal portrait of the Shah, with one of Khomeini, but I displayed neither.

It was common knowledge that many wealthy Iranians were leaving Iran on presumed vacations to the United States, Switzerland, or other European countries, but were not returning. This was true of several high-ranking executives in the company I worked for. Rumors were also circulated that a number of savings accounts in Iranian banks were being liquidated and the proceeds shipped to other countries.

In July 1978, I was leaving the U.S. Embassy on Takht-e-Jamskid Street in downtown Tehran, when I met a friend who lived in Kerman. He was a retired Air Force major by the name of Marty Berkowitz, who had flown F-4 Phantom jets in Vietnam and incurred injuries which prevented him from holding an FAA Aviation Medical Certificate. Not being able to continue a career in aviation, he decided to seek employment relating to his college degree in accounting. In this capacity, he worked for the Iranian National Copper Industries Company in Kerman.

Major Berkowitz lived with his charming wife in a large Western-style home in one of the suburbs of the city. The house, furnished by the copper company, was unusual in that it was smack in the middle of several run-down shacks, and surrounded by a high brick wall topped with pieces of sharp broken glass to discourage intruders.

I had spent several evenings as his house guest when on overnight flights to Kerman and enjoyed the hospitality offered by both he and his wife. We enjoyed after-dinner drinks while reminiscing about bygone days in the Air Force and service in Vietnam. Marty seemed to enjoy his life in Kerman, but I sensed that his wife was not as enthusiastic about living in Iran as her husband. Her discontent was most likely the result of a limited number of American women living nearby, as compared to the thousands of expatriate wives and foreign female workers residing in Tehran.

When I met Berkowitz in front of the U.S. Embassy, I asked him what brought him to Tehran. He told me that he had just returned from the United States after escorting his wife back home. He said she had felt increasingly more isolated and homesick, and with troubles brewing in Iran wished to return home. He said he was returning to Kerman to complete his two-year contract as he didn't wish to forfeit his contract completion bonus. He said he only had five more months to serve and would then join his wife back home in the U.S. I bid Marty farewell and he invited me to visit him during my next overnight trip to Kerman.

The next morning, I was shocked when I picked up the English edition of the Iranian *Kayhan* newspaper. The headline read, **"American Foreigner Slain in Kerman."** The article accompanying the headline told of a retired U.S. Air Force major, by the name of Marty Berkowitz, who was stabbed to death in the kitchen of his modern Western-style home in Kerman. The article went on to state that unknown assailants climbed the wall surrounding his house by throwing a mattress over sections of broken glass. They then surprised and attacked Mr. Berkowitz in his kitchen as he was preparing breakfast. He fought off his attackers, but was overpowered and stabbed repeatedly by two or more intruders.

According to the article, a Copper Industries Company limousine driver, parked in front of his house, heard a disturbance and upon examination, discovered Mr. Berkowitz lying on the kitchen floor in a pool of blood. The attackers apparently escaped over the same route taken to enter the house and the authorities had no clue as to their identity. His body was being shipped back to his wife, courtesy of the United States Embassy. His murder hit me hard as he was a friend and a retired Air Force pilot.

In early September 1978, there was a large demonstration in the streets of Tehran and in attempting to control the growing tension, Iranian army soldiers opened fire. Hundreds of demonstrators were killed including women and young children. Following this alleged slaughter, government workers throughout Iran started going out on strike, which threatened to cripple the infrastructure of the country.

With most government workers on strike, maintaining electrical power in downtown Tehran was becoming a serious problem. I would stand on the roof of my apartment building and at precisely 8:30 p.m. watch section after section of Tehran go dark. The time of the blackouts was no coincidence, as the only English program still being broadcast on Iranian TV was the nightly international news program which came on at 8:30.

One night, after the lights of the city had gone out, I was standing in a dark corner of my roof drinking a martini when my landlord walked up and in his limited English stated, "The Shah is finished." I didn't believe him at the time, but his simple statement proved to be acutely prophetic a short time later. When my landlord made this predictive comment, I sensed a note of satisfaction in his voice, and was one of the few times he attempted to speak to me in English. He was obviously gloating over the Shah's difficulties and wanted to share this vindictive pleasure with an infidel he had accused of violating the Koran and failed to eliminate.

The resistance to the Shah's attempts to modernize Iran was not limited to strikes and demonstrations by hard-line Muslim radicals. Some unexplained actions even infuriated people who normally supported his "White Revolution." One such ill-advised action, copied from the U.S., was "Daylight Saving Time." At the start of the "No Ruz" New Year's 13-day celebration in the spring of 1978, The Shah decided all clocks should be moved ahead one hour. The people were outraged as they didn't understand the necessity and accused the Shah of deliberately attempting to interfere with their daily periods set aside for prayer, especially the all-important one at noon. They refused to change their clocks and within a couple days the idea of "Daylight Saving Time' was canceled, but the resentment toward the Shah's stupid edict lingered on and fed into the growing resentment fueled by Khomeini's followers.

Chapter Fourteen --- Red Lion and Sun

The Iranian organization known as "the Red Lion and Sun" performed the same type of humanitarian functions as the International Red Cross, but with one marked distinction. In Iran its activities were closely controlled and not free to provide disaster assistance without first obtaining governmental approval.

From time to time, I flew Red Lion and Sun humanitarian medical evacuation flights which usually involved the use of the Rockwell *Turbo Commander*. The Rockwell *Commander* was capable of operating into smaller local airports, but was still fast enough to provide rapid evacuation. In addition, its operating costs were considerably less than the larger Fokker F-27 *Friendship* or the Dassault *Falcon* Jet.

The majority of my emergency flights were to airlift people injured in automobile accidents to hospitals in one of the major cities. Driving in Iran was a high-risk adventure and since everyone believed Allah controlled one's daily life in a preordained plan, standard safety precautions were considered unnecessary.

In the summer of 1978, I was dispatched to fly a F-27 to the Persian Gulf city of Bandar Abbas to evacuate a high ranking government official seriously injured in a highway accident. The authorization to use the larger Fokker *Friendship* to evacuate just one individual indicated that he must be a person of considerable importance.

When I reported to the flight operations center in preparation for the flight, I learned that the injured party was a personal friend of the Shah. My copilot for the flight was a good looking young Iranian and my two passengers were a medical doctor and uniformed nurse. A male flight attendant was assigned to assist where needed.

Since my aircraft was carrying a light load, I flew a direct course over the mountains and two and a half hours later landed at the Bandar Abbas Airport just before sunset. An ambulance was waiting to take my onboard doctor and nurse to a local hospital and prepare their patient for his flight back to Tehran. The doctor, before leaving, told me he should be back within the hour and requested we be ready to depart the minute he returned. I assured him that the aircraft would be refueled and ready, and once airborne we would be back in Tehran in about two and a half hours.

While the aircraft was being refueled, I visited flight operations, filed an instrument night flight plan, and was back at the aircraft in about 15 minutes. The refueling was nearly complete and good to my promise the aircraft was ready for departure with time to spare.

We were parked directly in front of the passenger terminal which provided a clear view of the main road leading to the airport. As soon as the red rotating light of an approaching ambulance was observed, I would be ready for a quick engine start. While we waited my young copilot requested permission to visit the airport terminal to make a quick telephone call to a local girl friend. I reminded him that we were literally standing-by for an immediate departure the minute our seriously injured passenger arrived. He acknowledged my concern, but pointed out that the terminal was only about 75 feet away and he would only be gone less than five minutes. I told him he could go and make his phone call, but if he wasn't back when the doctor arrived, I would fly back to Tehran without him. He said not to worry and went running toward the terminal.

A well dressed Iranian man, speaking excellent English, approached and identified himself as the airport control tower supervisor. He said he noted that I was flying to Tehran and wanted to know if his 16-year-old daughter could go with us. I told him I had plenty of room, but he would have to get permission from our operation's center in Tehran before I could allow her to board. I added that if he was going to seek permission from Tehran, I would need the authorization in writing and that time was critical as I would not delay my departure awaiting a response to his request. He headed for the terminal on a run, disappearing through the same swinging door my copilot had just used.

About 15 minutes later I observed a convoy of flashing lights approaching the airport. Before they rounded the terminal building, the control tower supervisor, in company with a very attractive young girl attired in Western-style dress, approached and handed me written authorization allowing his daughter passage to Tehran. I settled her down in a seat in the cabin as her father, in appreciation, slipped a 10,000 rial bank note ($140 or $530 when adjusted for inflation) into my shirt pocket.

A Red Lion and Sun ambulance escorted by two police cars soon arrived and stopped in front of the airplane. With the help from ground personnel we secured the victim's stretcher to anchor points in the forward section of the passenger cabin just behind the cockpit door. Seats were available for the doctor and nurse close to the patient. The doctor informed me that his patient's condition was critical and requested an immediate departure.

When I positioned myself in the captain's seat in the cockpit my copilot had not yet returned. Regardless, I instructed my male flight attendant to close the main entrance door and prepare the cabin for departure. He hesitated, reminding me that the copilot was not yet onboard. I responded that this was obvious, as I pointed to the empty copilot's seat. I told him again, **"Close the entrance door!"**

When the cockpit door open warning light went out, I pushed the starter button for the right engine. The Fokker F-27 turboprop Rolls-Royce engine, swinging a large four-blade Dowty Rotol propeller, produces a very distinct high pitch whine which grows increasingly louder as the engine comes up to idle speed. This ear-splitting sound can be heard from quite a distance and is so unpleasant that maintenance support personnel wear ear protectors when working around the aircraft. Obviously the sound of the engine coming to life reached my copilot's ears inside the terminal building. I observed him bursting through the door of the terminal and running toward the aircraft in an Olympic-style mad sprint. I purposely ignored him and kept my eyes directed inside the cockpit monitoring the right engine's rising temperatures and pressures.

Unable to catch my eye, he started pounding on the side of the fuselage, right below my cockpit side window. I allowed him to continue banging for a few seconds before I gave permission for the flight attendant to open the main entrance door and let him in. Before he settled down into the right seat, I had the left engine running and had accomplished the Before Taxi Checklist.

In an "out-of-breath" voice he asked me if I would have really departed Bandar Abbas without him. Responding in the affirmative, I wasn't sure if I had captured his hatred or loyalty, but from then on he was very attentive to his copilot duties.

About an hour and a half into the flight we were approaching the ancient city of Esfahan. It was a clear cloudless night and from 24,000 feet the flickering city lights were competing in glory with the bright stars filling the pollution-free night sky.

The cockpit door opened and the Iranian doctor requested permission to sit in the jump seat. As he sat down, I asked him how his patient was doing. He said he was in pretty bad shape, but was under a sedative and should sleep until we reached Tehran. He was very fluent in English and quite impressed with the brightness of the lights of Esfahan, the stars blinking above and the vast array of glowing instruments in the cockpit.

The doctor had only been in the cockpit about ten minutes when the door burst open. In a very excited voice the nurse requested that he return to the cabin. Although her request was in Farsi, the meaning was very clear. I instructed the copilot to monitor the operation of the aircraft and followed the doctor to the cabin.

The patient, who was stripped to the waist, was unconscious and the doctor began beating him frantically on the chest with his clenched fists. Apparently this was not doing the job, so he stuck a six-inch-long hypodermic needle directly into the area of his heart. More beating to the chest followed and finally, with the doctor wringing wet with perspiration, announced that his patient had died and covered his head with a white sheet. The solemnity of this final act was felt by everyone and not a word was spoken. We just stood there in silence for a few seconds.

My 16-year-old female hitchhiker had been observing the doctor's frantic life saving efforts, and shortly after he announced that the patient had died, she went into uncontrolled hysterics. She began shaking violently and sobbed out loud. I tried to talk to her, but couldn't get through the hysterical barrier she created. I finally slapped her quite hard on her cheek, which brought her out of her seizure.

When I had her attention, I took her to the cockpit and sat her down in the jump seat. My copilot with his headset covering both ears was snapping his fingers in obvious syncopation with music he was listening to on the radio. From past flights, I knew he was listening to a hard rock radio station. I took the headset off his head, turned up the volume, and placed it over the ears of my still sobbing young female passenger. My copilot seemed stunned by my action, but I told him to just fly the aircraft and I would explain later.

I returned to the cabin and asked the doctor if he wished to land at Esfahan, which we were just passing over, or continue on to Tehran which was about one hour flying time away. He said we might as well continue on to Tehran. He asked me not to radio ahead that his patient had died, as he would inform the proper government officials himself after we landed.

The remainder of the flight to Tehran was routine, but very quiet. My young distraught female passenger had finally got hold of herself and was just staring straight ahead, with no apparent visible emotion. She was probably mentally chastising her father for putting her on the flight. After parking and completing the Engine Shut Down Checklist, I politely excused myself and left the scene. My job for this flight was over.

I was on flight standby status in my apartment in late fall of 1978, and spent the entire day lounging, reading and listening for the telephone to ring. When on home standby, I was required to be available for call from early morning until 5 p.m., at which time I was to call dispatch to obtain my next day's flight schedule. Around 5:15 p.m. without being called, I was changing clothes and preparing to call the company and then head for the Army Officers' Club for dinner and a few games of pool.

When the telephone rang, I thought it must be my friend Captain Bill Aston wanting to know what time I would pick him up. However, the phone call was from the Chief Pilot. He acknowledged that I was officially off duty, but requested I fly an emergency Red Lion and Sun flight in a *Turbo Commander* to Abadan. He said the flight was to support victims of the disastrous fire in a Abadan movie theater, where more than 400 people had died, and hundreds had suffered serious burns.

The theater fire had been in the news the day before. According to reports, a serious fire erupted in a crowded movie theater creating panic on the part of movie patrons trying to escape the flames and smoke. However, when they attempted to use the emergency exits, they discovered them chain-locked closed from the outside. Dead bodies were stacked up around all the exits and the only survivors were people able to escape through the front door. The Iranian government blamed Islamic militant fundamentalists for the sabotage, and the demonstrators blamed the Savak (secret police). Regardless of who set the fire, there were hundreds of seriously injured victims needing immediate medical attention, which was the purpose of my emergency flight.

According to the Chief Pilot, I was to fly a load of whole blood to Abadan and depart Tehran as soon as possible. He said the aircraft was being prepared as we spoke and would be ready for departure by the time I arrived. I told him I would be there in about 30 minutes. After a quick change into my uniform, I was in my Volkswagen speeding through the streets of Tehran en route to the airport.

When I arrived at the dispatch center, I was informed that a flight plan had already been filed and my copilot was standing-by at the aircraft. Walking toward my assigned *Turbo Commander*, I noted the customary Red Lion and Sun white van parked nearby. Several people were loading boxes into the interior of the aircraft and at first glance, I wondered how they could be loading such a large number of containers into the passenger area. However, when I got closer, I noted that the passenger seats had been removed leaving an expansive open area for cargo.

I met my copilot who introduced me to the Red Lion and Sun official overseeing the loading. He didn't speak English, but according to my copilot he wanted to know the flying time to Abadan. Before I could respond, a heightened tone of excitement erupted between the supervisor and the personnel loading the cases of whole blood.

The supervisor opened several boxes and felt the outside of the bottles. This was followed by a tirade in Farsi at the people doing the loading. The loading process abruptly stopped and everyone began shouting at each other. I asked my copilot what was going on and he said that the Red Lion and Sun official was livid, as the cases of whole blood were room temperature and the van delivering them to the airport arrived without ice to keep them chilled.

The entire load of blood was declared unusable and the van would have to return to the hospital for a new batch. Using my copilot as an interpreter, I asked the supervisor how long this would take and was told about one hour. As my copilot and I walked to the pilot's lounge to wait for the new load of blood, I noted that we had about one hour of daylight remaining.

While relaxing in the pilot's lounge, I poured myself a cup of chay and offered one to my copilot. He declined, reminding me that it was the holy Muslim month of Ramadan and it was still daylight. I acknowledged with a nod, knowing that during Ramadan devout Muslims do not eat, drink, or engage in sex, from sunrise to sunset. I was just finishing my second cup of tea when the company dispatcher announced that the second load of blood had arrived and we should proceed to the aircraft.

When my copilot and I reached the aircraft, I could see that the last few cases of iced blood were being loaded. As ground handlers were securing a net over the cargo, I went through an abbreviated Before Start Engine Check and was ready to push the engine start buttons when I heard the main entrance door click shut. Both engines were soon up and running and as I taxied out for takeoff, the evening sun was just setting.

The encroaching hours of darkness is an important fact to note and will become evident during my landing approach to Abadan Airport.

The night flight to Abadan was uneventful and two hours later I was in contact with the Abadan control tower. I was pleased to note that the tower operator spoke understandable English and I requested the Abadan weather and approach clearance. The tower operator reported the weather was below published landing minimums with 100-foot overcast and one-quarter-mile visibility in blowing sand. He added that an Iran Air B-727 had just executed a missed approach and was returning to Tehran, since they did not expect the weather situation to improve.

Knowing that the delivery of my cargo was lifesaving for the critically injured theater fire victims, I informed the tower that I would attempt an approach. I was very familiar with the terrain surrounding the airport as I had made many landings there during daylight hours and felt comfortable in executing an approach under the present weather conditions.

The field elevation at Abadan is slightly above sea level and the surrounding area is flat desert. Also there were no high buildings or towers within miles of the airport, so I was confident I could sneak in safely, even if I had to descend below published landing minimums to successfully land. I requested the tower to turn the approach and runway lights up to maximum brightness and started a descent.

During the instrument approach I tuned the low frequency radio receiver (ADF) to the outer marker and the very high frequency radio (VHF) navigation receiver to the Instrument Landing System (ILS). When receiving strong signals on both radios, I settled down into my snug air-conditioned cockpit, and with a professional pilot's feeling of pride, experienced a rush of excitement in preparing to fly a perfect ILS in marginal weather conditions. My eagerness to successfully complete the approach was a combination of the importance of the mission and the fact that an Iran Air B-727 had failed to land, executed a missed approach and was now on its way back to Tehran. I knew the Iran Air pilot would be eagerly monitoring the success, or failure, of my approach on his radio. (He was probably hoping that I would be forced to execute a missed approach also, so he wouldn't feel like a loser. If I was in his position that is exactly what I would be doing.)

At 2,500 feet, I was flying on instruments in smooth air and did not yet have visual contact with lights on the ground. About ten miles out, I executed a final turn toward the airport and requested the copilot to lower the landing gear and set approach flaps. He took no action, so in a louder voice I repeated my call for landing gear and flaps. He reacted to my second command, but seemed to move in a sluggish unsure manner. However, in the dark cockpit, I wasn't able to devote much attention to the reason for his casual manner as I was becoming quite busy myself, due to an apparent instrument problem with my ILS system.

My glide slope needle (which provides descent guidance) started showing an "Off Flag" thereby denying me glide slope information. I asked my copilot if his glide slope needle was operational, but received no response. Wondering why, I glanced in his direction and observed him slumped over and apparently unconscious. The only thing that was keeping him from falling forward, against the flight controls, was his locked shoulder harness.

Knowing that I couldn't do anything for him unless I got the aircraft on the ground, it was necessary that I salvage what had started out to be a routine night ILS approach, but was now a "get-it-on-the-ground" necessity. I loosened my shoulder harness and by leaning across the cockpit felt relief when I discovered that the copilot's glide slope indicator was operating normally, and providing satisfactory descent guidance.

Flying off the copilot's instruments, I made a few abrupt maneuvers and was able to get back on the course center line and glide slope and continued the approach. When I passed through the published approach landing minimums, I was still in blowing sand, but at about 150 feet I caught a glimpse of the flashing stroboscope (high intensity) runway lead-in lights.

I continued my descent and at around 100 feet, I could see two blurred runway lights. I reduced power, continued the approach and allowed the aircraft to settle into a nose-high flare attitude. The landing was not one of my smoothest and the touchdown jolt caused my copilot to stir, but he did not come out of his stupor and remained slumped over in his seat.

When I taxied, albeit slowly due to restricted visibility, to the airport terminal, I could see a Red Lion and Sun van standing by with several eager ground handlers ready to unload my precious cargo of whole blood. As the engines were spooling down, I observed some movement from my copilot and with gentle slaps to his face asked him if he was OK. His one word answer was, **"Ramadan!"**

I asked him how long it had been since he had consumed any liquids or solid food. (I didn't ask him about his sexual activities.) He said, "Two days." According to his tale of woe he had gone to bed early the night before, when it was still daylight, with the intention of waking up during the hours of darkness when he would be allowed to eat and drink. However, he said he was very tired and slept the night through. When he awoke it was daylight, so naturally he couldn't eat or drink until the following night.

But, in the afternoon he was alerted for this flight and since we departed Tehran at sunset, he hadn't had a chance to consume any nourishment. (What I had on this critical night flight was a copilot who had passed out from dehydration and lack of nourishment, all in the interest of pleasing Allah and observing the ritual of fasting during the holy month of Ramadan.)

Since it was now good and dark, I helped him to a taxi and told him to go to the nearest restaurant and not come back until he had a full stomach and had drank at least a liter of water. I told him I would wait for him in the aircraft.

With the two rows of passenger seats removed, the back of the aircraft provided an excellent place for me to stretch out and rest. With the airport closed because the weather was below landing minimums, the field was very quiet. A cool night breeze was blowing in from the Trigris and Euphrates Rivers and I was soon sound asleep.

About two hours later my copilot was gently shaking me and I could see that he was a totally different person. He appeared alert and eager to go, so I let him fly the aircraft back to Tehran. He performed extremely well and executed a very nice night approach and landing. As we parted, I cautioned him to watch the Ramadan season as it could kill you. His response, "Insha Allah." (See Photo No. 10 of copilot.)

Other Red Lion and Sun operations I became involved with were humanitarian flights to a city in the northeastern Iranian Desert by the name of Tabas-e-Golshan. On September 16, 1978, Tabas and the surrounding area were severely damaged by a catastrophic evening earthquake. Eighty-five percent of the inhabitants (11,000 out of 13,000) perished. Total fatalities for the area was 25,000, with thousands more injured and homeless. Ninety villages were severely damaged and countless others lightly damaged.

Immediately following this catastrophe, Air Taxi joined the Iranian military and Red Lion and Sun in flying support missions to the stricken area. Initially, I flew two F-27 missions a day airlifting tents, food, blankets, portable heaters, medicine, doctors, nurses, stretchers, coffins, etc. Return flights were used to transport severely injured and dying victims to hospitals in Tehran or the city of Mashad.

The Iranian Army established a tent-city compound near an improvised landing strip of flat desert sand. One tent was designated as an operations center, where military dispatchers controlled the disposition of all incoming cargo and the scheduling of departing flights. After landing, I was required to check in with the operations center which would determine my departure time and exit cargo or passenger load.

Aircraft utilizing the desert runway produced huge clouds of billowing dust, especially during takeoff. The dust cloud behind departing Iranian military C-130s was massive and waiting for it to dissipate limited aircraft movements. Departures were restricted to no more than one every five to ten minutes. When the wind was from the north, the dust cloud would drift across the refugee camp creating confusion and discomfort for rescuers and survivors alike.

My participation in the Tabas-e-Golshan rescue missions made me feel like I was once again in the U.S. Air Force and flying combat support missions to war-ravaged South Vietnam. The activity in the Iranian Army tent city echoed, in almost every aspect, the scene one would find in an active war zone. Initially there were only about 50 olive-drab sand-covered tents set up in typical military alignment, but more were soon to follow.

Combat fatigue-dressed Iranian soldiers hustled about everywhere with some carrying stretchers while others carried sealed body bags, or victims covered with white sheets. Canvas water dispensers were scattered throughout the compound with lines of shabbily dressed refugees lining up for a drink. Jeeps, trucks and ambulances moved about with beeping horns to clear a path through the maze of human traffic. International photographers and journalists could be observed capturing the disaster for the evening world news. In the background, support aircraft were taking off or landing every five to ten minutes.

After obtaining my departure schedule, I would walk to my aircraft where passengers authorized to board would be forming a line. Walking refugees wore a boarding authorization tag around their necks, while stretcher-borne refugees had the tag attached to their chest bandages. They were allowed to board, one-by-one, after their entry tags were checked by an Iranian Army officer. To prevent the hundreds of other refugees milling about from attempting to board the aircraft, a cordon of soldiers circled the aircraft. Blowing dust, created during the engine start, tended to thin out the crowd to the rear of the aircraft, but the mass of refugees in front remained in place. Soldiers with fixed bayonets would force the milling crowd back far enough to provide sufficient space for me to taxi out to the sand-rolled runway for takeoff.

Once airborne, I would look back to observe the huge rolling dust cloud I created flowing across the runway and tent city, and felt sorry for the earthquake victims I made uncomfortable, but there was nothing I could do about it. The flight back to Tehran took about two hours. Busses and ambulances were waiting for my emaciated-looking injured passengers when I arrived. In a stark contrast, I went to my apartment for a martini, filet mignon steak and clean sheets.

The Tabas earthquake, in addition to killing thousands, made thousands more homeless. The Iranian Army tents provided temporary shelter for many, but there were not enough for everyone. Refugees crowded into these unheated enclosures like sardines in a can, in an attempt to protect themselves from the nighttime desert cold. However, the Iranian government was taking steps to alleviate this tragic situation.

Red Lion and Sun purchased hundreds of Japanese kerosene heaters and blankets which were shipped to Tehran by Japan Airlines B-747s. My task was to deliver them to Tabas via a Fokker F-27. I personally flew several missions with my cargo compartment filled to the ceiling with portable heaters and wool blankets.

Following one of my flights to Tabas, I was informed by the military operations officer that my return flight to Tehran would be delayed for several hours so I was free to take lunch in the senior officer's mess tent. It felt strange, after so many years, to eat once again from a military metal food tray. After lunch an Iranian Army colonel invited me to rest in his personal command tent. His tent was much larger than the others, and considering the circumstances, quite comfortable. Expensive Persian carpets covered the dirt floor, electricity was supplied by a Sony portable generator and several kerosene heaters were on the ready to ward off the nighttime cold. After squatting on the floor with a group of fatigue-clad high ranking Iranian Army officers, an Iranian soldier offered me and my companions a cup of steaming hot chay.

A major who had flown with me in the past asked if I had toured the earthquake damaged area of Tabas. I replied that I had observed the destruction from the air, but had not seen it from ground level. He said, from a historical concept, I should view the devastation and would secure a jeep and drive me through sections of the city hit the hardest.

As I climbed into the right seat of his jeep, he handed me a surgical face mask which he said I would need to help block out the scent of thousands of decaying bodies still trapped in the crumbled buildings.

As we drove through the city, I could understand why 85 percent of its inhabitants had been killed. Almost all of the buildings in the downtown area were constructed of mud block walls and wooden beam roofs. The earthquake struck during early evening without any pre-shock rumblings, and consequently caught almost all citizens at home eating dinner. The 30-second quake consisted of both a vertical and sidewise motion causing the buildings to collapse inward, which buried the people inside before they had an opportunity to escape.

Since the buildings had collapsed inward, the narrow streets were void of most debris and rescue vehicles, as well as our jeep, were able to drive through the town unimpeded. The stench of decaying bodies was overpowering and even with a face mask, I had to make a concerted effort to contain my lunch. (The fate that had befallen Tabas reminded me of the ruins of Pompeii, which was destroyed by the eruption of Mt. Vesuvius in the year 79 A.D.) By the time my military guide headed back toward the tent city, I was convinced I had seen and smelled enough of the destruction and my heart went out for the victims and survivors.

While we drove through the refugee camp, I commented to my Iranian Major guide that I didn't see many kerosene heaters or blankets in use by the earthquake victims. I added that I thought this strange, as I personally flew hundreds of heaters and crates of blankets to Tabas. His only response was a shrug of his shoulders and an "Insha Allah."

When inside the officer's tent, we sat cross-legged on Persian carpets while a young soldier poured us a cup of hot chay. Once again, I brought up the subject of the absence of heaters and blankets within the camp, and asked him why this was the case.

In a subdued voice, he told me that most of them were confiscated by the army generals and village chiefs and were hidden in mountain caves or private intact homes. He added that after the public notoriety of the earthquake had died down, and foreign newsmen left they would be sold on the black market. He requested that I not compromise his position by revealing where I had obtained this information. I assured him that I wouldn't violate his trust, but there was nothing I could do anyway, except feel sorry for the people forced to survive in such a harsh environment and be exposed to such disregard for their well-being by their own countrymen. (Unfortunately we experienced similar graft and corruption during our own catastrophe following hurricane *Katrina*.)

Several of my flights to Tabas were flown in the smaller Rockwell *Turbo Commander*. On these missions, I usually carried critical medical supplies or nurses and doctors. Prior to returning to Tehran, I was required to obtain a departure release from the command post in the same manner as when flying the larger Fokker F-27.

After one *Turbo Commander* flight, the command post operations officer asked me how many injured victims I could transport to Tehran. I told him five, but as I did, my copilot said he would like to speak to me out of earshot of the command post official. When we moved off to one side, he said, "Captain, we don't want to allow earthquake victims to board our VIP aircraft." When I asked him why, he said that they were dirty, hadn't bathed and might even leave blood stains on the seat cushions.

With total disgust at his lack of feelings for his fellow countrymen, I looked directly into his eyes and said, "If you wish to remain in Tabas you have my permission, and if you decide to stay, I'll inform the command post that I can carry six passengers, instead of five by putting one in the copilot's seat." He didn't say another word and quietly followed me to the aircraft and settled down in the copilot's seat for the flight back to Tehran.

One of my last humanitarian flights to Tabas was in a F-27, five days after the earthquake struck. When checking in with the command center, I was told to stand by as I would be flying a group of foreign journalists and photographers, as well as various disaster victims, back to Tehran.

The disaster refugee camp had by this time taken on an appearance of semi-normalcy as the roving crowds of angry refugees had subsided and the most seriously injured survivors had been evacuated. Water trucks had been brought in to water down the area so the choking clouds of dust were no longer a major problem. However, a quick review of the refugee tents still did not reveal many more kerosene heaters or wool blankets. (I guess the generals and tribal leaders were holding out for higher prices.)

Lining up to board my aircraft were about 20 shabby-looking male foreign journalists and photographers. Five days of "camp-out-style" living was evident by their dirty wrinkled clothes, five days growth of facial hair, and an obvious lack of sleep. Most were carrying bulging back packs and an array of cameras of every description were slung around their necks. They represented news outlets from various countries, but spoke with one voice in expressing a desire of returning to the civilized world. My aircraft, being the ticket to their escape made me very popular. As if in a formal receiving line, they all wanted to shake my hand as I made my way toward the cockpit.

The foreign journalists and photographers filled one side of the aircraft cabin while walking refugees occupied the opposite side. The Iranian Army ground controller gave me a "clear to start engine" signal, so I instructed the flight attendant to close the main entrance door. Noting that the group of armed guards was clear, I pushed the starter button for the right engine. With sunset fast approaching, I was eager to get going as the improvised desert runway was not equipped with lights.

Before the right engine came up to speed, my copilot called my attention to a military jeep, with its headlights flashing, racing toward our aircraft. It came to a screeching stop directly in front of the nose and an Iranian officer jumped out and started waving his arms in an obvious signal for me to abort the engine start, which of course I did.

An excited army major came to the cockpit and told me that rescuers had just uncovered a mother and her teenage daughter who had been buried in the rubble for five days. He said they were still alive, but very weak and it was imperative they reach a hospital as soon as possible. Since the nearest hospital was in Mashad, he wanted to know if I could proceed there before flying unto Tehran. I told him no problem, but we must hurry as it was getting dark. I added that as soon as the victims were on board, I would have them in Mashad in about one hour. I asked him to alert Mashad authorities by telephone to have an ambulance and medical assistance standing by at the airport. He said he would ensure that this would be accomplished and left stating he would return shortly with the injured evacuees.

A few minutes later a Red Lion and Sun ambulance was backing up to the aircraft and two stretchers were loaded through the front door. The two victims were bundled head to foot in bandages with intravenous feeding tubes providing nourishment. A nurse was tending to their needs and said that she would accompany them on the flight. I helped anchor the stretchers to the floor with nylon straps and with landing lights on, raced down the desert-sand runway five minutes later. The usual rolling dust cloud signaled my departure as I made a right turn in the darkening evening sky to the northeast, toward the city of Mashad about one hour flying time away.

After we landed at Mashad, the two seriously injured earthquake victims were placed in an ambulance and rushed to a nearby hospital. I was eager to depart for Tehran as soon as possible so as to reach my apartment before the 9 p.m. curfew went into effect. Otherwise, I would be forced to sleep in the Air Taxi dispatch office and not be allowed to leave until 7 a.m. the next morning. However, since flights in Iran during the hours of darkness required the filing of an instrument flight plan, and the aircraft had to be refueled, time was of the essence.

Since passengers were not allowed to remain on the aircraft during refueling, I ordered a bus to transport them to the nearby terminal. Before they left, I instructed my copilot to advise them not to leave the area as we would be departing in about 30 minutes. My copilot was going to remain with the aircraft to supervise the refueling while I went to the control tower to file an IFR flight plan for Tehran.

About 20 minutes later, I returned to the aircraft and was pleased to see the refueling truck pulling away. After being assured that the aircraft was ready for departure, I contacted the control tower and told them to have the waiting bus pick up my passengers standing-by in the terminal and transport them to the aircraft. When I observed the passenger bus approaching, I felt everything was humming along on schedule and reaching Tehran before the curfew went into effect was no problem.

However, when the bus stopped in front of the aircraft the only passengers getting off were the group of foreign journalists and photographers. I didn't see a single rag-tagged Iranian earthquake refugee among them. I went to the passenger cabin, and addressing one of the journalists stated, "What happened to the Iranians that were waiting with you in the terminal?" He said that he thought they had secured a bus and gone to a nearby mosque for evening prayers and to give thanks to Allah for sparing the lives of the rescued mother and her daughter. My quick departure plan was now in jeopardy and if we didn't find our passengers and get airborne within the next 30 minutes, we might have to spend the night in Mashad, a city of which I did not have fond memories since my ill-advised visit to the Muslim mosque earlier that same year with two "not-so-bright" young Iranian Navy copilots.

I instructed my copilot to commandeer the waiting passenger bus, proceed directly to the nearby mosque, and retrieve our passengers. I told him if he wasn't back in 30 minutes there was no need to hurry as we would be spending the night on the airport ramp. With my copilot urging the driver on, I watched the bus careen around the airport terminal en route to the mosque where I hoped our missing passengers were located.

About 25 minutes later the bus came racing around the terminal building heading toward the aircraft. As it came to a stop I pushed the starter button for the right engine and had it coming up to speed as my tardy passengers boarded through the left-side main entrance door and were taking their seats.

When the cockpit "cabin door open light" extinguished, I started the left engine and before my copilot was fully positioned in the right pilot's seat, commenced a fast taxi toward the runway. Mashad tower cleared me for an immediate takeoff and I accelerated down the runway before my copilot was fully mentally up-to-speed. (Col. Madina would have been proud of me!)

I leveled off at 20,000 feet and set engine power at maximum cruise. When we were on autopilot, I apologized to my copilot for the expedited takeoff, but emphasized that even now it was questionable if we would be able to land in Tehran in time for me to drive to my apartment before the 9 p.m. curfew went into effect. He said he understood and found the whole episode quite exciting.

After flying a super-fast straight-in approach, I parked in front of our company operations center at 8:30 p.m. I instructed my copilot to call for a bus for the passengers and turn in our post-flight report to dispatch as I grabbed my flight bag to make a mad dash for my Volkswagen.

As I was leaving the cockpit, he recommended that when driving into Tehran, I keep my uniform on and the windows open to be able to hear a challenge from Iranian soldiers enforcing the curfew. He also taught me the Farsi words for, "stop." As I left the cockpit he wished me good luck and the customary, "Insha Allah."

When I drove through the company security gate, I had 25 minutes to reach my apartment before the start of curfew. I wasn't sure if there was sufficient time for me to make the trip, before the soldiers started shooting, but thought I would see what the traffic conditions were like and if it appeared that I couldn't make it in time, I would return to the airport and sleep on a white leather sofa in the VIP room.

When I entered the main highway, I found I had the road almost to myself. In Iran speed limits were not enforced, so my little Volkswagen *Beetle* enjoyed the freedom of racing toward downtown Tehran like a thoroughbred race horse in the home stretch. The absence of traffic on normally congested roads was surreal, but I didn't wish to slow down to prolong the unusual experience. I only saw one or two other civilian cars during my drive into town and assumed they were also racing toward some unknown destination, with the hope of beating the curfew. I parked in front of my apartment at five minutes to nine and drew a big sigh of relief. At the same time I felt an unwinding rush of excitement, not unlike the winning of some athletic event, or a NASCAR auto race.

As I walked through my front door the clock struck nine o'clock. Shortly thereafter I could hear the crack of small arms fire starting to flare up throughout the city. I mixed a double martini and went to the roof to observe what was becoming my substitute for nightly English television entertainment, which had been discontinued by government order.

While I stood in the shadows, I could see various sections of the city going dark and hear single and automatic gun fire erupt from many quarters. At times, explosions would light up the night sky and tracers could be seen racing through the darkness like Roman candles. By the time I finished my martini, I was ready for a home-cooked meal and a good night's rest.

I felt I had put in a good productive day and was pleased in the fact that I probably helped save the lives of the woman and her daughter, had flown a group of foreign journalists and photographers back to civilization, and by racing through deserted Tehran streets in my Volkswagen reached home before the 9 p.m. curfew. Another exciting day of flying and living in turbulent Iran in 1978 was history.

Chapter Fifteen --- Black Sunday

Sunday, November 5th, 1978 was the most memorable day in my three years in Iran. I was scheduled to administer a Fokker F-27 line check to a Captain Ghanbari, on a turn-around flight to Bandar Abbas. I would occupy the right (copilot's) seat while an Iranian captain would occupy the left (captain's) seat. The flight to the Persian Gulf was routine and after lunch we headed back to Tehran.

When approaching the city, I attempted to contact our company dispatcher by radio, but was unable to get a response. I thought this strange as we were certainly within radio range and had always been able to contact them in the past at this distance. However, after several more attempts, I gave up and concluded that their radio must be inoperative.

When we were about 50 miles out, I attempted to contact Mehrabad Approach Control, but was unable to contact them either. I considered the possibility that both my radios were inoperative, even though this likelihood seemed remote. I then checked the aircraft electrical system and found it fully operational. Since the weather was clear with unlimited visibility, I instructed my student captain to continue on toward Tehran.

As we drew closer the panoramic view of the city seemed bizarre, but I wasn't able to ascertain why at first glance. However, when we started our descent it became clear as to what was different about the view of Tehran on this memorable day.

Clouds of black and white smoke were rising from sections too numerous to count. I didn't comprehend the significance of these unfamiliar smoke clouds, but without radio contact, I couldn't request clarification from the company. Not seeing, or hearing, any other aircraft in the area, I instructed my Iranian colleague to continue the approach and execute a "no-radio" landing on Runway 29 Right.

The final approach to the runway we normally used, when landing, required a low altitude flight path over the southern section of the city. In fact, I would usually inform my passengers sitting on the right side of the aircraft that they would have an excellent view of Tehran during the landing approach. Today, sitting in the right pilot's seat, I enjoyed this unrestricted panoramic view myself.

However, I couldn't believe the scene unfolding before my eyes. Numerous buildings were ablaze and large open fires were burning in the middle of streets throughout most of the city. There were thousands of people roaming the streets who, from the air, appeared like ants descending on a stream of sugar. (See Photo No. 18.)

Adjacent to the airport is Azadi Square where the famous "Shahyad Tower" sits in the middle of a large traffic roundabout. This 148-foot-high white marble spire was constructed by the Shah in 1971 to stand as a gateway symbol to Iran. It is often seen in publicity photos of Tehran and is the first and last memorable sight visitors see when visiting Iran.

Normally, Azadi Square is jammed with automobiles fighting their way around the traffic loop. However, today not a single automobile could have passed through, as the circlet was blocked by thousands of demonstrators. Even from the air I could see waving banners of various colors and men and women with raised fists shouting in obvious anger.

After landing we taxied to our company parking ramp, but the customary passenger bus was not there to meet us. My student captain and I decided to walk to our dispatch center. I instructed the flight attendants to remain with the passengers until we sent out a bus to pick them up.

The dispatch and company operations center was in complete turmoil. Pilots, flight attendants and company personnel were milling about aimlessly. The dispatcher said that the airport was without electrical power and tens of thousands of demonstrators were destroying Tehran.

Apparently, as the facts became known, the Shah had become thoroughly frustrated with the continuing unrest in Tehran. To demonstrate how destructive the revolutionary Islamic militants were, he ordered his soldiers to stand down for a period of time and not interfere.

The Shah was reported to have stated, "If they want to destroy their city let them suffer the consequences." However, the demonstrators grew to unexpected large numbers and the destruction was more widespread than anticipated. Later, with complete anarchy ruling the day, the Shah ordered his soldiers to restore order. This harsh directive resulted in scores being killed and many injured.

I turned in my post-flight paperwork to the dispatcher, instructed him to send a bus for my passengers and told him I was departing for my apartment. He attempted to stop me by stating that no one was allowed to go to town, as the managing director had directed that crew busses were not allowed to leave the company grounds. I told him I didn't require transportation as I had my own automobile and headed for the door.

When I approached my trusty white Volkswagen, I was intercepted by an English female flight attendant the company employed for high level *Falcon* VIP flights. I had never flown with her, but admired her beauty and poise. She was tall, trim and could have easily worked as a fashion model, hence the reason the company hired her.

She inquired if I was driving into town and when I said yes, asked if she could ride along. She said her apartment was not far from the airport and was concerned about her husband, since she couldn't get through to him on the telephone. I told her, "No problem, hop in."

When I entered the main highway, I noted vehicular traffic was light, and even though it was mid afternoon, all had their headlights on. I didn't know the reason, but decided to turn mine on as well. (I found out later that this was a good move as showing headlights implied sympathy for the dead and injured anti-Shah demonstrators.)

During the drive into town my English flight attendant friend asked me where I lived. When I told her in the downtown area, she asked why I was exposing myself to possible danger by driving into an area under siege. I told her I was concerned about a special friend of mine who worked in the Japanese Club, that I had over two million rials in a local bank, and was just plain curious as to what I might discover when reaching the center of the city where most of the chaos and destruction was taking place.

I dropped the flight attendant off at her apartment and was pleased when her husband, seeing her alight from the car, greeted her with a big smile and hug. They both gave me a wave of thanks as I departed.

I drove onto the Shahanshah (King of Kings) expressway (one of the few four lane highways in Tehran) and headed south toward the center of the city. The expressway was laid out in a valley, well below ground level, so my view of the downtown area was limited to distant skylines. I could see numerous plumes of smoke rising in the clear blue sky, but street-level scenes were blocked by the high sloping highway shoulders.

I exited the expressway onto a street that I normally used en route to my apartment. As I crested the uphill exit, my eyes bulged when I saw the pandemonium I had driven into. A military truck was on its side and burning fiercely. Not far away an Iranian Army jeep was turned upside down and also on fire. Roving gangs of youthful demonstrators were bending steel road signs back and forth until they broke off. They were using these steel rods as improvised crow bars to break open steel screens protecting shops and banks.

From the shops, already broken into, demonstrators were removing desks, chairs, file cabinets, paper records and anything else not nailed down, and throwing them into roaring fires in the middle of the street.

Motorists like myself, who had driven into this chaos, formed a slow moving single file on the north side of the street, where the melee seemed less violent. I took off my airline blouse and threw it to the floor in fear that some young bearded demonstrator, with eyes dilated with rage, would confuse me for a member of the Shah's hated military. Several demonstrators gave my car a curious once over, but I believe my Iranian license plates, and bright shining headlights, caused them to find mischief elsewhere, and moved on down the street.

I followed the slow moving line of cars while anxiously looking for an opportunity of escaping onto a side street. After a slow drive of about two blocks, I began to hear the "rat-a-tat-tat" of gun fire and could now see soldiers attempting to gain control of the mob. They were wearing gas masks, armed with fixed bayonets and firing tear gas into the unruly crowd that showed little signs of dispersing.

Clouds of tear gas began drifting into the open windows of my Volkswagen as I observed, through crying eyes, cars up ahead turning onto a side street. With a sigh of relief, I followed. The sound of gun fire and the din of shouting mobs was receding in the distance as I drove through several blocks of narrow back roads before finally reaching my apartment. I was not able to drive past my bank, so I had no idea of the status of my Iranian savings account. (I would have to check on this later.)

After safely reaching my apartment, I was pleased to learn that my telephone was still working and placed a call to Chieko. After some difficulty in getting through I was delighted to discover that she and her Japanese colleagues were safe and had sought refuge in their apartment building. I felt much relieved and decided a double martini was in order.

With a chilled martini in hand I went to the third story roof of my apartment building to see if I could determine the extent of the turmoil Tehran was going through. With the sun setting in a cloudless red tinted western sky, I felt as if a giant kaleidoscopic curtain was coming down at the conclusion of the final act of a cataclysmic revolutionary play. However, as if presenting an encore, gun fire was still coming from many sections of the city, smoke was still rising from countless fires and the shouts of rebellious crowds could still be heard far-off in the distance.

Fortunately, the streets in my immediate area seemed quiet, including the street leading to my bank. I decided that after dinner, I would venture out to explore the damage demonstrators had caused in and around my immediate neighborhood.

When I walked the back streets toward my bank it felt like everyone else in the area had left town. The unusual quiet street accentuated each click of my boot heals as they echoed off the back alley walls. Rounding a corner, I was pleased to note that the bank was still standing, but other signs of wanton destruction were clearly visible everywhere I looked.

The street in front of the bank was awash with smashed office debris of every description and countless fires were still smoldering and forming piles of black ash. The windows of the bank were covered with heavy sheets of plywood, which shielded any sign of activity that might be occurring inside.

Peering through a narrow crack between the overlay of plywood, I looked inside and noted that the interior was basically undisturbed, and the large steel vault door was closed. However, I could see that the frenzied demonstrators had been able to reek some damage. Apparently they had been able to reach through broken windows with long steel road sign rods and smashed office equipment near the front of the bank, but were unable to gain entrance to the bank itself. The heavy steel mesh screens, lowered for protection, were bent and damaged, but remained intact. Feeling that my $30,000 dollar account (Approximately $102,000 in today's dollars) was secure, I returned to my apartment somewhat relieved, but vowing I would check further the next day!

I awoke early the next morning to clear skies and a surprisingly quiet city. Normally the traffic noise filtering into my apartment was uncomfortably loud, but this morning it was as quiet as a cemetery. After contacting the company and being informed that I was not scheduled to fly, I decided to take another walk to my bank to check on its status. The back alleys and main streets were almost as deserted as the night before and my bank appeared as if it was still closed.

However, when I stood close to the plywood barriers covering the windows, I heard the muffled sound of activity inside. I went to the front door and knocked briskly on the sheet of wood concealment. My knocking was initially ignored, but after repeated attempts, it produced a response.

A male voice from inside, speaking in Farsi, was at last responding to my knocking. I didn't understand what he was saying, but recognized the voice as that of the bank president. I knew him as a friendly English-speaking man who had in the past invited me to sit down with him in his office to enjoy a cup of chay and a friendly conversation. He was a frustrated pilot who enjoyed discussions about aviation and life in the United States. Speaking in English, I identified myself and in response he unlocked the front door and invited me in. I noted that he was all alone. After I entered, he quickly locked the door behind me, while stating that he was pleased to see that I had survived the riots of the previous day unscathed. He invited me to sit down and enjoy a hot cup of chay.

As I had observed the night before, only portions of the interior of the bank, close to the front windows, were in disarray while the rear area was undisturbed. My bank president friend told me that he was in the bank during the heaviest demonstrations the day before and heard the hoard of militant rioters coming down the street toward his building.

However, much to his relief, armed soldiers arrived and dispersed the mob before they could do much damage to the bank. He assured me that my savings were safely locked-up in the vault. Relieved at this news, I asked him when I could make a withdrawal. He said probably in three or four days, but not until bank auditors had an opportunity to examine his books and authorize him to resume operations.

Soon after returning to my apartment, I received a call from Bill Aston. Bill said that the streets and sidewalks in the vicinity of his apartment were almost deserted and inquired about the situation in my neighborhood. I told him it was the same in my area and that even the street in front of my bank was deserted but still contained burning ruble.

He suggested I drive over to his apartment to pick him up and then go out somewhere for lunch. He added that it would be interesting to drive around Tehran to see the damage the demonstrators had caused. I agreed, stating that I would call Chieko to see if she would like to join us.

During my short drive to Bill's apartment, I didn't see any other civilian automobiles, just a few curious adventurous pedestrians and some Iranian military jeeps on patrol. However, the wild dogs were unimpressed with the revolution and were out in force looking for something to eat.

Bill was waiting for me in the doorway of his apartment and jumped in. I told him Chieko would be joining us, but before deciding on a place for lunch, we would drive through some major sections of the city.

After picking up Chieko we started our motor tour around noon on Monday, November 6th, 1978. We had the streets to ourselves and drove for blocks before seeing any other cars. The only impediments to driving were the remnants of large, still smoldering, street fires, broken office furniture, charred buildings, burned-out military vehicles, and smashed Mercedes-Benz and BMW automobiles. Empty tear gas canisters marked the sites where violent clashes with demonstrators had taken place.

Most luxury automobile dealerships, movie theaters, liquor stores and Western hotels were severely damaged and still smoking. It was sickening to peer into Mercedes-Benz and BMW garages, through broken bay windows, and see new automobiles as burnt-out skeletons. Strangely, our drive around the city did not seem to arose much interest and we were not challenged by the military or the few civilian onlookers. As a precaution I kept my headlights on and figured my Iranian license plates were still a factor in our favor.

It appeared that finding a place to eat lunch might be a problem as most shops and places of business were shuttered and obviously closed. As a last resort we decided to see if a Mexican restaurant, very popular with locals and foreigners alike, was open and serving lunch.

With no cars parked in front of the restaurant, I thought it must also be closed, but decided to go inside to check for sure. The front door was unlocked and upon entering, I noted that all the overhead lights were off. Not a single table was occupied and the absence of the usual Mexican music blaring out from loud speakers presented a weird picture. I was about to leave, when a waiter approached and asked if he could help me. I inquired if the restaurant was open for business. With some hesitation he said, "I guess so, as our kitchen staff is standing-by to prepare lunch!"

I returned to my car, gathered up Bill and Chieko and returned to the restaurant. As we entered, the house lights were turned on and the overhead speakers came alive with the customary Mexican music. The waiter told us to take a table of our choice as we were the only customers.

It was difficult to comprehend that we were the sole diners in this very popular Mexican restaurant at the height of the noon-time meal hour. Previous visits would have found every table filled and people standing at the front door waiting to be seated. We spent about an hour in the restaurant enjoying a long leisurely meal, several beers and didn't see any other customers until just before we were preparing to leave. Four male foreigners entered and appeared just as bewildered as ourselves in finding the restaurant open for business and took a seat while an Iranian waiter bid them welcome and presenting them with a menu.

I drove Chieko back to her Japanese enclave and Bill and I decided to head for the U.S. Army Officers' Club for a game or two of pool. However, the military base, like almost everything else in the city, was closed to visitors. I drove Bill back to his apartment and en route we exchanged thoughts about how the unchallenged demonstrations of the day before would affect our job. We were eager to make our daily telephone call to our dispatch center that evening to find out.

However, on November 7th, two days after Black Sunday, I was back in the cockpit with a flight to Khark Island and a relief flight to earthquake-ravaged Tabas. Although there was a sense of anxiety in the air, it appeared the country was struggling to survive. The Iranian Army's presence was now clearly visible, and British-made *Chieftain* tanks and sand-bagged machine gun nests were positioned at most major intersections. A 9 p.m. to 7 a.m. curfew was still in effect and it was announced that violators would be shot on sight. Cleanup crews put streets back in service, but there was a noticeable reduction in the number of vehicles using them. Stores and shops were once again open and if you avoided the burned-out buildings, things appeared normal.

When I returned to my apartment from my November 7th flight, I attempted to call Chieko to see how she and her Japanese colleagues were weathering the revolutionary storm. I became concerned when I couldn't get anybody to answer the phone at her residence, or the Japanese Club where she worked. Later that evening Chieko called and because the connection was not clear, I asked her where she was calling from. She said, "I'm safe in London, England, and having a good time."

She told me that the morning after our tour of ravaged Tehran, her manager informed all Japanese employees that they were evacuating Iran and must be ready to depart in two hours. They were driven by bus to Mehrabad Airport and departed on a British Airway's flight to London that afternoon. After a short company-paid holiday in England she and the rest of the staff would be flying back to Tokyo by Japan Airlines. I was relieved to learn that she was safe and on her way back home, but at the same time distressed that she was no longer living in Tehran. Her job in Iran, which she had fought so hard to obtain, lasted just 11 months.

I was determined to remain in Iran as long as possible for several reasons; chief among them was to complete my second two-year contract. I had one more year to go and upon completion would receive a "end-of-contract" bonus of $15,000. ($50,385 when adjusted for inflation.)

Secondly, I fully expected the Shah to survive, just like he did during previous attempts by Islamic Extremists to dethrone him. I didn't count on President Carter and the French government to abruptly withdraw their support, which I believe resulted in his eventual overthrow and the establishment of a ruthless fundamentalist Islamic theocracy, under the anti-American despotic leadership of Ayatollah Khomeini.

Thirdly, even though I was exposing myself to a certain amount of danger, I found being an eyewitness to a country undergoing a revolution quite interesting. I wanted to see the final chapter played out.

Surprisingly, in spite of the turmoil in Iran some aspects of life didn't seem to change. My copycat F-27 written-test buddy, Mohammad Ahmadi, invited me to a private party in downtown Tehran to celebrate his upgrade as an F-27 *Friendship* captain with Pars Air, a small charter company also located at Mehrabad Airport. Ahmadi was a likable 50-year-old man, but a mediocre pilot. The Air Taxi Chief Pilot decided not to upgrade him so he resigned and took a job with Pars Air, and to everyone's surprise, was checked out as a captain. I think he was just as shocked as his former colleagues and wished to celebrate this accomplishment with a grand party of food, booze and beautiful young female belly dancers. He told me that when he was 16-years-old he came home from school one day to find his house laden with strangers. He was informed that the gathering was celebrating his marriage to an eight-year-old girl he had never met. However, the marriage was not consummated until eight years later resulting in the birth of a daughter. He moved to New Jersey, divorced his wife, became a U.S. citizen, and obtained a Commercial Pilot's Certificate before returning to Iran.

Author's note: The 1986 TV mini-series On Wings of Eagles illustrates in remarkable realism the chaotic situation in Tehran during the overthrow of the Shah. It parrots my observations and I highly recommend it.

Chapter Sixteen --- It's My Money

In between flights I made several trips to my Iranian bank in an attempt to withdraw my savings. However, I either found the bank closed, or if open, was told that they were still waiting for an audit and couldn't close out my account. Such was the life in Iran in mid November 1978.

A week later, when I still hadn't been able to withdraw my money, I decided it was time to start acting like an Iranian and engage in some arm waving, foot stomping and loud shouting. The bank manager saw me marching firmly toward his office and before I could say a word, he said he had some good news.

He announced that the auditors had completed their investigation and his bank was now authorized to resume operations. I told him I welcomed the news and therefore would like to withdraw my money. After reviewing his bank records, he said my deposit balance was 2,100,000 rials (About $30,000 or $102,000 adjusted for inflation). I concurred with his figures and said I would like to have this amount in 10,000 rial ($140) notes.

I was surprised when he told me that the bank didn't have a sufficient number of large bills to meet my request, and if I decided to close out my account, it would have to be paid in a combination of small denomination rial notes. He questioned whether it would be wise to have this amount of unwieldy cash in my possession, especially with the country in such turmoil. He added, with a chuckle, "You certainly don't want to hide it under your mattress Mr. Martin!"

Since I was aware that my landlord frequently entered my apartment during my absence, I agreed that hiding large bulky sums of money anywhere in my apartment was not a good idea, and decided not to close out my account for cash at this time.

I suggested that a more appropriate measure of security would be for the bank to issue me international traveler's checks, as Iranian rials were still accepted foreign currency. He said he would like to oblige, but at the present time his bank, and in fact all banks in Iran, were temporarily prohibited from issuing traveler's checks or Western currency in exchange for rials. His advice was to leave my money in his bank where it was safe until banking restrictions were relaxed. I felt I had no other choice and left the bank, whose windows were still boarded, with an empty heart and empty pockets. (I believed that my banker friend was telling me the truth.)

Since I had the day off, I decided to walk to the American Embassy to review the bulletin board for any hot tips for U.S. citizens living in Iran. I didn't put much faith in finding any useful information, as President Carter's implied philosophy of, "head-in-the-sand, see-no-evil-approach" provided little useful information. I had been relying on the British, Canadian or Japanese Embassies in regard to areas in Tehran that should be avoided. (The U.S. Embassy bulletin board usually referenced the local newspapers as the only source of useful information.)

The sprawling 27-acre American Embassy compound was a brisk 30-minute walk from my apartment and I often walked instead of driving. Not only was walking more interesting and safer, but provided good exercise and eliminated the problem of trying to find a parking spot in one of the busiest sections of Tehran. The embassy was a popular place for Americans to visit as it had a football field, tennis courts, swimming pool, commissary and an excellent American-style snack bar. It was located on Takht-E-Jamshid Street, in the heart of Tehran's business district and close to most foreign banks, other embassies, and my favorite English-style pub where I would often meet my two English pilot colleagues for a game of darts and a pint or two of English beer.

When I approached the embassy, I observed a crowd of people milling around the entrance to the Saudi Arabian Bank. Looking farther down the street, I noted crowds gathered in front of other international banks. I elbowed my way into the lobby of the Saudi Bank and observed bank tellers accepting Iranian rials in exchange for traveler's checks, French francs, German Deutsche marks, English pound sterling, and U.S. dollars.

I asked a man leaving a teller's window for confirmation that the bank was accepting rials in exchange for foreign currency. He said that they were, but had a $1,000 per day limit and recorded the transaction in your passport. This was 180 degrees from what my friendly bank president had told me just a few minutes earlier. (A typical Iranian deception of diluting the truth which becomes a reality if the story is believed.)

I left the Saudi bank, hailed a taxi, and instructed the driver to drive me to my bank as quickly as possible. I don't think he understood my broken Farsi, but he certainly grasped the excited tone of my voice and my frantic arm waving in the direction I wanted him to drive.

I rushed into my bank and told the president that downtown banks were exchanging foreign currency for rials and I wanted to close out my account as quickly as possible. After conferring with one of his tellers, he told me that the bank did not have that much cash on-hand, but if I would come back the next day he would be able to accommodate my request.

"Bullshit," I answered. "I don't believe that your bank doesn't have this amount of money available! Get up off your fat ass and instruct one of your tellers to close out my account without any more screwing around."

This comment got his attention, and in response, he said what he could do would be to issue me a bank cashier's check, which I could take to their main branch near the U.S. Embassy for payment in large rial bank notes. He said if that was acceptable, he would personally call the main branch president informing him that I was on my way. I said, **"Do it!"**

About 20 minutes later, with a cashier's check for 2,100,000 rials in my pocket, I was back in a taxi and headed downtown. I had the name of the main branch bank president I was to see and didn't want to waste any time in converting my cashier's check into hard cash. As my taxi approached Tehran's business center, I was pleased to see crowds still milling around foreign banks.

Pushing my way past people waiting in line to exchange money, I walked directly into the bank president's office stating that he should be expecting me, as my local bank president had informed him that I was on my way. He nodded in agreement and in fairly fluent English requested the cashier's check issued by my bank.

He took the check and invited me to have a seat while he directed one of his teller's to prepare payment. He left his office and I observed him walk to a male teller and hand him the check. He briefly talked to him, pointed in my direction and returned to his office. Without saying a word, he sat down at his desk and started shuffling papers.

I kept my eye on the teller who had received my cashier's check, fully expecting him to start arranging a stack of rials which he would deliver to me. However, he continued to service people standing in line before his station and took no action toward assembling the rials needed to honor my check.

After he waited on three customers, without showing any indication of cashing my check, I left the president's office and bucked the line in front of his window. I told him I was not waiting any longer and wanted him to cash the cashier's check that the bank president had handed him 15 minutes earlier. In broken English, he told me, "I don't know what you are talking about Mister, as I don't have a cashier's check for you."

I stormed back into the president's office and banged my fist on his desk. He peered over his half moon glasses and asked me what was the problem. Hoping to display my anger in a way that he would understand, I told him that I had handed him a cashier's check, which I saw him give to one of his tellers for payment. But after not being paid, I inquired as to when he was going to cash it. However, the stupid ass said he didn't know what I was talking about! The bank president asked me to point out the teller I had talked to, and when I did, he left his office to talk to him himself. I noted considerable arm waving and pointing toward me during their heated discussion, which is normal conversational behavior in Iran.

He abruptly returned, escorted me to the front of the line at the teller's window, and said my check would be cashed without further delay. The teller swung open the metal bars in front of his station and began stacking bundles of rials on the counter. The bank notes he was stacking were all 500 and 1,000 denomination notes. ($7.00 and $14.00). I told him I preferred 10,000 rial notes, but with a snarl, he said he didn't have any larger bills and I could take it or leave it. I had no other choice, so I instructed him to continue the money-stacking process.

When he reached a count of 2,100,000, he had two stacks of money about one foot high each. I told him that there was no way I could stuff all this cash into my pockets and asked if he had some sort of container that I could use. He said he would see what he could find and came back with a large tattered paper grocery shopping bag.

As I began stuffing the bundles of cash into the bag, I asked him if I could purchase some foreign traveler's checks in exchange for a portion of my Iranian rials. It was obvious that I wasn't one of his favorite customers when he stated that he was sold out of foreign traveler's checks and couldn't help me. I decided to quit while I was ahead and left the bank lugging my bulging shopping bag full of Iranian cash.

When I emerged from the bank, I looked up and down the street and observed huge crowds still milling around the banks. Assuming that this indicated that they were still open for business, I walked into the nearest one to see what transactions were taking place.

From the melee inside, one would think the tellers were dispensing free money. However, the lines of people standing before each teller's window were waiting to exchange rials for any brand of Western currency or traveler's checks available. I asked a foreigner leaving a teller's window if they were accepting rials for foreign cash. He told me that the only exchange being made at this bank was rials for foreign traveler's checks. I quickly got into line to wait my turn.

When I finally reached the head of the line, I asked the teller how many rials I could exchange for U.S. dollar traveler's checks. He told me $1,000 dollars worth by presenting my passport. I dug into my shopping bag and through mental calculations extracted one thousand dollars worth of rials. When I handed them to the teller, he asked for my passport, which he date stamped to indicate I had exchanged one thousand dollars worth of rials. He then handed me ten 100 U.S. dollar traveler's checks along with an admonishment that my passport indicated I had exchanged rials for foreign currency on this date and wouldn't be authorized to exchange money again until the following day. I felt somewhat relieved in the success of my first exchange, but at the same time thought at this rate it would take me 29 more days to empty the shopping bag.

While I stood off to the side, I noted that the adjacent teller was issuing traveler's checks for Iranian rials without asking for passports. I got into his line and was able to exchange another $1,000. I watched this teller for a few minutes and noted that he was so engrossed in exchanging money that he wasn't eyeballing the customers standing before his window. Thinking he wouldn't recognize me (as all foreigners look alike), I got into his line again and was able to exchange another $1,000 without question. I got back into his line for the third time and when it came my turn, the teller said he was sold out of U.S. dollar traveler's checks, but could issue traveler's checks in German marks or Swiss franks. I told him I would take German marks and reached into my paper bag while mentally converting rials to marks to dollars to know how many rials I would have to extract from my paper-bag bank to satisfy the teller.

As I was thumbing through my cash reserves, the bank teller asked if I had exchanged money with him earlier. With the confidence of a truth-telling Iranian, I looked him straight in the eye and said that this was my first time through. After he issued the Deutsche mark traveler's checks, I moved off to the side to see if there was another teller I could use to exchange another $1,000 worth of rials.

I joined an irregular line of shoving foreigners waiting at a different teller's window and figured I would be able to complete another transaction before I was recognized as a repeat customer. However, just as the teller was about to accept my rials, the cashier I had previously dealt with came over and informed him that I had already changed money in their bank. I was therefore denied another exchange. Figuring that I had accomplished all I could in this bank, I left to seek help elsewhere knowing that I had $26,000 worth of rials to go before my shopping bag would be empty, but feeling good about my progress this far.

Departing the bank I noted that the streets were more crowded then before, and more panicky rial-holding foreigners were arriving every minute. It was obvious that there was a "run-on-the-banks" in progress and it was every man for himself.

I went to a different bank, got into line, and when it came my turn to exchange money, I asked the teller what type of foreign traveler's checks he had available for rials. He told me he only had Swiss francs. Going through another mental exercise of exchange rates I told him, I wanted $1,000 worth. As he was preparing the traveler's checks he asked for my passport. I held it open to a page far removed from the previous entry reflecting a money exchange. He stamped the page I held open without question and without thumbing through numerous pages of visas to check for another money exchange entry.

As I stepped away from his window, I faked a walk toward the door, but when the teller's attention was diverted to another customer, I joined another line. I was able to exchange another $3,000 before the tellers refused to exchange any more of my rials. I figured I now had about $22,000 left to exchange before declaring victory but wasn't exactly sure.

I continued working my way down the street exchanging two or three thousand dollars per bank. The traveler's checks and cash I was able to purchase included U.S. dollars, German marks, Swiss francs, French francs and Canadian dollars. My depository for this mix of foreign currency were the four outer and inner pockets of a blue Experimental Aircraft Association wind breaker I was fortunate enough to be wearing. The depository for my rials was still the paper shopping bag which through continuous use was becoming shopworn, but not bulging out like it was when I started my money exchanging adventure earlier in the day.

Just as I attempted to enter another bank, an attendant closed the door and pulled down a shade which stated, "Bank closed." At first, I feared that the Iranian government had stepped in and suspended all foreign money transactions, but then realized it was the standard afternoon closing between 2 and 4 p.m. for their afternoon siesta.

I had lost track of how many rials I had been able to exchange, but figured it must be considerable as my jacket pockets were bulging and my paper bag was much lighter. I decided to walk the short distance to the U.S. Embassy for lunch and take stock of my frantic money exchange endeavor up to this point.

At the U.S. embassy I went to the men's room and locked myself in a large handicapped toilet stall. In the privacy of the stall, I emptied my jacket pockets and spread out the various traveler's checks on the bare floor. I then counted the monetary value of the rials remaining in the paper bag. Unfortunately, I didn't have a calculator, but did have a pen and the paper bag to scribble on. Much to my surprise and satisfaction, I determined that I had exchanged approximately $21,000 worth of rials and had a like amount of various traveler's checks and Western cash in exchange. My mind was still reeling from all the mental calculations I had gone through, but I was certainly pleased with the results. I now had $9,000 worth of rials to go.

I stuffed the traveler's checks, foreign cash, and rials into the thinning paper bag and decided to treat myself to a double cheeseburger and thick chocolate malt in the embassy snack bar. Clutching my bag of cash I then took a taxi to my apartment to lay plans for when the banks reopened.

After stuffing the money I had exchanged under my mattress, and hoping my landlord wouldn't find it, I headed back downtown to continue exchanging my remaining rials into some form of Western currency. However, when I approached the area where most of the banks were located, I was struck by an absence of milling crowds of foreigners attempting to get inside. This was a stark contrast from what took place in the morning and I thought that all banks in Tehran may be closed.

When I reached the front door of one of the banks, the reason for the absence of people waiting to exchange money became patently clear. Displayed on the front door was a hand printed sign in English and Farsi stating that the bank would be closed until further notice. I went from bank to bank, located on the main business street of Takht-E-Jamshid, and observed the same message in all banks.

I was still carrying the paper bag of rials and the excitement of my morning success began to ebb. I thought I might be stuck with $9,000 worth of Iranian currency that was fast losing its exchange flexibility. However, I wasn't ready to give up without a fight. I remembered seeing some smaller banks on a back street not far from my apartment and hailed a taxi to take me there to see if they were also closed.

Alighting from the taxi in front of a small community bank, I could see that it was open for business and accommodating customers in an unpretentious normal flow. I went inside and within a few minutes was standing in front of a non-English-speaking teller. Through a combination of sign language and notes, I informed him that I wished to exchange rials for foreign traveler's checks. Following a short verbal struggle, he told me that his bank only had English pound sterling traveler's checks available, and I would only be able to purchase an amount equal to $1,000. Utilizing the Iranian practice of haggling, and telling the biggest lie, I pleaded with him to exchange $2,000 worth as I was leaving for America the next day and needed the cash to purchase an airline ticket. He bought my downhearted fairy tale and agreed to exchange $2,000 worth of rials. (Seven thousand to go!)

I proceeded to another small bank and was pleased to see only a couple Iranians in front of me at the teller's window. When I reached the front of the line, I found myself addressing a relatively young male cashier who spoke excellent English. His English, to my surprise, had a hint of a Texas accent which I commented on. He proudly told me that he had attended college in Texas near the city of Waco. We immediately struck up a friendly conversation when I told him that I had attended pilot training with the U.S. Air Force in Waco. He was eager to discuss his life in Texas and I felt I could "talk about Texas" with him until closing time, but I had more important things on my mind, namely exchanging money!

I told my Texas cashier friend that I would like to exchange some rials for U.S. dollar traveler's checks. He said this would be no problem, but the limit was $1,000 per day. I replayed my heart-wrenching story about leaving Iran the next day and needing enough cash to purchase an airline ticket, pay rent to my Iranian landlord and to pay for hotel rooms during my trip back home. I asked him if he could help a fellow displaced Texas friend and exchange $2,000 worth of rials. He bought my story and said, "As a gesture of good will to a former Waco, Texas partner, I'll exchange $2,000 worth." When he requested my passport I presented a random page which he stamped without question. (Five thousand to go!)

While he was preparing the traveler's checks, I asked him if he missed Texas. With a homesick far-away look in his eyes, he said he wished he was there right now as he was worried about the future of Iran. I asked him what he missed most. He replied, "Mexican food, long-legged Texas girls and Tequila." He added he hadn't tasted Tequila for several years and missed the tang it left in his mouth.

Looking for an opening to persuade him to exchange an additional amount of rials, I realized I couldn't do anything to satisfy his lust for long-legged Texas girls, or his desire for Mexican food, but I did have a full unopened bottle of Tequila in my apartment just a few blocks away. I told him that since I was leaving Iran the next day (not true, but a good opening) I wondered if he would like to have it. With a glee in his eye he said, "Yes, sah! I sure would!" I told him I would get the Tequila if he would sell me another $2,000 worth of U.S. traveler's checks. He agreed, but added that the bank was getting ready to close so when I returned, I should rap on a side door and insure the Tequila was enclosed in a paper bag so his boss wouldn't see it.

Fifteen minutes later I was tapping on the side door of his bank. My Texas cashier friend opened it with a, "You'll come on in here?" He was ready with $2,000 worth of traveler's checks and after a longing peek into the sack containing the Tequila, we completed the exchange without another stamp in my passport. (Three thousand to go!)

With the banks closed for the day, I went home and decided to drive my Volkswagen to the Army Officers' Club for dinner. As a last minute thought, I decided to take my remaining rials with me. As I entered the club, I noted several U.S. military officers waiting in line at the cashier's window. One of the men standing in line was a U.S. Army colonel I had played pool with in the past.

We exchanged pleasantries of the day and during the brief discussion, I asked him why he was standing in line at the cashier's window. He said that he had to purchase a couple thousand dollars worth of Iranian rials to buy some items he had on hold in a local jewelry shop, and to pay his house rent.

With the confidence of a used car salesman, I said, "Have I got a deal for you colonel!" I told him I had three thousand dollars worth of rials which I would sell at a discount. He told me, "Done, I'll take two thousand dollars worth, but will have to give you my personal check." He gave me his check, (which cleared with no problem) and in exchange, I gave him some well-worn rial bank notes. As I dug into my near empty paper shopping bag and handed him the rials, he asked if I had any notes of a larger denomination? With a chuckle I told him no. He shrugged his shoulders and replied, "That's OK it's all money."

Figuring I had put in a hard day, I thought I deserved a double martini and a large steak before heading home, with only $1,000 worth of rials left, which I could use myself. I tossed the well-worn empty shopping bag into a trash can and drove home eager to see what was in store for me the next day.

Later that week I retrieved the undisturbed traveler's checks and foreign cash hidden under my mattress and bundled them into three separate packages. I then sent them to my brother Hank's house in Eau Claire, Wisconsin, by registered mail, from the U.S. military post office.

Fortunately all three packages were delivered intact. My "Easter-egg-colored' **green** military ID carried the day once again!

Author's Note

The Islamic Revolutionary Guard converted the former United States Embassy compound in Tehran, which was made famous by the taking of American hostages on November 4, 1979, into a museum to showcase contempt for America. Most of the propaganda posters displayed depict the U.S. as the "Great Satan," while glorifying the Islamic fundamentalist theocracy.

Chapter Seventeen --- Living with the Revolution

By late November 1978, many of my flights were military missions involving the movement of Iranian troops and supplies to various cities and locations in Iran. If it hadn't been for my civilian airline uniform, I would have thought I was once again flying military combat support missions during the war in South Vietnam.

The Chief Pilot called me into his office stating that the company was dispatching two Navy F-27s to Bandar Abbas to transport 80 Iranian military electrical engineers to Tehran. He said that they were needed to take over control of the power generators from striking civilian government workers who were cutting off electrical power in Tehran almost every night. I was to fly one aircraft and an Iranian captain colleague was to fly the other aircraft.

The three-hour flight to Bandar Abbas was uneventful and after landing I found the Iranian Army engineers armed, dressed in full battle gear and waiting to board the aircraft for the return flight to Tehran. After refueling and a lunch of lamb, rice and chay, I departed Bandar Abbas with my Iranian captain associate following ten minutes behind.

Approaching Tehran, I was instructed by Air Traffic Control (ATC) to hold over a radio beacon 20 miles south of the city as I did not have authorization to land at Tehran's Mehrabad Airport. I thought this odd since the weather was excellent and the absence of radio transmissions indicated limited air traffic. I asked ATC how long I would be required to hold, but was instructed only to stand by. I continued circling and ten minutes later was joined by my Iranian colleague who set up a holding pattern 1,000 feet above my aircraft.

After circling for about 30 minutes without receiving further instructions, I felt something had to be done to break the stalemate. I instructed my copilot to inform ATC, in Farsi, that I was canceling my instrument flight plan and was going to land under visual flight rules. My copilot transmitted the message and they quickly responded, also in Farsi. Upon hearing their response, my copilot's face turned white and his eyes bulged as if he was in a state of fright. It was obvious he was not pleased with the answer he received!

I asked him to translate the controller's instructions to me into English. In a stuttering voice he said that they stated that if we attempted to land without permission at the Mehrabad Airport, we would be shot down. Not wishing to be directly involved in the government's rebellious dispute over providing electrical power for the city, I picked up the microphone and informed ATC that I was proceeding to the nearby Iranian army military airport of Dowshan Tappeh. A few seconds later my Iranian colleague, flying the second aircraft, announced he was also proceeding to the same army base and to cancel his instrument flight plan.

After landing at Dowshan Tappeh it was comforting to have my aircraft surrounded by friendly armed Iranian soldiers as my passengers and crew deplaned. I telephoned our operations center to inform them of my location and to request further instructions. I was surprised when the managing director, Mr. Djahanbani, answered instead of one of his regular dispatchers. He said that the reason he was manning the telephones was that his dispatchers were on a 24-hour sympathy strike with the Islamic militants, forcing him to fill in during their absence. I attempted to inform him of the reason I had landed at the Iranian army military base, but he interrupted stating he was already aware of my location and complimented me for my course of action.

He instructed me to leave the aircraft with my copilot on the military ramp and have an Iranian army crew bus transport myself and the two flight attendants to our respective residences in Tehran. He requested that I hand the telephone to a military official so he could coordinate the necessary instructions.

About ten minutes later, a small military bus arrived in front of the base operations building. The driver did not speak English, but my flight attendants were aware of our plan and relayed them to our young camouflage fatigue-clad driver. It was a short drive to the main gate, where we were stopped by armed guards who requested to inspect our identification badges and the driver's vehicle pass.

While the guard was performing his inspection, I noted that the main gate was blocked by a high steel barrier set on metal wheels and topped with barbed wire. It was obviously designed to roll back and forth on steel rails during the open/close operation. About 30 feet from each side of the gate were sandbagged machine gun nests with 50-caliber machine guns trained on the center of the opening. Both guns were manned by soldiers and belts of live ammunition could be seen hanging from their breaches. In addition there were about ten soldiers carrying M-1 carbines with fixed bayonets moving about the gate area.

When the guard was satisfied that the driver and his passengers were authorized to leave the base, he shouted instructions to the sergeant in-charge to open the gate in preparation for our departure. Soldiers began rolling the large steel door toward the open position, while guards with fixed bayonets came alive, put out their cigarettes and began moving into the widening open space created by the slowly moving gate. As the barrier started moving, the soldiers manning the machine guns also came alive and trained their weapons on the expanding opening.

Before the gate was halfway open, it became readily apparent why the Iranian military maintained such extreme security at the entrance to their base. Hundreds of angry demonstrators were assembled just outside the gate, shouting anti-government chants, and shaking their fists in defiant gestures. Their anger seemed boundless and increased in tempo and volume as the gate opening widened. The soldiers with fixed bayonets began a slow march toward the crowd with an obvious intention of creating a path through the milling crowd wide enough for our crew bus to pass. The unfolding rebellious scene directed toward the Shah's Army and all persons associated with it was something that I hadn't counted on when I was told to proceed to my apartment in downtown Tehran.

I jumped up from my seat in the bus and told the driver, "Enja," (stop) and with the help of my flight attendant's translation, ordered the sergeant controlling the operation to pull back his soldiers and close the gate. As the gate was closing some aggressive members of the demonstrators attempted to surge into the base, but were prevented from entering by the bayonet-armed soldiers. When the gate was finally closed, I instructed the driver to take us back to the base operations building. As we departed the area, I observed the soldiers and machine gun crews lighting up cigarettes and assuming a more typical military GI relaxed attitude.

As the crew bus approached base operations, I could see that my Iranian pilot colleague, who had been flying the second aircraft, was preparing to depart and in fact had already started his right engine. I grabbed my flight bag and ran to the front of his aircraft. When he opened his cockpit window, I asked him where he was going. He replied Bandar Abbas. I requested that he have one of his crew members open the aircraft's rear door as I was going with him. With the aid of a helpful crew member, I was hoisted aboard and took a seat in the cabin.

The next day, I was lounging next to the Navy Officers' Club swimming pool when an Iranian sailor told me I had a telephone call from Tehran. The Air Taxi Managing Director wanted to know what I was doing in Bandar Abbas. I told him, "Breathing!"

I explained why I was in Southern Iran and he said he fully understood. I asked him about my copilot and flight attendants I had left at the military base. He said they were OK, had spent the night at the base, but were now in their homes safe and sound. He suggested I take a couple days off and catch a ride back to Tehran when I was ready. He added that the Shah appreciated the delivery of the army electrical engineers to Tehran as the power generators were now back on line.

Two days later, I returned to Tehran and found a city with all the trappings of a city under siege. Military vehicles patrolled the streets on a regular basis and armed and manned English *Chieftain* tanks guarded most major intersections. Machine gun nests protected by sandbag enclosures were everywhere, pedestrian and vehicular traffic was considerably reduced and a 9 p.m. to 7 a.m. curfew was still in effect.

Sporadic gun fire could still be heard both day and night, but large-scale demonstrations, so common a few weeks earlier, were no longer in evidence. The Shah had decided to take a much more aggressive stance toward demonstrators in his struggling effort to remain in power. Tehran had become an armed camp and no matter where you went, you knew you were being watched by armed soldiers.

Foreigners were openly concerned about their safety and offered different opinions about whether or not the Shah would survive. I probably displayed a greater sense of optimistic hope than good sense and thought he would weather this storm like so many he weathered in the past. Supporting this belief was an unsubstantiated CIA report in September 1978 stating that the Shah had a stable regime and would continue to hold power for at least 10 to 15 years. However, I didn't count on the crumbling support he would receive from the United States and France. I was hoping that my interesting and lucrative job would continue.

After returning to Tehran from a military support flight to Southern Iran, I was preparing to depart the dispatch center for my apartment when Captain Fritz Grunt, the pilot from Vienna, Austria, asked if he could ride into town with me. During the drive, I asked Fritz if he had any plans for dinner. When he said no, I asked him if he would care to join me for dinner at the Kansular restaurant. He said he had heard about the Kansular and since he had never been there would like to go. I suggested we make a short stop at my apartment, which would allow me to call for a reservation, and while waiting we could enjoy a German beer or two.

The Kansular restaurant was very popular among foreigners and upper class Iranians. Not only was the food good, but they served alcohol and their menus were in English. Pita bread was baked fresh in a red-hot oven right before your eyes, indigenous musicians entertained you with authentic Middle East music, and the decorum was rich with Persian carpets and hand-made brass ornaments. Due to its popularity, reservations were required, especially if you wished to secure a table where you could observe the pits bread oven and the authentic Iranian musicians pumping out their weird style of Middle East musicology.

I called the Restaurant and requested dinner reservations for two at 6 p.m., but was told the earliest table available was at seven. Even though this would require eating hurriedly so as to be home before the 9 p.m. curfew, I made reservations anyway so Fritz could have the opportunity of visiting this unique ethnic Iranian eating establishment. We had two hours to kill before leaving, so we decided to indulge in some authentic German Lowenbrau beer which I knew Fritz would enjoy.

Several beers later we were fully engaged in exchanging stories (mostly true) about skiing and partying in Austria and Germany and didn't pay much attention to the passing time. When we noticed the clock approaching seven we were feeling the effects of the beer and I didn't think it was wise for me to drive under these conditions.

It was dangerous enough to drive in Tehran in broad daylight, stone sober, but to do so at night after drinking would put a strain on Allah's protective oversight. I suggested that we forget the Kansular and burn a couple burgers in my apartment instead. Fritz agreed, and after a few more beers and a home-cooked meal, he left by taxi to reach his apartment before the start of the 9 p.m. curfew.

On the way to the airport the next morning, I stopped to buy a copy of the English edition of the *Tehran Kayhan* Newspaper. The headline read, **"Several foreigners killed when terrorists bomb the Kansular restaurant."** The details of the attack stated that unknown terrorists had thrown a large bomb into the lobby of the restaurant instantly killing several foreigners waiting to be seated. The time of the attack was 7 p.m. Had Fritz and I kept our reservation appointment we would have been standing in the lobby waiting to be seated and would most likely have been among the victims. I guess after nearly three years in Iran, Allah was actually starting to look after me, "Insha Allah."

In late November 1978, both English and Iranian magazines featured graphic color pictures of the Jonestown, Guyana mass murder-suicide of 900 radical followers of "Jim Jones." His followers, including 270 children, were persuaded to drink cyanide-laced Kool-aid. According to the article their self-inflicted deaths would ensure that they received a first-class ticket to Paradise.

This apocalyptic event created considerable discussion among my Iranian Muslim colleagues. Their main point of contention was that since the Jonestown victims were not Muslims, it was blasphemous to suggest that they would go directly to Paradise after committing suicide for a cause not relating to Allah. They asked me my opinion. I told them that I thought Paradise was big enough to accommodate both Muslim and Jonestown victims. They didn't agree, thinking that the bizarre incident involving 900 American infidels could cause a problem in Valhalla.

By late November 1978, long gas lines were again appearing at city gas stations. I thought this very strange in a country awash with oil, but my copilots told me that it was an artificial shortage created by the Shah to dampen civil movement and unrest.

On the way home from work, I took my place in a long line of cars waiting at a government-operated gas station. I was positioned directly behind an older American Chevrolet *Caprice* which dwarfed my little Volkswagen. I knew the driver of the Chevrolet in front of me was very short, because I couldn't see his head through his rear window.

Suddenly, without warning, he began to back up at a high rate of speed. I couldn't get out of his way because of automobiles directly behind me and the frantic sounding of my weak six-volt Volkswagen horn was not loud enough to warn him of his imminent stupid mistake. With a loud thump he backed into the front of my car, and stopped only after his rear bumper was half way up the slanted hood of my Volkswagen.

A small middle-age man emerged from the *Caprice*, surveyed the damage he had caused and began shaking his head. He was no more than five feet five inches tall which explained why he couldn't see me in his rear view mirror. I didn't think he was Iranian and after struggling with his broken English, I learned that he was Armenian. His automobile was owned by a local taxi company in Tehran.

The accident caught the attention of a couple Iranian army soldiers manning a machine gun nest nearby, but other than curious looks, they made no effort to investigate. He apologized for backing into me and stated that his company would make all repairs to my automobile.

I told him that I wanted to call the Iranian police, which caused him to turn white with fear. The Iranians and Armenians hated each other and I knew this. He suggested I talk to his boss on his car radio who would confirm that his company would fix my car and that it was not necessary to involve the police. His boss told me to follow his driver to his shop where my car would be repaired. With the help of a couple onlookers, we dislodged his automobile from mine and I followed him to his company's garage. When I drove my damaged car into their garage I think the owner was surprised when I appeared in my airline captain's uniform. He looked at the damage and said to leave the car with him for a few days and he would straighten out and repaint the front end. I accepted his offer and with the help of a couple strong men and a crow bar, pried open the caved in front trunk area so I could retrieve my flight bag.

In true Iranian custom, I told him that if I left the car, I would be without transportation and his company would have to provide me with a taxi until my car was fixed. After some haggling, he agreed. I then told him that I was also concerned about paint match, and wanted the whole car painted. He resisted until I threatened to call the police. When I left his shop he said he would have my car ready in about five days. Good to his promise (he wasn't an Iranian), I had the use of a taxi wherever I went. Five days later I picked up my 1966 Volkswagen which looked brand new. (Unfortunately, I would be forced to abandon it just a few weeks later when I would make my hurried escape from Iran, See Photo No. 15.)

The heavy concentration of armed troops openly visible in most major cities prevented the gathering of large groups of demonstrators. However, it did not soothe the ever increasing boldness and dissatisfaction of a large percentage of the people and the revolution started to resemble a guerrilla-type war of resistance. Demonstrators set fire to government and foreign buildings, while an ever increasing number of Iranian soldiers were allowing citizens to place flowers into the barrels of their weapons. While it was becoming clear that the city infrastructure was beginning to crumble, surprisingly, shops were still stocked with food, and by waiting in long lines, gas for automobiles was still available.

By early December 1978, most of the foreign Air Taxi pilots had departed Iran and Captain Bill Aston and I were the only ones left. Although I was still flying trips, the frequency had dropped off to about two or three per week. This reduced flight schedule provided many days of free time, but with a 9 p.m. to 7 a.m. curfew, I found myself confined to my apartment night after night. Television and radio stations no longer carried programs in English, and due to the curfew, house parties were scarce or discontinued altogether. Not wishing to become an alcoholic required diligent self control.

I became a frequent visitor to the U.S. Embassy with the goal of keeping my survival liquor cabinet full and to check the bulletin board for any cautionary alerts for American citizens. I found the liquor store well stocked, but the bulletin board bare of any useful information. With "twenty-twenty" hind sight I believe that the Embassy was following President Carter's philosophy of encouraging its citizens to take a "head-in-the-sand, don't worry" approach and to ease the pain, stay inebriated and "don't make waves." My English pilot friend, Bill Aston, kept me fully apprised on the expanding Iranian insurrection provided him by his Embassy. Without these daily alerts I wouldn't have been able to maintain an understanding of how serious my remaining in Iran could be.

During the entire Iranian revolutionary period of 1978, the U.S. Embassy was silent in regard to potential anti-government demonstrations that should be avoided. I and the thousands of Americans, still living in Iran, were on our own. Fortunately, the British, Japanese and Canadian Embassies did not adhere to this unresponsive approach to the Iranian revolution that was about to overthrow the Shah (an American ally) and presented useful alerts for Western expatriates.

Unfortunately, in some respects I don't think the U.S. State Department has significantly improved. According to reports only six of the 1,000 employees in the U.S. Embassy in Baghdad, Iraq speak Arabic. This is shocking since it's possible to learn a foreign language in only six months.

Chapter Eighteen --- Time to Leave Iran

In early December 1978, militant Muslim demonstrators seized several government buildings, smashed offices and set numerous fires. Before the Iranian Army was able to regain control many protesters were killed. It appeared that the attempted overthrow of the Shah was breaking out anew with an increased effort in bringing their efforts to fruition.

My flight schedule was reduced considerably and during the month of December. I flew only seven trips. Walking the streets of Tehran, even in daylight, became more menacing. Roving gangs of young militant Iranians would shout "Death to America," while displaying the Western-style insult of a raised middle finger. There were reliable reports that demonstrators were painting an "orange circle" on apartments or homes occupied by Americans. The U.S. military was sending its dependents and nonessential members home and reducing its overall presence in Iran. In spite of these menacing indicators, the U.S. Embassy was still following a "head-in-the-sand" approach and not issuing warnings or alerts to American citizens living in Iran.

Around the 10th of December, Captain Aston and I were paid our salary for the month of November. With about $4,000 worth of rials in our pockets we drove my freshly painted Volkswagen to downtown Tehran with the hope of exchanging some or all of our questionable Iranian rials into Western currency. We visited the American Express office and several banks, but found them either closed, or if open, not accepting rials in exchange for other currencies. We gave up and stuffed what now appeared to be nothing more than "Monopoly money" into our pockets. (I utilized a portion of these rials in paying my rent and figured on spending the rest in enjoying what was left of the finer aspects of Tehran's luxuries.)

Bill and I were still able to get in a few games of pool in the Army Officers' Club and due to the military cutback had the game room almost to ourselves. However, we had to pay close attention to the 9 p.m. curfew and head for our individual apartments by eight-thirty. After hunkering down in my apartment and missing Chieko, boredom would once again set in. Reading was not a good option to relieve the monotony as electrical power was once again abruptly shut off soon after the start of the nightly curfew. One diversion that had no bounds was to mix a martini and go to the roof of my apartment building to take in the nightly small arms fireworks display.

December also saw an increase in militant demonstrators playing anti-Shah cassette tapes over loud speakers poking out through open windows. From my roof-top perch, I could hear these propaganda broadcasts blaring out from many different sections of the city. The Iranian military's attempts to silence them consisted of jeeps, equipped with strong search lights and 50-caliber machine guns, cruising up and down the streets. When they located an active loud speaker, they would pinpoint it with the search light and silence it with a burst of machine gun fire. As the Christmas season of 1978 approached, I entertained thoughts of leaving Iran, but was still hopeful the Shah would survive and I would be able to finish my second two-year contract. However, my decision to "hang-in-there" abruptly changed after being exposed to three chilling events.

The first one occurred when I visited a local market to shop for fresh fruit. As I left the store, several young thugs surrounded me and started the usual loud chants of "Death to America," along with the raised middle finger, but this time several shouted in English, "We follow you and kill you." They stuck with me until I sought refuge among soldiers manning a machine gun nest at a nearby corner.

After my young admirers left, I thanked the two soldiers manning the machine gun for providing me sanctuary and walked to my apartment. When arriving home, I spotted an orange circle painted underneath my apartment window. In spite of exhaustive efforts to scrub it off with soap and water, its ominous stain was still clearly visible.

The third eye-opening, heart-wrenching event occurred the next night. Bill Aston had been over for dinner and drinks and after a hurried meal left for his own apartment to beat the 9 p.m. curfew. I had a few more drinks, but when electrical power was cut off I went to bed.

I was just dozing off when I heard a loud speaker blaring out anti-Shah propaganda. From the volume and clarity, I thought it must be across the street from my apartment. I attempted to ignore the ear-shattering noise and tried to go back to sleep by covering my head with a pillow, but it didn't help much, as the volume was too loud and shrill.

Suddenly, a long blast of machine gun fire erupted with such lucidity and volume that it sounded like it was in the next room. My bed vibrated with the staccato of each explosive round and I shook violently from the concussions. My military training took over and I instinctively rolled out of bed and cowered on the hard cold floor. I laid there for several seconds with my pounding heart competing with the "rat-a-tat-tat-tat" sound of the machine gun.

As quickly as it began, the firing stopped and along with it, the blaring loudspeaker. I laid on the floor several minutes before climbing back into bed with the resolve that I didn't wish to relive the Vietnam War. Once was enough, especially since I was now a volunteer civilian pilot.

The next morning I called Mr. Djahanbani, the managing director of Air Taxi, and requested permission to take a 120-day leave of absence. He understood completely, approved my request, wished me well and said he hoped things would settle down to the point that I would be able to return sometime soon. He requested I keep him informed of my address and telephone number in the United States.

Subsequent to the violent public demonstrations that erupted in early September, I had purchased several KLM open airline discount tickets in case I needed to leave Iran in a hurry. I had also obtained an Iranian exit visa required by all foreigners when departing Tehran. The airline tickets and exit visa were a contingency move I was glad that I had taken.

I called the Tehran Royal Dutch Airline (KLM) ticket office and to my surprise got right through to an English-speaking Dutch female. I told her that I wished to make a reservation for KLM's next day flight to Amsterdam. She asked if I was Canadian or American. I told her I was an American pilot working in Iran, but figured it was time for me to leave. She understood, but said departing Tehran might be a problem as all flights were oversold. However, she added that recently most flights, in spite of the over booking, were departing with empty seats.

Apparently, Iranians wishing to leave Iran were making reservations, but not possessing valid exit visas, were not allowed to board the aircraft. She said she would put me on a standby list and although she couldn't guarantee a seat, she didn't think I would have a problem if I went to the airport about two hours or more early.

Due to time constraints and a desire to travel light, I packed only a carry-on bag. Under the chaotic conditions I knew would exist at the Mehrabad Airport, I didn't wish to trust the airline with checked baggage.

I then crammed personal items like my stereo set, clothes, cooking utensils, television, etc., into several cardboard boxes and placed them in a corner of my apartment for safe keeping and possible use in the event I was able to return to complete my second two-year contract and garner a sizable cash bonus.

I then informed my landlord, through his English-speaking niece, that I was leaving Iran for an extended period, but due to the changing political situation may not be able to return. Using some of my unused Iranian rials, I gave him two months advance rent stating that this would allow me time to evaluate whether or not I would return. If I didn't, the extra month's rent, plus my security deposit, would satisfy all rental contract commitments. He agreed that the arrangement was very fair.

There was one more item that required attention. I asked him if it would be OK to leave my freshly painted white Volkswagen parked on the street directly in front of his apartment. If I decided not to return, I would have one of my Iranian pilot colleagues pick it up for sale. He said that this would be fine and would ensure it was looked after, so having no choice but to believe him I gave him the keys. (See Photo No. 15.)

I then called my good friend Bill Aston, told him about the machine gun blast in front of my apartment the night before, and said I was planning on departing for Amsterdam the next day. He attempted to get me to change my mind. He said he was remaining with the hope that things would get better and suggested I remain in Iran also. However, I told him I figured it was time for me to leave, wished him good luck in future pool games and gave him a stateside contact address and telephone number.

The next morning I took a commercial taxi to the airport, arriving three hours early. The entrance to the terminal was so packed with cars and crowds of milling people that my taxi was not able to drive to the normal passenger drop-off point. I paid my driver and began a long difficult elbow-wrestling trek to the inside of the terminal. Exhausted and ruffled, I finally made my way to the KLM passenger counter. After a long wait, I was at the front of the line.

A KLM agent examined my ticket, passport and exit visa, and without hesitation asked if I desired a window or aisle seat. I said, "Window please," and was issued a seat assignment without a hassle.

I elbowed my way toward the boarding gate which was manned by armed Iranian soldiers. After an exhaustive and detailed examination of my carry-on suitcase and boarding documents, I was allowed to proceed to a secure holding area. When the flight was called, I boarded a KLM DC-8 only half-filled with mostly ecstatic foreign passengers and a few Iranians obviously delighted that they were able to escape Iran.

Five hours later, I was in Amsterdam where I planned on spending a few days unwinding before departing for the United States. Walking the streets of Amsterdam, void of sandbagged machine gun nests and English *Chieftain* tanks, was a welcome change from life in Tehran.

Another stark contrast was that the young men walking the streets were not sporting thick unkempt beards, were not shouting "Death to America" and were not threatening to follow me to my hotel and kill me. While drinking Tuborg beer and eating delicious Vienerschnitizel, I wondered if I would be able to return to Iran anytime soon.

Chapter Nineteen --- Safe in the United States

On January 16, 1979, it was announced that the Shah and his immediate family had left Tehran for Cairo, Egypt, where he became a temporary guest of President Anwar Sadat. When the Shah, exhausted and visibly drawn, arrived in Cairo President Sadat stepped forward, kissed him on both cheeks and said, "Rest assured, Mohammad, you are in your country and with your people and brothers." The Shah's eyes filled with tears as he walked past hundreds of well wishers who came out to greet him and his family at the airport.

On February 1, 1979, Ayatollah Khomeini triumphantly arrived in Tehran from his exile in Paris, France, on an Air France B-747 *Jumbo* Jet. He received a rousing welcome from approximately three million hysterical Iranians who mobbed the airport and filled the streets to welcome him. The crowds were so enthusiastically unruly, and large, that he had to be flown to his downtown headquarters by helicopter.

Many high-ranking military and government holdovers from the Shah's regime who remained in Iran felt they could mount a coup d'état against Khomeini. However, within a week hard-line Muslim religious leaders and followers of Khomeini took over control of all government and military functions. Hope of a plot against the popular Ayatollah quickly faded.

The revolutionary government started arresting key government and military supporters of the Shah, which was followed by a vigorous campaign of summary trials and expeditious executions by firing squad.

It became very clear that I would not be returning to my flying job in Iran. This decision was based on two factors, the turmoil in Tehran being fermented by the ruthless Ayatollah Khomeini, and that my employer, which was owned by the despised Shah, would certainly not be looked upon favorably by the Khomeini regime.

I sent a registered letter to my landlord in Tehran, Mr. Amini, advising him that I would not be returning to Iran. I requested, in accordance with our rental contract and verbal agreement, that he consider my letter as notice of lease termination. In the letter I also advised him that I would arrange for an Iranian pilot colleague to pickup my Volkswagen and the personal effects I had left in my apartment.

Making international telephone calls to Tehran, even before the revolution, was difficult, but I didn't expect the problem to manifest itself tenfold. Day after day, I would sit by the telephone attempting to make contact with my Iranian friend Captain Mohammad Rezi Mousavi.

Captain Mousavi was a respected colleague and well liked by all foreign pilots. As previously mentioned he was a former jet fighter pilot for the Iranian Air Force and had attended pilot training in the United States. He was also my instructor pilot when I checked out in the French *Falcon* jet and during the transition we developed a warm professional relationship. He espoused a Western-style philosophy and, although he didn't openly engage in political discussions, it was obvious he supported the Shah. I thought if I could contact him, he would help me retrieve some of the personal items stored in my apartment and sell my Volkswagen. However, repeated telephone calls to the number I had for him were not answered, nor could I get through to the main information switchboard in Tehran.

In desperation, I decided to try to contact Mr. Djahanbani, the managing director of Air Taxi. Surprisingly, I got right through. Mr. Djahanbani's voice was clear, but very weak. He sounded like someone awakened from a sound sleep. I thought this strange as the time I called was midday in Iran.

I identified myself as Captain Martin and that I was calling from the United States. He responded weakly with, "Hello, Captain Martin. I can't talk to you right now." I asked him if I had woken him up, and if I had I was sorry. His response was, "No you didn't wake me up, but they executed my father by firing squad this morning and I don't feel like talking to anyone right now!"

Mr. Djahanbani's father was a retired Iranian Air Force General who I had seen from a distance many times when he visited his son at the airport. He was a handsome man in his late forties or early fifties and drove a white Mercedes-Benz sedan, which in itself would automatically mark him as an enemy of Khomeini.

I expressed sympathy regarding the death of his father, but asked if he could give me the telephone number of Captain Mousavi, as the number I had was apparently incorrect. Still the gentleman, in spite of his great loss, he told me to stand by while he looked it up. He came back on the line and gave me Captain Mousavi's new telephone number and stated that everything in Tehran was a mess and advised me not to plan on returning. I again expressed condolences for his loss and said I was disappointed that I wouldn't be able to return, as I enjoyed my job with Air Taxi and working for him. I wished him well and hung-up.

The next day I called Captain Mousavi who was surprised to hear from me, but pleased to learn that I was safe in the United States. He told me that Tehran was in turmoil and I wouldn't recognize it. He said I should not plan on returning.

I told him about my conversation with Mr. Djahanbani and the fate of his father. He was not aware that General Djahanbani had been executed, but wasn't surprised. He said that executions were occurring almost every day, including some Air Taxi pilots and VIP passengers we both knew, but couldn't say more over the telephone.

I asked Mohammad if he could do me a favor. He responded, "Absolutely. Just name it Captain Martin." I told him that my Volkswagen was parked in front of my apartment at 33 Ladan Alley and that my landlord, Mr. Amini, had agreed to look after it until I returned, or I arranged for someone to pick it up for sale. I Told Mohammad that I estimated it to be worth about $5,000 (approximately $18,000 today) and if he could sell it he could keep $1,000 for himself. He thought this was too generous, but when I insisted, he agreed and said he would attempt to retrieve it from Mr. Amini's care.

I also told Captain Mousavi that there were several boxes of personal items stored in my apartment that he was welcome to have as an expression of friendship. I said these items included a set of china, a small television, a stereo, cassette tapes, sheets and blankets, a portable typewriter, two airline uniforms, a couple civilian suits, some sport shirts, and miscellaneous cooking utensils. I thought that since we were about the same size, the uniforms and civilian clothes should fit him quite well. He offered to pay me for these items, but I insisted that he accept them as a gift since I could not ship them back to the United States. He expressed extreme gratitude for my generosity and said that since Khomeini's arrival, there was very little flying, so he should be able to visit my apartment straight away to pickup my car and personal items.

Before we hung up, I asked him if he knew who I should contact regarding unpaid company wages. I also mentioned that the only item I would like to have from my apartment was a small box labeled "personal papers." He wished me well and said he would call back soon.

About two weeks later Captain Mousavi called and said he had some good and bad news. He had visited my landlord and was allowed to retrieve the personal items I had left, but they did not include a television or stereo set. He said that when he asked my landlord about them, he was told that Mr. Martin must have taken them with him. (Not true.) He was allowed to pickup the other items, including the clothes, which he greatly appreciated. He also located the box of "personal papers" and said he would send them to me, but wasn't sure how or when.

Regarding my Volkswagen, he said it was still parked in front of my apartment, but my landlord wouldn't allow him to take it. He said Mr. Amini stated that I had broken my lease agreement when I departed and demanded a payment equal to $1,000 before he would release the car. I told Mohammad that it was a rip-off, but we had no choice but to meet his extortion demands. I suggested he deduct the ransom payment from the price received from the sale, but his commission of $1,000 would still stand. He thanked me again and said that once he had the car in his possession, it should sell easily and at a good price as cars were in high demand, especially Volkswagens, since the revolution.

Mohammad said he had checked with the company regarding my unpaid wages and I should send a letter to Mr. Dashti in Air Taxi. He wished me well and said he would call me again soon.

I sent a registered letter to Mr. Dashti, outlining in detail, that Air Taxi owed me $9,000 ($30,000 in current value) in unpaid wages and bonus, and requested his help in ensuring I receive full payment. He did not respond and about two months later I sent another registered letter. Neither letter was answered, nor did I receive any money. I gave up and considered it a lost cause to pursue the matter any further by letter.

A few weeks later Captain Mousavi called and said he had visited my apartment again and informed my landlord that I had agreed to meet his demand for an extra $1,000 payment. However, he now stated that before releasing the car, I would have to provide him with a notarized statement, issued by an Iranian Consulate Office in the U.S., granting Captain Mousavi "Power of Attorney" for disposing of my Volkswagen. (It was obvious that my landlord was attempting to move the goal posts to a position where it would be impossible for us to score.)

Mohammad and I agreed that we might never win this battle, but decided, as two former Air Force jet pilots, to see it through as a personal challenge against my former landlord. He provided me with his birth place and date, his father's name, and his current address. I told him I would check into obtaining an Iranian power of attorney and get back to him.

I contacted the Iranian Consulate General's Office in Chicago and explained what I needed. They told me that I would have to provide a notarized letter granting Mr. Mousavi limited power of attorney to sell my car in Iran. They demanded that the letter must be in English and Farsi and identify the automobile by serial number. With the help of an Iranian college exchange student, I sent the required documents to Chicago.

A couple weeks later the Iranian Consulate General's Office returned my limited power of attorney letter, stamped approved, which contained the required Revolutionary Government of Iran raised seal. I promptly forwarded it to Captain Mousavi in Tehran by registered mail.

Several months passed with no additional word from Mohammad and my telephone calls to him went unanswered. I began to worry about his well-being, since following the turmoil in Iran, I had seen newspaper pictures of some of my former passengers and a couple pilot colleagues who had been executed by the Khomeini regime. I prayed that my friend Captain Mousavi was not among them as punishment for his efforts in assisting an American infidel colleague in the United States.

My fears for the safety of Captain Mousavi were somewhat relieved when I received a package, postmarked New Jersey, which contained the personal papers I had asked Mohammad to pickup from my Tehran apartment. The package did not contain a return address or name, just a short note inside stating that the sender was an Iranian pilot and our mutual friend Captain Mousavi asked him to send these papers to me when he arrived safely in the United States.

Hearing nothing more from Captain Mousavi, I decided once again to attempt to contact Mr. Djahanbani. After several failed attempts, I finally got through to him on the telephone. I asked him how he was doing personally and the status of the company. He told me he was doing as well as could be expected, but in addition to losing his father, many of his friends were either in prison or had also been executed.

I told him that I had been working with Captain Mousavi in an attempt to clear up my affairs in Tehran, but I hadn't heard from him for several months. Mr. Djahanbani said that obviously I hadn't heard that Captain Mousavi had been killed in an aircraft accident north of Tehran. He also told me that due to unbelievable complications I should not expect to receive any unpaid salaries or bonus payments.

I wished Mr. Djahanbani well and with a tear in my eye over the death of Captain Mousavi, I prayed his soul was happy in Paradise. I knew he had done his best in attempting to help a fellow American pilot. I gave up on attempting to recover anything more from Tehran at this time, and hoped that the crazy traffic in Iran would zero in on my Volkswagen and destroy it in a big fiery crash at one of Tehran's busy intersections.

Chapter Twenty --- Do Not Return to Iran

By early May 1979, news reports indicated that the worst of the turmoil heralded by Ayatollah Khomeini's triumphant arrival in Tehran was over. Also the United States Embassy in Iran, which had been invaded by Islamic Militants in February 1979, was back in American hands. Reviewing the situation, I thought it might be safe for me to return to Tehran for a brief visit. My desire to return was a combination of curiosity and a desire to see if I could recoup some of my financial losses.

I still possessed two open KLM round trip tickets to Tehran, via Amsterdam and Rome. My plan was to treat my 18-year-old son Michael to a springtime visit to these two fascinating cities. When we reached Rome, I would visit the Iranian Consulate Office to request a visa to visit Tehran. If I was successful in obtaining a visa, I would give my son the option of waiting in Rome until I returned from Iran, or returning to the United States on his own.

At first my son was not too keen on leaving his teenage friends in Wisconsin for a two-to-three-week visit to Europe. However, after I explained the wonders and excitement of the trip, he relented and agreed to accompany me. We drove from Northern Wisconsin to Chicago, parked our car in a long term parking lot, and were soon on a nonstop KLM *Jumbo* Jet flight to Amsterdam.

I always enjoyed the cultural excitement of Amsterdam and we took a room in a quaint downtown hotel that I had stayed in during previous visits. I escorted my son around town taking in all the sights, including scrumptious meals in fine restaurants, wandering through interesting museums, the Anne Frank House and a canal boat trip. Four days later, we departed on a flight for Rome, Italy.

Rome, without a doubt, is my favorite European City. Its four million citizens are extremely friendly and possess an exciting lust for living from dawn until the wee hours of the morning. With my son in tow, we visited the Coliseum, the Roman Forum, early Christian places of worship, the Fountains of Rome and my favorite restaurant "Alfredo di Roma."

Mr. Alfredo di Lelio opened his restaurant in 1914, and in addition to other fine culinary achievements, was the originator of "Fettuccine Alfredo." He concocted this egg noodle dish, heavy with fresh cream, butter and parmesan cheese, to temp the palate of his pregnant wife, who had lost her appetite. Alfredo di Roma was the restaurant movie stars, prominent business executives, German & American Generals and celebrities of all walks of life, felt obligated to visit, and have their picture added to the restaurant wall. Alfredo was a great showman and a colorful man with a bubbling personality. He was especially proud of a large, solid gold fork and spoon set presented to him by silent movie stars Douglas Fairbanks Sr. and his wife Mary Pickford when they visited his restaurant on their honeymoon in 1927. He proudly displayed them in a glass case in his restaurant. For special customers, he would remove the gold fork and spoon set from their protective case and use them in a flamboyant table-side mixing ceremony, of his famous Fettuccine noodles. After the mixing was complete, which was accomplished with flowing arm movements and off-key singing, he would dish out equal amounts of Fettuccine to dinner guests seated around the table, except one! Alfredo would then set the large plate he used in the mixing ritual in front of the person he chose as the table leader. This would be accompanied by a cheer and applause from customers seated at adjacent tables, who had been observing this entertaining performance.

I'm proud to state that when I was in the Air Force, I visited Alfredo's restaurant so often, and brought in so many customers, that he would honor me with his gold fork and spoon table-side mixing and set the large platter in front of me. This would be accompanied by a beaming smile, from underneath his flowing six-inch mustache and a "Bon appetite."

I'm sure Mr. Alfredo is now mixing Fettuccine for St. Peter and his band of angels in heaven, but without his gold fork and spoon, since it still hangs on the wall in his original restaurant in Rome.

In addition to being able to take my son to the original Alfredo restaurant, we enjoyed long interesting walks on 2,000-year-old streets. Michael thought this was very interesting, but wanted to know when we would visit the Vatican City. I told him we would spend a full day visiting the Vatican after we returned from a trip to Naples and the ruins of Pompeii. However, I first wanted to visit the Iranian Consulate Office to make an application for a visa to visit Tehran.

Walking into the Iranian Consulate was a trip back in time. All of the male employees were wearing full beards, dull-looking rumpled suits, and no neck ties. The few female workers employed were dressed in full-length black chadors. Large pictures of Ayatollah Kohomini were hanging from the walls in every dingy looking room.

What a change from the days when the Shah was the leader of Iran. These same picture frames had been used to display colorful pictures of him, and the drab, plainly dressed, no-necktie men working there would have been clean shaven and dressed in neat business suits. The female workers would have been wearing businesslike Western-style dresses and modern hair styles.

I completed my visa application and presented it, along with my passport, to one of the shaggy bearded men. He asked me why I wished to visit Tehran. When I told him I had been a pilot for the Air Taxi Company and wished to inquire about unpaid wages and the liquidation of a Volkswagen I had left behind with my Iranian landlord, he seemed interested. He told me that my visa request would be considered and I should come back in three days. He never smiled once during my short visit and left me with the impression that had his face displayed even a hint of a smile, he would have suffered a heart attack.

My son and I took a bus to Naples and spent a couple days visiting the ruins of Pompeii and the surrounding area. Michael really enjoyed Pompeii and was coming out of his teenage, anti-older-generation slump, and we were starting to enjoy each other's company. I was truly glad I had insisted he accompany me on the trip.

After returning to Rome, I went directly to the Iranian Consulate Office and was informed that my visa application had been approved for a seven-day visit to Tehran. My passport was stamped accordingly and I joined my son waiting in a taxi outside. I told him we would now spend a day or so visiting the Vatican and other sights before I left for Tehran.

No matter how many times I visited St. Peter's Basilica, I still looked forward to touring it again. We spent nearly a full-day wandering through the Vatican museums, walking silently through the Sistine (Michelangelo) Chapel, gazing at sarcophaguses of dead popes, and walking around the famous open Piazza San Pietro Square in front of the Basilica.

While standing in the square, I pointed out to Mike the 435-foot-high cupola atop the dome, stating that this would be the highlight of our visit to the Vatican. I was standing in the middle of the square with an out-stretched arm pointing toward the top of St. Peter's Basilica when a neatly dressed man and his young son approached us.

In English, with an accent I didn't immediately recognize, he said, "Excuse me, sir, can you tell me how we can get to the observation area on top of the church." I told him that my son and I were going there now and if he wished to accompany us, he was welcome. He thanked me for the offer, but seemed somewhat reluctant to accept the invitation. When I repeated it, he said, "We would like to accept your kind offer, sir, but wonder, since we are Muslims, if we would be allowed to go with you." I told him that the entire Vatican complex was open to people of all faiths and he and his son were more than welcome to accompany us.

I added that since it was obvious that this was their first visit to the Vatican he owed it to himself and his son to take in all the sights, including the world famous Saint Peter's Basilica.

We took an elevator part-way up and then climbed 320 stone steps through a narrow spiral stairway to the top of the dome. Once outside, we were greeted with a panoramic view of Rome, St. Peter's Square and the Via Della Conciliazione below. It was a breathtaking sight and I sensed that my new Muslim friends were impressed and glad they had made the trip. As I pointed out various sections of the Basilica, they began verbalizing the experience in their native language. I recognized that they were conversing in Iranian Farsi and asked him if they were Iranian? In a hesitant manner, he said, "Yes."

I shook his hand while stating, "Salam-u-Alaikum (Peace)." My Farsi greeting surprised him and he asked how it was I knew Farsi. When I told him I had lived in Iran for three years he shook my hand with an obvious warmth of friendship. He said that he and his son wanted to visit the inside of St. Peters Basilica, but again were hesitant since they were Muslim. He suggested that if I and my son accompany them, they would like to repay our kind deed by taking us out for lunch. I agreed.

After escorting them on a tour of the Basilica, we secured a table in the garden of a pleasant Italian restaurant. The scent of fresh flowers, simmering tomato sauce and pasta and the gentle rays of a spring sun, reaffirmed my strong attachment to the peaceful lifestyle of Rome.

My new found Iranian friend introduced himself as Mohammad Baharlu. I introduced myself as Captain Martin. He recalled that I had mentioned working as a pilot for the Air Taxi Company in Tehran and asked if I had known General Djahanbani, the father of Air Taxi's managing director. When I told him that I knew of the General, but had never met him, he asked if I knew he had been executed by Khomeini loyalists. I told him yes, that I had learned of his death during a telephone conversation with his son a couple months ago. He then told me that several of General Djahanbani's military colleagues had also been summarily executed and his son, my former boss, was fearful for his own life.

To my surprise, he was very familiar with the operation of Air Taxi and identified by name several VIPs who had been my passengers. When I responded that I recognized many of the men he mentioned, he told me that many of them had also been either executed or were in prison.

I asked Mohammad how it was that he was so knowledgeable of the Air Taxi Company and what he and his son were doing in Rome. He told me that he had owned an import/export business in Tehran and frequently flew on Air Taxi aircraft, but apparently never on one of my flights or he would have remembered me.

In regard to his presence in Rome, he told me that immediately following the Shah's hurried exit, he quickly liquidated as much of his business as he could and flew to Rome with his wife and son. They had been in Italy for several months awaiting a visa to enter the United States, where he hoped to someday reside.

I told Mr. Baharlu of my plan to return to Tehran and that the Iranian Consulate Office in Rome had granted me a visa. His jaw dropped and looking me straight in the eye said, **"Captain Martin, do not return to Tehran!"** He added that the Iranian Revolutionary Consulate office in Rome did not have the authority to issue me a visa without first obtaining permission from Islamic officials in Tehran. He was sure that since I had been a pilot for the Shah's Air Taxi Company, and was approved for employment by the hated Savak secret police, Khomenini's Islamic Militant Revolutionary Supporters would certainly want to talk to me.

He said I would surely be placed under arrest the minute I set foot in Iran. He added that even as a U.S. citizen, I couldn't expect much help from the American Embassy in Tehran. According to Mohammad the temporary invasion the U.S. Embassy experienced in February 1979 resulted in them adopting a "day-by-day" attitude of getting along with Khomeini. And since they were assisting in the Shah's protection they were reluctant to do anything to ruffle his revolutionary government.

Mr. Baharlu went on to state that if I was locked up, they would probably throw away the keys and I would have a devil of a time getting released. He also thought, as a U.S. citizen, they would probably hold me until I was forced to admit to some form of anti-Khomenin, pro-Shah activity. He added that even if I was released after a period of confinement, I would have no chance of recovering my Volkswagen or unpaid wages from Air Taxi as it was now under Islamic management.

He suggested that I spend a few more days with my son in the sunshine of Rome before heading back to the United States, the country he was trying so desperately to visit himself.

I thanked Mr. Baharlu for the lunch, the timely advice, and said I felt very fortunate that I had met him and his son. I wished him success in obtaining a U.S. visa and gave him my address and telephone number in Wisconsin in case he was successful. We parted with a handshake, and in true Iranian custom, I bid him, "Khoda Hafez, Insha Allah." (Good-bye and Allah's blessing.) I never heard from Mr. Baharlu again.

My son and I spent a few more enjoyable days in Rome and then flew back to the United States. I considered my exciting three years in Iran a closed chapter of my stimulating life as a charter pilot for the Shah.

Author's Post Script:

When the Shah and his family departed Iran on January 16, 1979, their first stop was Cairo, Egypt. After a brief stay they moved to Morocco, then to the Bahamas and later to Mexico.

From Mexico he went to New York on October 22, 1979, for medical treatment for lymphatic cancer. His visit to the U.S. infuriated Ayatollah Khomeinin's Islamic Militant Revolutionary Government who demanded he be extradited to Iran to stand trail for treason. (I believe had he been sent back to Iran he would have faced a short show trial followed by execution by firing squad.) Khomeini's extradition request was denied.

Two weeks later Iranian militants seized the U.S. Embassy in Tehran and took more than 50 Americans hostage, demanding the extradition of the Shah in return for the hostage's release. His extradition was still refused, but the Shah left the U.S. for Panama and then back to Cairo, where he was granted asylum by President Anwar Sadat. He died in Cairo on July 27, 1980 at age 60. The Shah is survived by his wife, Queen Farah, Empress of Iran, his 45-year-old son Reza and a daughter.

Note: Information relating to the Shah's post Iran travel was extracted from The Encyclopedia Britannica. Comments about possible execution are those of the author.

Epilogue

It is my belief that the political pendulum in Iran is swinging toward another regime change, but the shift will be slow. The Islamic theocracy established by Ayatollah Khomeini is not popular with the average Iranian citizen. His influence is declining and this is of concern to the militant fundamentalist Muslim Mullahs. The Smithsonian Magazine stated, "Iranians might be the least anti-American populace in the Muslim world, with the largest discontent among the younger generation." Because of the huge loss of adult males during the eight-year Iran/Iraq war, 70 percent of Iran's population are under 35-years-of-age. It is this generation who are fed up with Iran's anti-Western strain of Islam. Gender separation in schools, having to pass a test on the Muslim faith to attend college, the banning of alcohol, Western music, TV satellite dishes, men not being allowed to wear T-shirts, females required to wear long black garments and unmarried couples subject to flogging for having sex ---- all have run their course. Punishment for violating these assaults on freedom is severe and administered by roving members of the "Thought Police."

Similar to demonstrations that opposed the Shah, Iranians have marched in ever greater numbers in protest. (More than 10,000 recently protested outside the Tehran University, the same campus that witnessed demonstrations against the Shah in 1978.) In retaliation Islamic militants smashed their way into the university dormitories and beat up sleeping students, which resulted in an increase in public demonstrations.

Government authorities reacted by banning political protest marches and arrested several hundred participants, but have not forcibly blocked them. In December 2006 Iranian students disrupted a speech by the radical Iranian President Ahmadinejad at a Tehran University, setting fire to his picture and shouting "Death to the dictator." So far there has been limited loss of life, but it's just a matter of time before there will be demonstrators killed. Many Iranians are of the persuasion that dying, when pursuing a religious cause, provides them with a guaranteed ticket to Paradise and 72 virgins. The Muslim motto is "Victory or Martyrdom."

The Iranian National Security Council has, to some degree, given in to the demonstrators. They reversed the death sentence of Hashem Aghajari, a popular reform university lecturer, and lifted the house arrest of 81-year-old Grand Ayatollah Hossein Ali Montazeri, Iran's most senior dissident arrested in 1997 for criticizing Ayatollah Khomeini's successor. His release was the result of intense pressure from reformist lawmakers, who support a more pro-Western-style government. However, Iran's ruling clerics have not abandoned their goal of maintaining total control over Iranian citizens. Pursuing this objective they have closed opposition newspapers and denied political reformers a chance to air disagreement.

In October 2003, Shirin Ebadi, an Iranian activist lawyer and the first female judge appointed by the late Shah, was awarded the Nobel Peace Prize. She was an outspoken critic of the Islamic Republic and sent to prison for fostering her views. Her award was criticized by Iranian Islamic radicals, who accused the Nobel Peace Prize Committee of meddling in Iran's internal affairs, especially since the award was given to a female.

The fact that demonstrations are allowed is a marked contrast from the restraint on dissent enforced by the former Iraqi dictator, Saddam Hussein. His secret police descended on offenders who were sent to prison, tortured and often executed. These harsh measures were the only way he remained in power. However, he met the same fate when he was hanged in Baghdad on December 30, 2006. The long struggle with any successful revolution begins when authorities acquiesce to the demands of street mobs, which tend to grow in number. News outlets give the impression that the majority of Iranians support President Ahmadinejad's plan of enriching uranium. However, they would prefer that the money be spent on reducing the 30% unemployment rate and providing Western luxuries they see on TV. They resent paying $600 for a cell phone!

The Iranian Islamic leaders stated that they were attempting to provide thousands of new jobs by converting the Persian Gulf Island of Kish into a posh resort. But many obstacles cast doubt on the success of this venture, chief among them: the restrictions against gambling, consuming alcohol, dancing and men and women restricted to separate beaches. This is hardly the atmosphere for an inviting Western vacation spot.

Other dubious enterprises engineered by the Islamic leaders were the building of a new international airport, which cost billions of dollars; the impeachment of the transport minister; and providing very few new jobs.

The recent Iranian/Syrian alliance is a PR ploy and poses no additional direct threat to the U.S. Iranians are of the "Aryan" race and 80% Shiite Muslim, while Syrians are of the "Arabic" race and 85% Sunni. These two distinct religious groups have been feuding for 1,400 years, and won't be smoking a peace pipe anytime soon, especially with the possibility of an emerging democratic Iraq between them, where 30% of the 275 members of Iraq's new national assembly are women. (An abhorrent concept to both countries.) In addition, Syrians, after the assignation of the former Lebanese Prime Minister Rofik Hariri, were forced, by massive demonstrations in Beirut, to withdraw their troops from Lebanon.

As a witness to the overthrow of the Shah, who enjoyed a certain amount of international support, I think the present Iranian leaders are in for some rough times. The elections in Afghanistan and Iraq are watched closely in Iran. If democratic leaders emerge from these elections, it could expedite a regime change in Iran and other Middle East countries. The elections in Iraq, in January, October, and December 2005, were critical "tipping points." The Muslim hard-liners in Iran fear more than anything else freely elected governments on their eastern and western borders.

The decision to join Europe in offering concessions to Iran is a mistake. President Bush stated, "As you stand for liberty, America stands with you." This statement, if not fulfilled, will dissuade Iranians from seeking a regime change from within. Solving the terrorist problem in Iraq will not be easy, but progress is being made. The fact that 82% of eligible voters had the courage to risk their lives in order to vote was encouraging. There are problems but they are solvable. Defense Secretary Donald Rumsfeld put it well during a talk to U.S. troops in Mosul, Iraq, when he said, in part:

"When it looks bleak, when one worries about how it's going to come out, when one reads and hears the naysayers and the doubters say it can't be done, and that we're in a quagmire, one should recall that there have been such doubters throughout every conflict in the history of the world."

In countries where we support non-democratic leaders, the citizens have a low opinion of the U.S. i.e., Egypt, Jordan, Pakistan, Saudi Arabia, and Turkey. However, where we criticize despotic leaders, popular support for the U.S. is paradoxically higher, i.e., Iran and Syria.

Soliciting assistance from Iran and Syria in solving the war in Iraq would be a mistake. If these two Muslim countries had an interest in solving the Iraqi enigma they would not be assisting the insurgents in their war against the elected Iraqi government and in the killing of Americans.

Iran and Syria would most likely publicly agree to assist in solving the Iraqi situation, but their demands for aid would be high. And, once we acquiesce to their demands we can be sure that their pledge would not be honored. Iran has been negotiating to suspend nuclear enrichment for three years; yet we are not close to a solution. Iran's demands for assistance would probably be for the U.S. to discontinue criticism of their nuclear program and a promise not to engage in any military action against them. We can't trust a leader who denies the existence of a the Holocaust, actively supports the Hezbollah and vows to erase Israel from the face of the earth. Syria's demands would most likely be returning the Golan Heights to the Palestinians, free-run in Lebanon, being accepted as a member of the European community and, like Iran, a promise that the U.S. will never take military action against them.

The 2006 Iraq Study Group Report (ISG) is nothing but a "feel-good" document. Only one member of the ISG ventured outside the protected Green-Zone when visiting Baghdad. They could have received the same presentation without ever leaving Washington. President Bush's plan of a "surge" of 21,500 more troops is not the answer. Unrelenting brutal military force, without charging U.S. marines with murder when killing the enemy, is the only way to defeat fanatical jihadists whose goal is to die while seeking an Islamic world under "Sharia" (Muslim law). Their missive to infidels is to convert to the Islamic religion, pay an exorbitant tax or face death by decapitation. These are the only options they extend to infidels. We are attempting to fight a ruthless war without killing people. War is hell and the more brutal we make it the sooner it will be over. This is the doctrine our enemy is presently following and they seem to be winning.

Glossary

Airborne radar--------------------Radar set installed in the aircraft.
Aircraft flight manual:-----------Manual instructing how the pilot should operate the aircraft.
Aircraft type rating:-------------Official authorization for pilots to act as PIC in a large aircraft, or a turbojet of US registry.
Airline transport license:------Highest level of pilot's license.
Admiral Hornblower:-----------Famous British (Fictional) Admiral.
Allah Akbar:----------------------Farsi for "God is great."
Armenian:------------------------Native of former country northwest of Iran.
Ayatollah Khomeini:-----------Religious leader of Iran's Shiites. He became Iran's sole power after the Shah.
Bakhsheesh:--------------------Under-the-table payment.
Base Operations:--------------Military term for operations center.
Bazaar:--------------------------Term for shopping center in Middle East.
Beefeater Gin:------------------Famous London dry gin.
Brown nosing:------------------Colloquial expression used for people courting favors from superiors.
Bucket seats:-------------------Seats inside cargo aircraft.
Chador:--------------------------Long head-to-toe black flowing robe worn by Iranian women.
Charter company:-------------As used in "Wings over Persia" a company leasing aircraft and pilots for flight.
Chay:-----------------------------Strong Iranian tea.
Checklist:------------------------List of items requiring review.

Chief Pilot:------------------------Supervisory pilot.
Chelo Kabab:--------------------Roasted lamb on rice bed.
Civilian Aeronautics Board:----Forerunner of Federal Aviation Administration.
Cockpit Resource Mgt:----------Procedures for efficient utilization of crew members.
Compressor stalls:---------------A jet engine being starved of sufficient air, and excess fuel, results in "backfires."
Controls free & normal:--------A check pilots make to ensure flight control surfaces move freely in all directions.
Deadheading:--------------------A crew member flying who is not a member of the regularly assigned crew.
DME:------------------------------Onboard electronic equipment which measures distance to a station.
Empress Farah:------------------The Queen of Iran, Shah's wife.
Expatriate:-------------------------A person who leaves one's country for another.
Farsi:-------------------------------Iranian language.
Feather propeller:---------------Causing the propeller blade to streamline to the relative air flow. (minimum drag)
First Class Medical:-------------Highest level of medical rating by pilots. Requires updating every six months.
Flagellate:-------------------------As used in text to punish one's self by whipping with steel whips.
Flat pitch propeller:-------------A propeller in the lowest blade angle possible. Required at low RPM in turboprops.

Foreign clearance code:------A numerical code issued which allows an aircraft to penetrate another countries airspace.
Freon air conditioning:--------An air conditioning system in the FH-227.
Geodetic survey:---------------Relating to geography of country.
Gust locks:----------------------Mechanical locks installed on flight control surfaces to prevent them from flapping in ground winds.
Gust lock removal rods:------A series of metal rods that, when assembled, provides a means of removing or installing gust locks.
Hajib:-----------------------------Head scarf for covering a woman's hair.
High Altitude Chart:-----------An air navigation chart used for flight above 18,000 feet.
ILS:-------------------------------Instrument landing system that provides both course and height guidance during landing.
IFR:-------------------------------Flying by instrument flight rules.
Iman:-----------------------------Prayer leader of a Muslim mosque.
IMC:------------------------------Instrument meteorological conditions. (no visual reference)
Infidel:---------------------------A non believer of the Muslim faith.
Inbound course:---------------The course leading to runway.
Insha Allah:---------------------Expression in Farsi meaning "If Allah wishes."
Instrument flight plan:--------Document filed with the FAA which authorizes the aircraft to fly under IMC.
Islam:----------------------------Submission to God.
Jeppesen:----------------------Pilot supply company, best noted for aeronautical publications.

Jumbo Jet:------------------------Large aircraft, normally used in describing a B-747.

Kamikaze:-------------------------Reference to Japanese pilots who committed suicide by diving their own aircraft into the target.

Khoda hafez, Insha Allah:-----Good bye with Allah's blessing.

KLM:--------------------------------Royal Dutch Airlines.

Koran:------------------------------Book of composed writings accepted by Muslims. Also spelled (Quran.)

Kurts:-------------------------------Indian style male flowing gown.

Latrine:-----------------------------Military term for toilet area.

Line check:------------------------Flight check administered to pilots while flying the line.

Log Book:-------------------------As used, means reference to a log relating to flights performed.

Machine gun nest:--------------As used refers to a series of sandbags surrounding a machine gun.

Martini:-----------------------------A cocktail composed of mostly gin.

MEA:--------------------------------Minimum En route Altitude on instrument flight plans.

Mehrabad Airport:---------------Tehran International airport.

Mohammad:-----------------------As used in the text, would pertain to the founder of the Muslim religion who lived from 570 to 632 AD

Mosque:----------------------------Building used for public prayers by Muslims.

Muslim:-----------------------------An adherent to Islam, one who surrenders to God.

Naft:---------------------------------Farsi word for kerosene.

No-radio landing:----------------Landing at an airport without being able to contact the tower.
No Ruz:---------------------------Iranian New Year, or equinox. Thirteen days of celebration that begins around the 19th or 21st of March.
Obento:---------------------------Japanese-style box lunch.
OMEGA:--------------------------Computerized navigation unit. Accuracy was obtained from eight radio stations located throughout the world. This system was discontinued in 1997 and replaced by GPS.
Off flag:---------------------------A small red flag located inside an instrument that appears when the unit is inoperative.
Oversold:-------------------------A term used by airlines when tickets sold exceed capacity
Paykan:---------------------------Iranian small car based on the English Hillman and assembled from kits.
Pahlavi:---------------------------Family name of the Shah and his father.
Persia:----------------------------Name for ancient Iran. In 1935 the government officially changed the name of the country to Iran.
Pilot-in-command:---------------Term used to identify the pilot in command of the aircraft. (PIC)
Piper-Cub:-----------------------Small 65 HP single engine aircraft built by, Piper Aircraft.
Pita bread:-----------------------Flat circular bread baked daily and served in round disks.
Preflight:--------------------------As used in text, refers to inspecting an aircraft before flight.
Princess Ashraf:-----------------The Shah's twin sister.
Premier Zhou Enlai:-------------Founding emperor of the Chinese Communist dynasty who died in 1976.

Prophet:----------------------------As used in the text refers to one who utters divinely inspired revelations.

Ramadan:--------------------------The month when Muslims do not eat, drink or engage in sex from sunrise to sunset.

Refueling tanker:-----------------Aircraft configured to refuel other aircraft in flight.

Rial:---------------------------------Iranian currency. In 1978 one U.S. dollar equaled 70 rials.

Roughneck:------------------------Refers to oil field workers.

Saddam Hussein:-----------------Military dictator of Iraq until 2003.

Sake:--------------------------------Japanese rice wine, served warm.

Salam-u-Alaikum:-----------------God be with you in peace.

Sari:---------------------------------Indian-style female silk dress.

Savak:------------------------------Iranian secret police.

Shah:-------------------------------Iranian leader (king) until 1979.

Sheik:------------------------------An Arab chief. A man supposed to be irresistible to women.

Shiite:------------------------------Muslim religious sect who declared Mohammad's son-in-law as their new leader.

Single-pilot flight:-----------------Flying without a copilot. Used in TC-690A only.

Space-available ticket:-----------Airline ticket which allows a seat only if the aircraft is not full.

Speed brakes:---------------------Drag device on jet aircraft.

Stall:---------------------------------Speed at which aircraft weight vector is greater then airfoil lift.

Steep turn:-------------------------Training and testing maneuver involving a 360 degree circle in a bank angle of 45 degrees without a loss of altitude.

Strobe lead-in lights:-------------Flashing ground strobe lights that lead to landing runway.

Sunni:-------------------------------Muslim religious sect who declared Mohammad's disciple as their new leader.

Sushi:-------------------------------Japanese food delicacy of raw fish, wrapped in seaweed, rice and vegetables.

Susir:---------------------------------Indian-style flute.

Tantu Vadya:----------------------Indian-style two-string instrument

Tequila:-----------------------------Mexican hard liquor.

Touch and go landing:----------After landing, the pilot makes another takeoff without taxiing back to the end of the runway.

Turboprop aircraft:---------------Aircraft powered by jet engines connected to propellers.

Turnaround flight:----------------Aircraft returning to departure airport after making one or more en route stops.

Type rating:-----------------------License for pilots to act as PIC in aircraft over 12,500 pounds.

VFR:---------------------------------Flying by visual flight rules.

VMC:--------------------------------Visual meteorological conditions.

V1:-----------------------------------Decision speed during takeoff at which the takeoff may be either aborted or continued.

Abbreviated Keyword Index

D

E

F

G

ISBN 141200107-2

9 781412 001076